INVASION

INVASION

Defending Britain from Attack

DAN CRUICKSHANK

BOXTREE

Endpapers: *An 1803 French fantasy of a co-ordinated, combined operations, attack upon England. The French forces come not only by sea - with gun-boats in the forefront, but by balloon and via a secret tunnel cut beneath the Channel. The Royal Navy is shown as the first hurdle to cross while the English appear to be sending up 'anti-aircraft' kites carrying kamikazi-minded musketeers.*

Frontispiece: *Lindisfarne Castle seen from down beside the causeway that links the island to the mainland.*

First published 2001 by Boxtree
an imprint of Pan Macmillan Ltd
Pan Macmillan, 20 New Wharf Road, London N1 9RR
Basingstoke and Oxford
Associated companies throughout the world
www.panmacmillan.com

ISBN 0 7522 2029 2

Text copyright © Dan Cruickshank 2001

Designed and typeset by
Dan Newman/Perfect Bound Ltd
Colour reproduction by Aylesbury Studios, Kent
Printed and bound by Bath Press

With thanks to the following people for permission to reproduce their images:
BBC/ Ed Bazalgette 173
BBC/Charlie Mason 172
BBC/Dan Cruickshank 106, 113 top, 162, 167
BBC/Tim Cuff 7, 125
The Bridgeman Art Library 4, 8, 57 bottom, 90, 91, 92-3, 97, 98, 110, 112, 113 bottom, 114
British Library 51, 59
Carmarthen Museum 102
Corbis 177
David Rose 165 and inset
Dover Museum 118, 119
English Heritage Photo Library 9, 19, 23, 24, 40, 41, 128, 129
Historic Scotland 80
Imperial War Museum 141, 143, 149, 152, 153, 156-7, 160
Mrs Daphne Lovegrove 29
Murray King 60
Mary Evans Picture Library 12, 13, 15, 16, 26, 34, 36, 43, 57 top, 64, 67, 74, 83, 84, 132, 135, 139, 159, 163, endpapers
Much/Albatros 144
Munday/Albatros 146
National Maritime Museum 86, 127
Malcolm Pratt, Town Clerk of Winchelsea 30
Public Records Office 31, 53, 55
The Royal Armouries 45, 122, 123

CONTENTS

INTRODUCTION

The last time an invading force conquered England was in 1066. But for nearly 1000 years after that date the fear of invasion, and the massive precautions taken to prevent it, have had a profound influence on life in the British Isles.

William Shakespeare offered an image of England that has a potent and romantic appeal.

> '...this scept'red Isle... This fortress built by nature for herself against infection and the hand of war...this little world, this precious stone set in the silver sea, which serves it in the office of a wall, or as a moat defensive to a house, against the envy of less happier lands; this blessed plot, this earth, this realm, this England...bound in with the triumphant sea, whose rocky shore beats back the envious siege.' *(Richard II, Act 2, Scene 1)*.

But in reality Shakespeare's view was wishful thinking – no more than a fanciful myth. The coastal inlets of the British coast, its many secret and secluded bays, estuaries and rivers almost proved its undoing. Far from being a protective moat, the waters around Britain, and its rivers, were invasion highways tempting intruders to penetrate to the very vitals of the nation.

This had been the case for the 1000 years before the Norman invasion in 1066. Ever since Julius Caesar first set foot on England's shore in 55BC, a constant stream of invaders inexorably followed. The Romans returned in 43AD, followed by north German 'barbarian' tribes after 400AD – most notably the Angles, Saxons and Jutes – and lastly, the Vikings from the eighth century. Each new wave settled, inter-mingled with the natives and became – in their turn – prey to the next invader. This process of repeated invasion saw the transformation of England from a confederation of tribes of Romano-Britons into Germanic mini-kingdoms, a dual Anglo-Saxon and Danish realm and, eventually, into a united 'England.'

The physical memorials to these ancient invaders are few but architecturally significant – Hadrian's Wall on the Scottish border, Offa's Dyke on the Welsh border, the Roman shore forts in Sussex and East Anglia,

the defensive towers of Anglo-Saxon coastal churches. Significantly, these were all anti-invasion works built by invaders who had learned, through their own experience, how vulnerable the British Isles was to invasion.

The Norman victory in 1066 changed nothing. Invasion – or at least violent raids by hostile foreign powers – remained a ghastly but inescapable fact of life. Within 150 years of Hastings there had been a dozen major invasion attempts or incursions in force by would-be conquerors. The terror of these years – and their influence on the architectural and social history of Britain – have now been almost forgotten. But for much of the last 1000 years invasion has been a way of life and the inhabitants of the British Isles have honed a deep-rooted terror of attack from the sea and, for the last 100 years, from the sky. Indeed the shared fear of invasion has, in many ways, helped to forge the disparate peoples inhabiting Britain into a single nation.

But not all invaders brought terror. Sometimes they were accepted or even welcomed and were, in essence, a challenge to the fragile notions of nationhood and national identity. The Tudor dynasty – which did much to create the idea of a distinct and characteristic English nation – was born out of invasion when, in 1485, a French-sponsored invading army swept Henry VII on to the throne. Just as dramatically, the 'Glorious Revolution' of 1688 - which saw the final demise of Stuart despotism, an increase in Parliamentary power and of much-prized individual liberty - started with a Dutch invasion headed by William of Orange. Other invasions – threatened by far less benign foreign powers - were welcomed by sections of British society for religious or political reasons. The Spanish-led Roman Catholic crusade against England in the second half of the 16th century raised the spectre of an 'enemy within', when the state feared that English Catholics would put faith above nationalism and aid the Spanish cause. Again, in the 1790s, the British authorities were driven to a frenzy of fear because they imagined that large sections of society – thrilled by the egalitarian principles of the French Revolution – would form a Fifth Column to pave the way for French invasion.

The story of invasion after 1066 offers a crucial insight into the making of the British character – at once defiant and deeply fearful of foreign influence, expansive yet profoundly insular. The story also reveals the forces that fueled Britain's social, political and industrial revolutions and brings into focus a wide range of objects and technologies – ships, guns, aircraft and building materials – relevant to the defence of the British Isles. It presents a vignette of British architecture that gives meaning to much of the built fabric of the British Isles. The purposes behind the coastal gun-towers and batteries, the inland systems of pillboxes and the other architectural oddities that lie scattered throughout Britain are explained by an understanding of the fear of invasion that has gripped succeeding generations of the British.

This book tells the story of invasion in a chronological order – any other approach would prove too confusing. It juxtaposes the broad historical story with highly detailed accounts of individual actions – notably the French rape of Winchelsea in 1360, the Spanish molestation of Mousehole in 1595, the American attack on Whitehaven in 1778, and the French invasion of Fishguard in 1797. Through these it is possible to see how, over the centuries, the threat of invasion or incursion has affected the lives of ordinary people.

Several themes emerge throughout the book, not least the weather which – far more than Britain's island isolation – has time and again saved the nation from invasion. The most famous example of divine intervention in the form of storms and high sea is the dismal fate suffered by the Spanish Armada in 1588. But various earlier invasion fleets were blown adrift, as were French and Spanish attempts on England and Ireland in the eighteenth century. Most dramatic was the French invasion of Bantry Bay in December 1796 when the seas were so rough that the large French force could not get ashore and was eventually blown back out to sea. Another recurring theme is the Royal Navy. England was protected by armed merchant fleets during the Middle Ages – notably that of the Cinque Ports – but from the early sixteenth century, under the patronage of Henry VIII, the Royal Navy emerged as a powerful fighting force with control of the Channel – the principal

Hadrian's Wall at Cawfields, built on the orders of Emperor Hadrian after he came to Britain in 122AD. It is Britain's earliest masonry-built anti-invasion fortification.

invasion route into England – its main concern. The English navy achieved its first great triumph when it saved the country from the Spanish Armada in 1588 and, for the next 350 years became Britain's first and great line of defence against invasion.

The story of the battle to repel the invader offers a fascinating social and architectural history of Britain and the British.

PART ONE

INVASION AS A WAY OF LIFE

CHAPTER ONE

THE NORMAN CONQUEST AND ITS AFTERMATH

The Norman invasion changed England for ever. The consequences were dramatic and far-reaching for monarchy, ruling elite, language of government, social system, architecture, and landscape. However, one consequence of the Battle of Hastings is often overlooked: the dramatic shift in England's position in Europe. Instead of remaining within the orbit of a greater Scandinavian empire, England was dragged into mainland continental politics, with new enemies to fear.

When the English king Edward the Confessor died in 1066, there were several claimants to the throne. Norman sources state that Edward had nominated William, Duke of Normandy, as his successor as early as 1051. William himself claimed that Harold, Earl of Wessex, had been sent to him in 1064 to confirm Edward's grant. However, evidence from the *Anglo-Saxon Chronicle* and the Bayeux Tapestry suggests that Edward entrusted the kingdom to Harold on his deathbed, a decision that was to be ratified by the Witan, the assembly of England's leading nobles. Another rival was the Norwegian king, Harald Hardrada, who had a distant claim via a pact made with Edward's predecessor Harald Harefoot in the 1040s; while Edgar the Aethling's presence at the English court was a reminder of his direct descent from the old Anglo-Saxon royal family exiled in 1016.

But it was Harold who prevailed and was crowned king on 6 January 1066, the same day that Edward was buried. Yet Harold knew that by seizing the crown he would be forced to struggle to keep it, and he began to make preparations for what he assumed would be an imminent invasion.

Spies quickly informed William of Harold's coronation. The Norman chronicler William of Jumièges describes the Duke's rage at the news, probably because William had already announced to the world that he was to be England's next king. He immediately made plans to invade – the Bayeux Tapestry vividly depicts the felling of trees and shaping of countless vessels to carry troops, warhorses and armour. However, William's aristocracy questioned the wisdom of such an expedition, refusing to serve outside Normandy. William countered by obtaining a papal blessing for the enterprise, which turned it into a virtual 'crusade' to reform the English church, and found supporters flocking to his banner. More compelling, however, was the promise of

Above and opposite: *Detail from the Bayeux Tapestry. On the left, spies tell William that Harold has been crowned. On the right, trees are felled and William's invasion fleet is built and launched.*

rich plunder. Throughout the spring and early summer of 1066 William built a fleet of about 400 ships at the Dives estuary at the mouth of the River Somme to carry an invasion force of up to 10,000 men, 3,000 horses, three prefabricated forts, arms, armour, supplies and equipment.

In England, Harold's first move was to secure the support of his northern earls, the brothers Edwin and Morcar, by marrying their sister. He then set about the defence of the vulnerable south coast against the danger from across the Channel. As well as his navy, stationed chiefly at the Isle of Wight, Harold kept 3,000 professional soldiers forming an elite bodyguard (*huscarls*) plus an additional 12,000 part-time, irregular and untrained warriors (the *fyrd*) on alert throughout the summer along the south coast. These would have manned the ancient coastal defences, such as the old Roman forts and Anglo-Saxon fortified towns (*burghs*), but neither Edward nor his predecessors had formulated an integrated system of anti-invasion works. This lack made Harold particularly vulnerable to Norman aggression. In addition, the *fyrd* was required to serve for only a maximum of forty days each year.

Defensive units were concentrated in Hampshire, which makes it clear that the ancient capital of Winchester was Harold's prime concern. It also suggests that he hoped to march out to meet an invader wherever he landed, rather than secure the entire stretch of coast.

William's invasion would have been a very different story if he had managed to set sail when his preparations at Dives were complete in early August. Scouts had probably assessed where the best place to land the massive fleet would be – along the Sussex coast – but throughout the summer the English fleet was active in these waters, ready to harass the flotilla of vessels. Furthermore, it is unlikely that William would have landed unopposed, and Harold would have had a great opportunity to strangle the invasion at birth. But the absence of southerly winds prevented William from sailing to probable defeat. Either by fortuitous coincidence – or great forward planning – 8 September marked the expiration of the forty days' service that Harold could reasonably demand from the *fyrd*. With the harvest approaching, and no sign of an invasion, he was forced to stand down both the army and the navy and let his men disperse to their homes and villages to attend to their crops.

Four days later William finally gained the necessary wind, seized his opportunity, and set sail. However, the attempted crossing was a disaster. The wind shifted and began to blow from the west so strongly that the fleet was forced into the mouth of the Somme and anchored at the port of St Valéry, where it remained for a further two weeks. It is highly likely that a number of ships and men were lost, and provisions were running out – at this stage, the campaign was in danger of collapse.

Yet England was still invaded – not in the south, as expected, but in the north. On 19 September news reached Harold in London that a massive Norse army had landed in Northumbria, led jointly by Harold's exiled brother Tostig and Harald Hardrada. About 300 ships had transported up to 10,000 warriors, who advanced on York, a traditional Scandinavian bastion, and routed a hastily assembled army led by Edwin and Morcar at Gate Fulford on 20 September. Harold had already decided to march north to meet this unexpected threat, and with impressive speed led his *huscarls* and remobilized *fyrd* to the gates of York by 24 September. The Battle of Stamford Bridge on the following day has always been overshadowed by the events at Hastings, but it was one of the most decisive actions ever fought on English soil: the Norwegian army was slaughtered, with both Hardrada and Tostig slain. Only twenty-four ships were required to transport home the survivors, who promised never to return.

Perversely, at this moment of greatest triumph came the worst possible news. A southerly wind had returned to the Channel, allowing the Norman host to set sail on 28 September. They made for Pevensey Bay, which in the eleventh century was wide and flat-bottomed with good beaches. Harold's fleet was further down the coast near the Isle of Wight, and was powerless to prevent the Norman army landing unopposed. A prefabricated fort was quickly assembled in the disused Roman fort on the headland, and William's forces initially camped around it. After several reconnaissance missions, the army found no immediate threat to its position, and moved north into the marshy Sussex countryside, terrorizing the local people, burning houses and plundering food, provisions and whatever riches could be found. News of the events in the north soon reached William, and within days the army established a new base to the north of Hastings. Although marshland, hills and woods hemmed in the Hastings peninsula, potentially isolating the Norman forces, William refused to march further on to the strategically important London to Dover road. Further fortifications were constructed at Hastings and, unmolested by defensive forces, the Normans continued to mount raids into the surrounding countryside.

These events forced Harold to march back south as quickly as possible with the remnants of his exhausted and battle-scarred army. The surviving *huscarls* moved with him, but it is unlikely that many of the *fyrd* were forced to follow at the same pace. The northern earls were instructed to regroup their army and follow south as quickly as possible. Harold arrived back in London in early October, and allowed a brief time to rest and regroup his army. Although the full potential of the *fyrd* was lost to him – estimated at a maximum of 30–40,000 soldiers – sufficient numbers continued to materialize at the muster during the following ten days.

Time was clearly on Harold's side. The longer he waited, the more of his army would reappear, in particular the forces of the northern earls Edwin and Morcar. The shortened campaigning season, plus the routine of government that required William's presence back in Normandy, made a cat-and-mouse stalemate more likely to result in a favourable outcome to the English. Yet Harold made a pivotal decision to leave London and march on the Norman forces encamped in Sussex. This decision was probably reached through a combination of factors: the news brought by scouts of the looting and plundering inflicted in the heartland of his own estates, as depicted in the Bayeux Tapestry; the need to defend the validity of his crown against a potential 'usurper'; and a large dash of confidence after his heroic victory at Stamford Bridge. On 11 October Harold commanded his still-growing army to march the sixty miles from London to within six miles of the invaders.

Norman sources claim that there was diplomatic contact between the sides: William of Jumièges states that Harold sent envoys to William, demanding to know why 'he had invaded his land with an arrogant temerity beyond comprehension' and that he should 'withdraw from his land'; in reply, William reasserted his lawful claim to the throne, and stated that he was 'ready to wage my life against his that the English kingdom by right falls to me rather than him'. Fateful confrontation was only hours away.

Early on the morning of Saturday 14 October the Norman army began the march from Hastings, across the peninsula towards the London road, along which Harold's troops were approaching. It is likely that this manoeuvre caught Harold slightly unawares, as his intention of moving towards Hastings may have been to keep the Norman troops bottled up rather than to provoke a battle. However, he was able to find a strong defensive position on the high ridge of Caldebec Hill, backed by woodland and surrounded on either side by marshy ground that prevented flanking attacks from developing in strength. Harold planted his standard, the Fighting Man, by an old apple tree at the top of the ridge, and began to draw his forces into battle lines. By 8 a.m., scouts would have informed William of Harold's arrival, and his own troops began to move over Telham Hill into the valley in front of the assembled English host.

The armies would have been fairly evenly matched in numerical terms, with about 6–7,000 troops each. The core of Harold's force consisted of 3,000 *huscarls*, fighting with the two-handed heavy axes that had carved up the Norsemen two weeks before. A further 3–4,000 *fyrd* brought their support, fighting with javelins and axes. The entire army was arranged in lines up to eight deep strung across the crest of the hill, protected behind a shield-wall. Harold, with his personal troops and the bulk of *huscarls*, was situated in the middle, with his two brothers Leofwine and Gyrth each commanding one of the flanks. Their tactics were standard for infantry battles – to grind down the Norman forces, reduce their numbers, prevent them breaking through to the roads that led to London, and to sweep them from the field when they weakened. While the English army would only increase in size as reinforcements arrived from the north, Norman losses sustained in battle could not be replaced as easily, and the invaders could thus be driven back to the coast where the English fleet was now waiting.

William could count on up to 3,000 mounted knights, a similar number of foot soldiers wielding swords and spears, plus units of archers. The Normans took position in the centre with their Duke, surrounded by Bretons led by Count Alain of Brittany on the left flank, and Flemish under the command of Eustace of Boulogne on the right. William had placed the archers at the front, followed by the heavily armed infantry, with the cavalry at the rear waiting for the signal to charge at the English shield-wall – the first time the English would have had to face such an onslaught by mounted opponents. For William, the battle was an all-or-nothing gamble, God's judgement on his claim to England.

The sources for the events are many and varied. Contemporary Norman chroniclers such as William of Jumièges and William of Poitiers (who admits he was not actually present) wrote the most vivid accounts; whereas the Bayeux Tapestry clearly depicts the savagery of the battle in a prolonged sequence of frames. The *Carmen de Hastingae Proelio* provides another detailed account, but it is not clear when this was written, and therefore doubt has been cast on its accuracy. The *Anglo-Saxon Chronicle* provides a short and terse

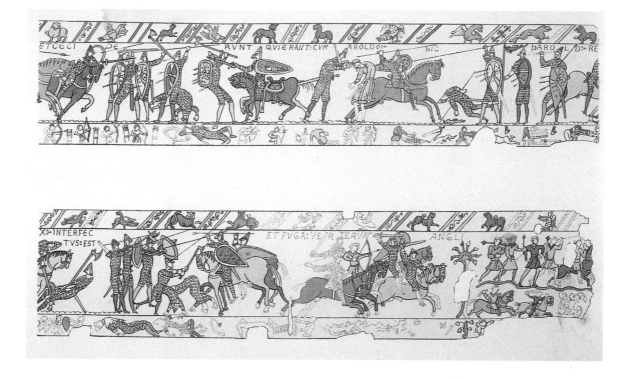

The Bayeux Tapestry – (top) the English army is cut to pieces, and Harold is fatally wounded by an arrow through the eye; (bottom) the Norman horsemen pursue the survivors.

report of the outcome, while later Anglo-Norman authors such as William of Malmesbury, Florence of Worcester and Orderic Vitalis were able to give a more balanced commentary, if chronologically distant. Nevertheless, the basic sequence of events is as follows.

After preparatory prayers from the Normans, and rowdy taunts and songs from the English, battle was joined with a blast of trumpets shortly after 9 a.m. The conflict was to last all day and into the early evening, one of the longest battles in medieval history. William initiated the first attack, deploying his archers to fire up the hill into the massed ranks of the English. It is unlikely that this caused many casualties, protected as they were by the shield-wall. Then the infantry advanced, and the English countered with a hail of 'spears and javelins and weapons of all kinds together with axes and stones fastened to pieces of wood' (William of Poitiers). The Normans suffered the most casualties, yet made little impression on the massed ranks of axe-wielding defenders. The cavalry was probably next deployed in the attack, but was equally unsuccessful, and forced to wheel away from the shield-wall.

At about 9.45 a.m. a critical moment was reached – the point at which most medieval battles were won or lost. 'The foot soldiers and the Breton knights, panic-stricken by the violence of the assault, broke in flight before the English' (William of Poitiers). With the left flank under pressure, the centre and right also began to give ground under the English onslaught. It is at this point that William was unhorsed, and the general cry began to go up among the Normans that their leader had fallen. At this one crucial juncture, Harold failed to press home his advantage with a decisive counter-attack – perhaps because it was at this point in the battle that his brothers Gyrth and Leofwine were killed in the mêlée. A full-scale assault by the entire

An early eighteenth-century portrait of William I. This romantic view of William, with his Domesday Book, emphasises his role as a lawmaker who stabilised England and laid the foundations of its future greatness.

English line would probably have led to a slaughter of the Norman archers and infantry, much as the Norse troops had been slain at Stamford Bridge. However, the main line held its position, while the right flank charged down the hill after the fleeing Normans.

The indecision allowed William to obtain another horse, identify himself to his troops and prevent the full flight of his army. After a brief period of regrouping, William personally led a counter-charge by the Norman cavalry that routed the English who had swarmed down the hill on the right, isolated from their defensive position, and put pressure on the line still on the ridge. This was another critical moment, but the shield-wall held in the face of the counter-charge and the Normans were forced back down the hill once again.

In all, only about two hours had elapsed, and the usual decisive moments of medieval battles had passed. The damage to the English right flank had given the Normans a definite numerical advantage, and effectively condemned Harold to a defensive battle. However, the Normans were still unable to break through the English line, which stoutly held its position on the ridge. From here on, we have little knowledge of the actual course of events – 'an unknown sort of battle' according to William of Poitiers – where a virtual stalemate continued for another seven hours at least. The Normans would have alternated between cavalry charges and infantry advances, while the English maintained their stubborn resistance punctuated with occasional sorties and counter-attacks.

In an attempt to break the deadlock, William appears to have employed the device of the feigned flight on two occasions, encouraged by the unexpected success during the crisis of the first hour of battle and realizing that battering the shield-wall was having little direct effect. Each time that the Normans simulated a retreat, English troops, probably from the less-disciplined *fyrd*, broke ranks and followed, only to be cut down by the cavalry. The gradual erosion of the English numbers made it increasingly difficult for Harold to maintain the defence of the hill with his fatigued troops. Yet with daylight ebbing away, it looked as though the battle would be inconclusive. At about 7 p.m. William decided on one final onslaught and, mirroring his first attack, recalled his archers. It is likely that they had more effect this time, creating gaps in the shield-wall; and it is at this point that Harold received the infamous wound to his eye. It may not have been fatal, but word spread that the king had fallen. Without a natural leader, morale and discipline among the *fyrd* were lost.

The Norman infantry moved forward against the shield-wall, which for the first time began to buckle. Eustace of Boulogne began to make telling inroads on the right, with the result that the entire line started to break. Although most of the *fyrd* began to flee, the *huscarls* retained their discipline and fell back along the isthmus, maybe with Harold still among their ranks. William led a final cavalry assault on their increasingly isolated and hopeless position, scattering some and cutting down the remainder. It is here that Harold was finally dispatched, hacked to pieces, according to the Bayeux Tapestry, by the Norman knights. Yet in the pursuit of the fleeing English, a large group of cavalry plunged to their deaths in the growing darkness in a ravine called the Malfosse.

William was thus the victor of Hastings. As well as being one of the longest battles of the Middle Ages, it was also one of the most decisive. The entire royal house of Godwin was killed, as were many of the leading nobles or *thegns*. William had won his kingdom at a single stroke, and God's judgement was thus delivered.

However, the scale of his victory would not have been obvious to William. After the battle he marched on Dover, where he fortified its defences and built a castle – the first of many throughout England. William then spent time suppressing the immediate countryside, moving west through Guildford, while a detachment of cavalry was sent to burn Southwark. He crossed the Thames at Wallingford and, after receiving reinforcements, he began to move towards London. At Little Berkhampstead William was met by the magnates of London, who surrendered the city and made him the offer of the crown of England.

Consolidating conquest

Over the next twenty years England was conquered and colonized by William's followers and was victim to an almost continuous sequence of counter-invasions and raids. The transition from an invading army to lawful rulers was painful and painstaking, and the period 1067–72 saw the fruits of the victory at Hastings hang in the balance.

William quickly realized the need to impose his authority within England but his reluctant subjects challenged his actions. For example, many Norman troops were killed at Exeter in 1067 before the town was handed over to the king, and in the following two years the dead King Harold's sons made two abortive invasion attempts from Ireland to recapture their former lands in the west country. The real danger to William lay in the old Anglo-Danish heartland of the northern earls Edwin and Morcar, who had not fought at Hastings and were allowed to retain their possessions. Other English were granted lands in the north and east, highlighting a clear geographical division between the old and new regimes.

After crushing the revolt in the south-west, William heard rumours of a plot among the English earls and was forced to march north, building castles as he went at Nottingham, York and Lincoln and leaving an army of occupation garrisoned at each. This caused massive resentment, as did the appointment in 1068 of the Norman Robert de Comines as Earl of Northumberland without local consent. In a ferocious uprising that united all the northern lords, Comines was killed, his garrison at Durham massacred and the newly constructed castle at York destroyed. To make things worse for William, the Anglo-Saxon prince Edgar the Aethling, who had a legitimate claim to the throne, invaded England from Scotland at the invitation of the northerners. Once more William countered the threat with force, sacking York and killing as many locals as he could. Edgar fled back across the border.

The stakes were raised still further in 1069. Memories of 1066 were revived when a huge Scandinavian fleet of 240 ships containing several thousand warriors landed in the Humber estuary, led by three sons of the Danish king Swein Estrithson, Harold's cousin. Whereas previously Edwin and Morcar had met the threat of Harald Hardrada with force, albeit unsuccessfully, they now greeted the new invaders with open arms, and were quickly joined by the Aethling in a strong coalition of disgruntled parties who had a vested interest in the overthrow of William.

The willingness of the English to give support to their erstwhile Danish masters realized William's worst fears. As the invaders once more reduced the castle of York to rubble, William returned north, wreaking devastation in his path, and drove the Danes back to their ships. However, they merely holed up in the Humber, and returned the following year under the leadership of Swein himself. William brought military pressure to bear once again; the Danes were bought off with treasure and returned home, and without their support the revolt lost its potency; by 1071 it had collapsed.

The immediate threat of invasion had thus been dealt with, but William's draconian 'final solution' to the separatist north earned him condemnation from both Anglo-Saxon and Norman chronicles alike. During the suppression of the 1069 uprising, William killed anyone who stood in his path, regardless of age or sex. Crops and livestock were burnt and villages totally destroyed north of York across Northumbria and Cumbria. Contemporary sources estimated that between 10,000 and 20,000 people starved to death as a direct consequence of the ensuing famine. Yet on a purely political level the 'Harrowing of the North' was a success, and effectively marked the realistic end to hopes of a new Anglo-Danish realm.

Nevertheless, two more invasions were planned. In 1075, as part of an Anglo-Norman revolt, the Danish fleet reappeared once again on the east coast, but was driven away before it could join with the land forces. A more serious threat arose in 1085, when Swein's son Cnut allied with Normandy's enemy, Robert Count of Flanders. William acted decisively and, according to the Chronicle, 'fared into England with as great a force of riding and marching men of France and Brittany as ever before sought this land… the king let the land by the sea be laid waste, so that if his enemies came up they would have nothing that could be taken quickly'. The scorched earth policy shows that the lessons of 1069–71 had been learnt, although in the event the invasion never materialised.

The war of attrition waged by the Normans on their new subjects between 1067 and 1072 changed the face of the English landscape. Castles were the main Norman device for stamping their authority on a hostile land, and were constructed in great numbers, whether simple earthwork fortifications or massive stone keeps. Indeed, William's first act as king was to begin work on the Tower of London to defend his capital. Wherever he rode with his army, castles would appear in his wake, garrisoned with metal-clad troops who were always

Launceston Castle, Cornwall, is a typical Norman creation. An artificial mound – a motte – supports a shell keep and is defended by a ditch. All was originally set within a walled enclosure, called a bailey.

ready to sally forth on warhorses to suppress native insurrection. To the local population, the castle represented the physical embodiment of an oppressive military force of occupation. This new and intimidating style of government, prevalent on the Continent, allowed the Normans to dominate large areas from a few strategic centres.

William's conquest of England created a new and powerful entity in Western Europe. His nearest neighbours and rivals – Anjou, Flanders and the essentially weak French crown – had cause to fear the combined resources of an Anglo-Norman state. The Channel had become an important line of communication between the two realms, rather than a natural form of defence, which allowed William to ferry across English troops for his campaigns against Maine in 1073 and Brittany in 1076. England now found itself protected by the Norman ports that had proved to be so threatening in 1066. On William's death in 1087, the Anglo-Norman realm was divided according to his wishes between his eldest surviving sons, Robert (Duke of Normandy) and William II (King of England). Henry, the youngest, was given cash that he immediately used to buy Norman lands from Robert. The period 1087–1106 is best viewed as a three-way fight between the brothers in an attempt to reunite the two territories, into which England was occasionally dragged through the intrigues of the cross-Channel aristocracy who found themselves in the uncomfortable position of owing bonds of loyalty to warring lords. Thus isolated rebellions broke out in England in favour of Robert of Normandy in 1088, 1095 and again with the accession of Henry I after the death of William.

This last revolt was the most serious disturbance of all: treachery among the English sailors allowed Robert to invade from Le Tréport and land a strong force of cavalry, archers and infantry at Portsmouth on 21 July 1101. Henry had clearly expected trouble; William of Malmesbury reports that the king personally trained the shire-levies in the techniques of opposing a cavalry charge. However, the English defensive troops were stationed at Pevensey, and consequently Henry was forced to march after his brother, who had made for London. They confronted each other at Alton; a treaty was agreed and Robert left England. However, the bulk of the fighting was conducted in Normandy, which had slipped into a state of near anarchy under the weak rule of Robert. After ridding England of the more troublesome cross-Channel lords, Henry launched a decisive counter-invasion on Normandy. On 28 September 1106 the brothers met in battle at Tinchebrai; the Norman army was decisively beaten and Robert taken captive. Forty years to the day after William I had landed for the first time in England, the Anglo-Norman realm was united under a single ruler once more.

England was thus secure for the remainder of Henry I's reign, a virtual spectator as he waged war against his neighbours on the continent. But when the Channel claimed the life of his son William in the wreck of the *White Ship* in 1120, Henry's daughter Matilda was left as his heir apparent. This was not a tempting proposition; her marriage to the Emperor Henry V raised the fearful proposition of absorption of both England and Normandy into the German empire; and after the emperor's death in 1125 she married Geoffrey Martel, the heir to Anjou, Normandy's oldest enemy. Therefore when Henry I died on 1 December 1135 and his nephew Stephen of Blois seized the crown of England, the Norman barons acknowledged him as their duke.

Stephen's reign was an unmitigated disaster. He failed to retain the support of the Norman barons, and the effects were felt in England as the cross-Channel magnates began to choose sides under pressure from Matilda. Once again, the Anglo-Norman realm was fractured by family warfare; the difference was that Matilda's invasion of England in 1139 brought the full horrors of continental castle warfare across the Channel. Regional anarchy, private wars and the emergence of independent baronial mini-states were all features of the 1140s, with Stephen able to claim royal authority over only the north and east while Matilda established her power base in the south-west.

The slow descent into civil war was hastened by the conquest of Normandy by Geoffrey of Anjou in 1145. The Channel became a means of supply for Matilda's forces in England, and in 1147 her son Henry joined the fray. He returned via Scotland in 1149, and soon took over the war in person. In 1150 he was created Duke of Normandy, and on his father's death in 1151 he added the title of Count of Anjou. His spectacular marriage to Eleanor, heiress to the Duchy of Aquitaine, in 1152 made him one of the most powerful men in Europe.

Henry invaded once more in 1153, but the English barons avoided a final confrontation and were largely responsible for bringing the two sides to terms. Henry was recognized as Stephen's heir by the Treaty of Winchester, and when the king died suddenly on 25 October 1154 Henry II was undisputed master of an empire that stretched from the borders of Scotland in the north to the Pyrenees in the south, with his continental lands engulfing an area that covered nearly two-thirds of modern France. With the creation of the 'Angevin Empire', England was once more safe from external invasion and its southern frontier was no longer the Channel but effectively a disputed territory on the French/Norman border called the Vexin.

The only moment of danger occurred during another family 'squabble' in 1173–4. England was faced with simultaneous invasion from the north by William the Lion of Scotland – who was captured when his horse fell on him, ending the incursion – and, more seriously, from the east. A planned invasion by the Count of Flanders saw two advance parties of Flemish mercenaries land, first in 1173 at Walton, Suffolk, and then at Orwell in 1174. The Walton raiders were cut to pieces outside Bury St Edmunds, but the second party, led by the Earl of Norfolk, managed to capture Norwich. Henry II moved quickly to suppress the revolt before the Count could sail with reinforcements, and thereafter the theatre of war moved back to the continent.

The emergence of France

A subtle shift in the balance of power between the Angevins and the Capetian kings of France had occurred with the accession of Philip Augustus in 1180. Under his leadership, France began to emerge as a serious force for the first time in centuries; Philip had an increasingly large pool of resources at his disposal to translate nominal overlordship into the beginnings of a strong centralized state. In an attempt to weaken his overmighty vassals, Philip waged war on Henry II and his son Richard I for most of his life, and in response greater measures were required to defend the Norman border.

By the time of Richard I's death in 1199, castle-building had so drained the Duchy of Normandy's coffers that regular drafts of money were being ferried across the Channel; and the cost of manning the defences actually exceeded the duke's entire Norman demesne revenue. Thus the Anglo-Norman frontier became a militarized zone in the Angevin–Capetian struggle, dotted with strategic castles that were essential to guarantee the security of the duchy and of England. At the centre was Château Gaillard, constructed by Richard from 1196 to 1198 and thought by contemporaries to be impregnable, the ultimate defensive fortification.

Although England was safe from direct attack, its defences were not neglected. Henry II began work on Dover Castle in 1179, which was completed in 1191. It formed a key defensive position on the English coast, guarding the Channel from potential marauders and acting as the centre of communications for Richard's all-consuming French campaigns. Its strategic value was soon to be put to the test. In 1203, during the reign of King John, the political map of Western Europe was turned on its head when Philip launched a successful invasion of Normandy. John fled from the continent, and one by one his castles fell to the invader until the entire duchy, plus Anjou and parts of Aquitaine, were in Capetian hands. By 1204, all that remained were the Channel Islands and Poitou. The heart had been ripped out of the Angevin empire; and for the first time in a century and a half England lay exposed to a powerful enemy across the sea, and the Channel was once again a defensive ditch rather than an Anglo-Norman lake.

Immediately after the capitulation of Normandy, English coastal castles were put on a state of full alert against the threat of invasion. In January 1205 plans for the defence of the entire realm were unveiled, to be organized by constables in every hundred (the subdivision of a shire) and borough. In response to information that Philip was ready to sail, a muster was authorized on 3 April 1205, with severe penalties for non-attendance.

John at least realized the new importance attached to the Channel. English naval defences were woefully inadequate, the complacent legacy of years of protection afforded by control of the northern and western coast of France. The first line of defence was now the sea, and John set about assembling a strong fleet. By February 1206 he was confident enough to mobilize his navy for a counter-attack, landing at La Rochelle and making limited gains.

Yet the grand prize was Normandy. For the next few years John feverishly devoted his energies to raising sufficient money to launch a full-scale invasion, and rebuilding a vast coalition of continental powers that shared a vested interest in halting the advances of Philip's France. However, in 1208 John incurred the wrath of the Papacy, which resulted in the imposition of an Interdict on the whole of England. This was just the excuse that Philip Augustus required, and in April 1213 he decided to launch a full-scale invasion, armed with the knowledge that God and the Pope were on his side. A fleet and an army were making final preparations at Gravelines when the news arrived that the Pope was now John's feudal overlord and protector, the contrite monarch having surrendered England into his hands as part of a settlement.

John spent the spring of 1213 personally supervising the defence of the coast, mobilizing the army on Barham Down between Canterbury and Dover, and assembling his fleet at Portsmouth. French shipping was attacked in the Seine and Dieppe was burnt, and in May John found the French fleet unattended at Damme. The English won a comprehensive victory, and many French ships were captured or burnt. With the threat of invasion removed, John, working in collaboration with Emperor Otto IV, finalized his own plans for reconquest.

In 1214 a two-pronged counter-attack was launched but ended in disaster with the defeat of the Emperor at the Battle of Bouvines on 27 July 1214. With Philip's decisive victory, John's hopes of regaining his lost continental possessions finally expired, and he returned to England to await the consequences of his actions.

Although Bouvines was fought on foreign soil, its outcome was as important to English history as Hastings, for it confirmed the reverses of 1204 and finally re-established the Channel as the front line between the nations. In addition, by returning in defeat, John was defenceless against the political opposition that was finally unleashed after years of arbitrary government. His rejection of Magna Carta in 1215 provoked outright civil war. The rebellious barons seized London, and appealed to Philip for help. Although technically at peace, Philip authorized his son Louis to undertake a campaign of conquest. John was aware of Louis's plans, but was unable to prevent the French fleet landing in Thanet on 21 May 1216. Louis quickly joined the rebels in London, and John's initial gains in the south-east were quickly reversed. Canterbury and Rochester fell to the invader, and Louis marched west to capture Winchester. Dover, however, remained loyal to John, and without this strategically important castle Louis could not guarantee his lines of communication with France.

Dover Castle was England's answer to Château Gaillard, and as such can rightly be described as one of the great fortresses of Western Europe. It dominated the cliffs overlooking the straits of Dover, with a tall square keep that mirrored that of the Tower of London – a symbol of royal power and prestige. The castle was defended by the Justiciar, Hubert de Burgh, with a garrison of about 140 knights and many other men-at-arms, and Louis could not leave this potential centre of resistance intact. His first move was to surround the castle and prepare earthworks, before fully investing it in mid-July. Half of his troops occupied the town, whilst the remainder conducted the siege itself. Louis's navy completed the encirclement with a sea blockade.

The key to winning Dover Castle was through the north gate that lay within the defensive D-shaped barbican, protected by a wooden palisade and ditch; the entire complex stood at the end of the spur of land on which the castle was constructed. After a fierce fight involving massive stone-throwing catapults and mobile siege towers, the walls were stormed and Louis's men were able to pour through the breach to occupy the barbican. This led to the next and crucial stage of the operation – taking the north gate itself.

Miners were employed underneath the twin towers of the north gate. The aim of the exercise was to tunnel into the foundations, light fires and generate enough heat to crack the stones and bring down the dangerously undermined walls. Yet the castle had its own maze of underground passages that were designed to counter this threat. Louis's miners simply dug deeper, and were able to bring down one of the towers of the north gate. This was the critical moment: troops were sent into the breach, where they met stiff resistance as the defenders

Opposite: *Dover Castle on its cliff-top site commanding the port. In the centre is Henry II's keep of 1179-91, surrounded by two sets of defensive walls – the first expression of this type of concentric fortification built in Britain. On the lower right is the remains of the North Gate.*

The moment of crisis during the siege of Dover Castle in 1216. After one of the towers of the North Gate has been undermined and has collapsed, the French storm into the breach that is stoutly defended by the English garrison.

attempted to prevent entry into the next stage of the castle's ring of concentric defences. The attackers were driven back and Louis, ultimately frustrated, signed a truce with de Burgh on 14 October 1216.

Four days later, John did everyone a favour by dying at Newark Castle, removing the main cause of English opposition and leaving his infant son Henry III as king. Undeterred, Louis invested Dover once more on 12 May 1217 where he constructed a trebuchet, a giant catapult, in an attempt to batter the castle into submission. But a decisive defeat for his troops at the Battle of Lincoln on 20 May damaged his position still further, while incoming reinforcements were crushed in a naval battle at Sandwich on 24 August. Without the support of the rebel barons, Louis gave up his attempt for the throne, and withdrew from England.

The crown had been saved but the empire was lost – and the unresolved relationship between England and France was to lead to generations of conflict and invasion.

CHAPTER TWO

THE HUNDRED YEARS' WAR AND THE RAPE OF WINCHELSEA

Immediately after the retreat of the French invader from England in 1217, relations between the two kingdoms were, for the time being, relatively placid. The Treaty of Paris in 1259 settled the terms by which England held part of the Duchy of Aquitaine – Gascony – from the king of France. In effect Henry III of England became the feudal vassal of Louis IX and, beside the humiliation of having to kneel before and swear allegiance to a brother king, Henry was forbidden from supporting Louis's enemies, and moreover was required to provide troops to defend France from attack. Non-compliance would provide Louis with legal justification to confiscate Gascony. In short, Henry had mortgaged England's right to an independent foreign policy.

The anomaly of having a king as the feudal vassal of another became ever more dangerous under Edward I. Gascony was a vital source of trade and customs revenue to England, but was increasingly coveted by the French kings who wished to increase their influence and power within France. Gascony's natural allies lay to the south of the Pyrenees in the kingdoms of Aragon and Castile, but when the French threatened them Edward was unable to lend assistance.

England had therefore been committed to a foreign policy that made good relations with the Spanish kingdoms essential, yet paradoxically difficult to achieve. The Channel became ever more important as a means of communication with Gascony as tension with France rose. Occasional piracy between English and French vessels was not unknown, but in 1294 a full-scale naval conflict broke out in the Channel between a Norman fleet and another mainly consisting of Gascons. The diplomatic situation collapsed; Philip IV of France confiscated Gascony, Edward responded with force and war erupted. Although a peace treaty was signed in 1303, by which Gascony was restored to England, this eventually was to cause later trouble – the ensuing marriage of Prince Edward (later Edward II) to Isabella, the daughter of Philip IV of France, gave Edward III his claim to the French throne.

Further war between 1324 and 1327 saw England lose half of Gascony, and the strategically important Franco-Scottish alliance was forged in the early 1330s. Threats to England therefore existed on two fronts; French raids were planned in 1333, and in 1336 the entire French fleet was moved to the Channel and mobilized for a full-scale invasion. This did not materialize, but English shipping off the Isle of Wight was

Bataille de Crecy

attacked, followed by all-out war when in 1337 Philip VI yet again confiscated Gascony. In October the same year Edward publicly reasserted his claim to the French throne and so heralded the real start of the Hundred Years' War.

The immediate French riposte was a raid on Portsmouth, which was burnt with only the church and hospital surviving. The fleet of the Cinque Ports – England's traditional first line of naval defence – failed to prevent this attack.

Worse was to come, with the spring of 1338 proving a particularly bad time. The Isle of Wight was plundered, Guernsey temporarily lost and Portsmouth attacked again; but the most serious casualty was Southampton. Froissart describes what happened in his *Chronicle*: 'They came on a Sunday in the forenoon to the haven of Hampton [Southampton], while the people were at mass, and the Normans, Picards and Spaniards entered into the town and robbed and pillaged the town, and slew divers people and defiled maidens and enforced [raped] wives, and charged their vessels with the pillage, and so entered again into their ships.'

This type of brutal raid, an opportunistic search for personal plunder more than a military exercise or act of invasion in a national war, became typical of the next 100 years of life on the south coast of England.

In 1339 another full-scale French invasion was planned, thwarted only by Edward's spectacular naval victory at Sluys in 1340 which destroyed the French fleet. The capture of Calais by the English in 1347 gave English vessels a port on the northern coast of France and a foothold on the mainland from which to launch invasions into France. But if the English became the masters in the use of a large-scale invasion army, the French became the exponents of the deadly hit-and-run raid. This was partly because French vessels – flat-bottomed galleys powered by oar and sail – were able to make inroads into English waterways far more easily than larger English vessels could penetrate French rivers. For the inhabitants of parts of England's south coast, invasion and bloody raiding became a fearful thread running through their history – it became a way of life. In these circumstances, castles, fortified manor houses and towns along the south coast became the front line against French incursion.

The town of Winchelsea

The fate of Winchelsea reveals much about the defence of England during the fourteenth and fifteenth centuries. Its story begins in the reign of Edward I, one of the greatest 'builders' of the medieval era. The mighty ring of castles he built during the late thirteenth century to subjugate and hold Wales are arguably among the finest ever constructed, and the decision to rebuild the ancient fortified trading town and port of Winchelsea was a typically ambitious exercise.

Although the old town had played a vital role in the defence and prosperity of England, by the end of the thirteenth century it was in danger of being swept into the sea. A commission sent to investigate reported back to the king in 1282; he decided to finance a complete rebuild on a new site. Plans were drawn up and were well under way by 1288; in 1292 the inhabitants were ready to move into their new town.

The layout, in which the king may well have taken a hand, was inspired by the walled and fortified towns called *bastides* that the English had built to hold south-west France. The town of Monsegur near Bordeaux seems to have been a particular influence on the design of Winchelsea, which was organized round a regular orthogonal grid of streets set within an encircling wall, made of stone, earth and timber and protected by a wide ditch. Great stone gates kept the town secure.

Opposite: *A French view of the Battle of Crecy of 1346 in which 9,000 English defeated 30,000 French. This was one of the major English triumphs during the Hundred Years' War, but while victories were achieved in France, vulnerable English coastal towns were brutally sacked.*

This layout may have been inspired originally by a remote knowledge of Roman fortified camps and towns, and adopted techniques pioneered by planned towns such as Salisbury, which was laid out in grid plan in about 1200. It is certainly far removed from the sort of organic, meandering and chaotic street plans generally associated with medieval towns and cities. A regular grid-plan allowed entire blocks of buildings to be dedicated to a specific use; thus public buildings or markets could be grouped together, while troops could be moved quickly through the wide straight streets when sections of the outer walls were threatened, making the town easier to defend. Two new churches were constructed, with St Thomas's intended to be on a huge scale to reflect the wealth and aspirations of the new town.

Merchants and townspeople would have been responsible for the construction of their private dwellings, which were mainly timber-framed or made of stone. In addition, many merchant houses incorporated stone-built wine-storage vaults at extra cost to themselves, although some were subsidized by Crown money. About thirty-two of these vaulted undercrofts are still accessible, invariably under later or much altered houses. A particularly fine example survives below the remains of the former Salutation Inn on the corner of Mill Street and Castle Street. It dates from around 1300, and incorporates carved details including a corbel embellished with an Atlas-like figure that carries the vault ribs upon his back; while another shows a man and woman locked in close embrace. This undercroft, in its bold scale and decorative style, offers a glimpse of the wealth and architectural ambition of the long-lost buildings of late thirteenth-century Winchelsea.

During the early fourteenth century, Winchelsea prospered behind its ramparts and strong stone-built gates, quickly expanding to fill the entire area within the town walls and supporting a population of around 6,000. But when attack came, neither economic prosperity nor stone walls were to be of any use.

The rape of the town

Winchelsea suffered seven major attacks during the Hundred Years' War; on virtually every occasion the French entered the town and burnt, killed and plundered. The first attack came in 1337, but the worst – and most destructive – came in 1360. This particular attack seems to have had two distinct aims. It was a deliberate act of revenge for the destruction that marauding English armies had recently visited on much of north France, as well as forming part of an invasion plan aimed at liberating the French King John II, who had been held in England since his capture in 1356 during the Battle of Poitiers.

The Patent Roll of 13 March 1360 makes it clear that English intelligence took the French invasion very seriously indeed. 'Considering the great peril of invasion and of the king's enemies now on the sea in a great fleet with horses', the king was granted a subsidy by Parliament for the defence of the country.

The French landed at Rye on Sunday 15 March 1360, disembarking on the banks of the River Rother without opposition. Contemporary accounts suggest that there were around 2,000 soldiers with horses in addition to the 1,000 or so men from the ships. Few were men-at-arms (trained professional soldiers); most were bowmen and foot soldiers from towns in Normandy, Picardy and Flanders. Some of these men came from areas that were suffering most from English aggression in France, and this may go some way towards explaining the savagery of what was about to happen.

The first blow of the invasion campaign fell on Winchelsea, just a mile or so from the French beachhead. The French entered the town early in the morning by slipping over the undefended wall or by passing through one of the town gates – the New Gate or the Strand Gate – which may have been left open for them. Treachery on the part of an English inhabitant or the work of a French agent? No one ever found out.

When it was learned that the French had entered the town, much of the population fled to the two churches – St Thomas's and St Giles's. Thomas of Walsingham, a contemporary chronicler, gives a good account of what

1 The Harbour.	24 Grey Friars.
2 Grindepepper Well.	25 Le Bocherie &
3 St Leonard's Well.	Little Monday
4 Sloghidam.	Market.
5 The Quay.	26 Town Hall.
6 Pipewell Gate.	27 Hundred Place.
7 The Stone Mill.	28 Court House &
8 The King's Field.	Prison
9 Le Trecherie.	29 Market Place.
10 Salutation Inn.	30 South Gate.
11 Three King's Inn.	31 Gate
12 [Modern Court	32 Mongysellers.
Hall].	33 Icklesham Ditch.
13 The street of	34 Town Ditch.
the Bakers.	35 Postern.
14 St Leonard's Ch.	36 Hospital of
15 West Gate.	St John.
16 Town of Iham.	37 Pewes Marsh.
17 Strand Gate.	38 Hospital of
18 St Thomas Ch.	Holy Cross
19 The King's High	39 Hospital of
Way .	St Bartholomew.
20 St Leonard's	40 Town Ditch
Creek.	41 New Gate.
21 Postern.	The position . of house
22 St Giles' Ch.	is not known & they
23 Postern.	cannot be inserted.

SCALE

NEW WINCHELSEA
CIRCA 1300

H.Lovegrove fecit.1947.   after W.McL. Homan.

Winchelsea as laid out in about 1285, and as built by 1300. The orthogonal grid of streets meant that the town's buildings could be grouped in an orderly manner and allowed soldiers to speed along the straight streets to threatened sections of the wall and surrounding ditch.

happened next: 'They … burnt the greater part of it. They killed all that resisted them regardless of sex, age or station. Also they took captive to the ships married ladies, girls and women who pleased their eyes … When the French landed many of the inhabitants were in the church at the time of mass. The invaders ran to the church with all haste, killing many and despoiling the church.'

On the edge of Winchelsea is a track, running down to the fields on the west side of the town. It is still called Dead Man's Lane, its name a testament to the horrors enacted in Winchelsea on that frightful Sunday. So many were killed that the lane was heaped with corpses that overflowed from the neighbouring St Giles's church yard where the survivors of the raid had started to bury the heaps of dead.

Many of these bodies would have been dragged from St Giles's Church itself, for the townspeople who cowered there were massacred – but not before at least two young women were raped and murdered in front of the terrified people. The names of these poor victims – and others subjected to this terrible assault – are now unknown, as are the names of the attackers. Also unknown are the reasons that turned a legitimate act of war and plunder against a declared enemy into such a barbaric and devilish assault. Clearly there was a thirst for revenge against the English who were capable of perpetrating similar ghastly acts on French civilians. The fact that the attackers and their victims were fellow Christians did nothing to check this primitive savagery. Indeed, the attackers seem to have been particularly brutal to those who took refuge in church, as if they saw this evocation of the protection of religion as an intolerable and provocative act of hypocrisy.

But killing was not enough for the French – having destroyed the people in the churches, they then seem to have set about the destruction of the churches themselves. St Giles's Church was despoiled, and perhaps

Above: *The chancel is all that remains of the once large and magnificent St Thomas's Church. The transepts are in ruins and the nave obliterated – the victims of invasion.*

seriously damaged. It seems that it was forever tainted by the terrible scenes that were enacted within it during that Sunday in 1360, and was gradually abandoned and fell into ruin. It has now been entirely obliterated. St Thomas's Church now lacks its nave while its transepts are ruins with only the chancel at the east end surviving. This destruction may be the result of later fourteenth-century raids or could, in part at least, be the work of the raiders of 1360.

While the French were squabbling over the distribution of their booty, about 300 horsemen of the Sussex county levies turned up outside the town gates. They were not strong enough to attack the raiders but the French were alarmed. More English were arriving and it was time either to fight to reach the king or to retreat. In the absence of accurate maps or information, the French were at a loss to know how exactly to find King John. When they were told by prisoners that he had been taken to Scotland (which was not true – he was still at Somerton in Somerset), they decided to return to their ships.

The retreat seems to have been a tricky business. Thomas of Walsingham wrote simply that the French 'carried away much loot and went away without any damage being done to them', but this does not seem to have been quite the case. Much looting took place, but it did not go entirely unpunished. Some French, still looting in the burning town after the main force had retreated, were cut down by the English levies,

Above: *A page from the 'Schedule of Decayed Rents' of 1363 shows that 409 properties in Winchelsea were still in ruins, with their owners unable to pay their rent to the Crown.*

while others were attacked on the beach when the French defensive formation broke up as men made for their respective ships. It was said at the time that about 300 French were killed and two ships abandoned in the retreat.

Winchelsea had been brought to its knees by invasion. A 'Schedule of Decayed Rents' for 1358, now in the Public Record Office, shows 184 properties in Winchelsea as 'waste and uninhabited'. About a third of the town was in ruins as the result of earlier French raids and the Black Death of 1348. But, as the records show, much worse was to come. The schedule drawn up in 1363 shows that 409 properties – just over half the town – were in ruins, with owners unable to pay their rent to the Crown. This was the terrible physical legacy of the raid of 1360.

Recovery was painfully slow. The schedule of 1370 shows that of the 409 properties in ruins in 1363, only thirty-six had been rebuilt. When the port started to silt up during the fifteenth century the work of physical and economic destruction started by the French accelerated, and the proud new town slowly died. By the end of the fifteenth century the southern end of the town had been abandoned, cut off from the rest by a new ditch. The haunting evidence of this dramatic decline can still be clearly seen in Winchelsea. The fields to the south of the town centre are crossed by tracks that were once broad streets, and contain strange bumps that must be the remains of cellars and foundations of long-lost houses. And within fields and spanning across a sunken lane is the mighty New Gate that once marked the southern edge of the walled town but now stands in rustic isolation.

What could have been one of England's great commercial cities is now nothing more than a few houses huddled around the gaunt remains of a once mighty church.

The undefended shore

The raid caused a sensation in England. Alarm was provoked not just because the French had managed to land and inflict such destruction but also – more worrying still – they had controlled an important town and portion of the south coast for more than twenty-four hours, without challenge. And landing in strength and coming with horses, it was obvious that the French could easily have turned their raid into a full-scale invasion. The English levies came too late to prevent mischief and were not strong enough when they did arrive to restrain or fully punish the invaders, whose losses seem to have been a consequence more of their own incompetence than of English military prowess.

The Government's response was feeble: it merely ordered that all ships should be hauled out of the water far enough to make them safe. So, it seems, there was no hope of fighting to save property from the French – the only hope was to hide it. While England's armies were triumphant in France they were clearly very weak at home. But then there was no real policy of defence. Armies were recruited for aggressive wars of conquest and fired by the prospect of pillage. By comparison, service in England offered few attractions and certainly little prospect of wealth. Worse still, the English had no coherently organized standing navy to compare with those of Castile, France, Genoa or Portugal. All the Government could do was to requisition the commercial fleets of the Cinque Ports. But by the time it managed to collect what ships it could, the ad hoc fleet of merchantmen was usually too late to play a decisive defensive role. It was to be nearly 150 years before England had a royal navy worth mentioning.

The absence of a coherent policy of defence meant that the threat of a full-scale invasion hung over England in 1385, 1386 and 1387. Each time it came to nothing, but the fear of French troops on English soil was actually realized in 1400, when a sizeable party landed to provide support to Owen Glendower's revolt in Wales and played an active role in hostilities deep in Herefordshire. The resumption of war on French soil under Henry IV and Henry V in the early fifteenth century greatly reduced the menace from the seas. Once Normandy had been invaded, captured and settled from 1415, the Channel resumed its position as the naval highway – the English lake – in the briefly reconstituted Anglo-Norman realm, providing security for England's coasts and shipping.

Even the erosion of the English advantage in the 1430s was not met with renewed French naval raids, as resources were concentrated on attacks on the English possessions within France. It was the loss of Aquitaine from 1451–3 that once again converted the Channel into the front line between the rival nations: England's first line of defence and yet her great weakness. The last French-sponsored invasion of Britain during the medieval period came in 1485 when Henry Tudor, backed by money and troops from Charles VIII of France, landed in Wales. Despite the gratitude the new Tudor dynasty owed to France, it was Henry's son – Henry VIII – who was to set in train a course of events that was to lead to virtually another 100 years of invasion-haunted war with first France and then Spain.

Chapter Three

Tudor Warfare and Defence

As the Lancastrian and Yorkist dynasties ripped each other apart during the Wars of the Roses, continental politics and invasion played an important role in the outcome. From 1461 Edward IV fostered good relations with Burgundy to counter Henry VI's marriage ties with France; it was there that Edward fled after Warwick (the Kingmaker) invaded England with French support in 1470 to restore Henry VI. Edward also used France as his base for a successful counter-invasion in 1471.

Following the deaths of Henry VI and his son Edward, Henry Tudor found himself the last 'best hope' of the Lancastrian cause, and promptly fled to Brittany. Yet his years in exile allowed him to plot his return. In 1483 he attempted to join Buckingham's abortive revolt against Richard III; and two years later, with French money and troops – albeit convicts promised freedom in return for military service – launched his own invasion. He sailed from Harfleur and landed at Milford Haven in west Wales on 8 August, and two weeks later emerged victorious from the Battle of Bosworth.

Henry's success established the Tudor dynasty and effectively ended the Wars of the Roses. But his many years as the 'pretender to the throne' left an indelible fear that his regime would one day meet the same fate that he visited on Richard III. Henry's paranoia was well founded, as first Lambert Simnel (1487) and then Perkin Warbeck (1496) launched invasions to seize his crown. Warbeck's incursion was particularly serious as it came from Scotland and was supported by the Holy Roman Emperor Maximilian. In 1497 Warbeck tried again, landing in Cornwall at the head of 3,000 troops – only to flee when Henry marched to meet him at Exeter. Warbeck was eventually captured, imprisoned and in 1499 executed.

The loss of French possessions under Henry VI, and years of internal strife, had reduced England to a lesser player on the international stage. This was the age when nations formed leagues against common enemies, and of international war, when no state could afford to stand on its own against another. France had emerged from the turmoil of the Hundred Years' War as a powerful force; its principal adversary was the Holy Roman Empire, which found staunch support from the kingdoms of Spain; and the prize they fought over was Italy. Henry VII's greatest achievement was to maintain cordial relations with all parties, although fitful French

MARCI 16
ITE IN MVDVM VNIVIRSV ETPREDICATE
EVANGELIVM OMNI CREATVRE

support for his enemies led him to favour the Habsburgs, cemented by Catherine of Aragon's marriages with his sons, first Arthur and then Henry. In 1508 the League of Cambrai brought a temporary peace in Europe, and Henry's attempt to keep England out of European conflicts would appear to have been vindicated.

This was the diplomatic world into which Henry VIII emerged on his accession in 1509; and he was determined to put England back on to the European map. Encouraged by his Spanish in-laws, and dazzled by the prize of the French crown dangled in front of him by the Pope, Henry rushed headlong into war with France. The result was a brief campaign in 1513 that revived the cross-Channel raiding traditions of the Hundred Years' War (Brighton was burnt in 1514) and secured for England the towns of Thérouanne, after a skirmish grandly called the Battle of the Spurs, and Tournai.

The venture also exposed England's Achilles heel, as James IV of Scotland took advantage of Henry's absence to launch an invasion in support of his French allies. Under Queen Catherine's direction, the Earl of Surrey met the Scottish army at Flodden in 1513 and utterly routed them in a bloody encounter, during which the Scottish king and most of his aristocracy were slain. Although the battle was a spectacular triumph – far overshadowing Henry's French exploits – it brought home the fact that England could deal with France only if the threat from the north was neutralized.

The rise of Thomas Wolsey tempered Henry's bellicose nature somewhat, as did the exorbitant cost of war – England was simply unable to afford to compete with the 'big players' of France, Spain and the Empire. During Wolsey's grip on power between 1514 and 1529, England re-entered the intricate world of continental diplomacy instead. The highlight of the period was the 'European peace' negotiated in the Treaty of London in 1519, followed in 1520 by the meeting of Henry and Francis I of France in the splendour of the Field of the Cloth of Gold. Yet Henry was always looking for an excuse to launch another French invasion, and finally got his wish in 1522 – but only after conducting a series of raids across the Scottish border in an attempt to nullify the 'Auld Alliance' first. Lessons had been learnt.

The war spluttered on with the tacit support of the Emperor Charles V; but when he defeated and captured Francis I at Pavia in 1525, the balance of power in Europe dramatically altered. Charles's vision of Europe was vastly different from Henry's, and in a double snub to his ally he refused to partition France (Henry's 'Grand Design') or marry Henry's sister Mary. The prize was Italy, and in Charles's eyes England was a willing pawn to be used when necessary.

Stung by this humiliating turn of events, Wolsey orchestrated a dramatic U-turn in English foreign policy, openly anti-Habsburg and crowned by an alliance with France in 1527. It was no coincidence that Henry chose this moment to announce his desire to divorce Catherine of Aragon, Charles's aunt. This decision brought Henry into direct confrontation not just with the Papacy, now under the control of Charles after the Sack of Rome in 1527, but also the might of the entire Habsburg dynasty, which effectively controlled the Holy Roman Empire, Spain and the Low Countries.

The divorce negotiations dragged on for two years, and ultimately cost Wolsey his life. Thereafter Henry found himself both outmanoeuvred and increasingly isolated in the international arena, and in desperation he sought, and finally obtained, French support in 1532. The stakes were raised in 1533 when the Pope threatened Henry with excommunication; in the past, the consequence of such a sentence had been international deposition and the threat of invasion. Henry rose to the bait, pressed on regardless and in 1534 broke with Rome.

Opposite: *Henry VIII in his pride and power. Through his policies and aggression, Henry was to bring England to the brink of disaster through invasion, and to launch the country on a path to military greatness.*

An early nineteenth-century view of the decisive and bloody 1513 Battle of Flodden during which the Scottish King James IV and most of his aristocracy were slain.

It is difficult to overstate the significance of this event. England had stepped outside the established international community, the protection of the Holy Roman Empire and the fellowship of Christian kings. Henry himself had been all too quick to join a Holy League when the Papacy had decreed Louis XII of France to be schismatic, gladly accepting the offer of the French crown in 1512. Now Henry had stepped into Louis's shoes, and in doing so placed England in exactly the same danger.

The declaration of peace between the Empire and France in 1539 triggered plans for a simultaneous triple invasion of England from Scotland, the Low Countries and Spain. Preparations to repel the imminent Catholic crusade were hastily set in motion. Musters were levied in each county; defensive works were strengthened in Calais and on the Scottish border; the navy was mobilized to counter the fleet that was massing at Antwerp and Boulogne to carry invasion forces over from the Low Countries; and in the south-east ditches were dug and barricades, ramparts and palisades assembled in case a landing occurred.

In the event, the invasion never materialized, and neither Francis nor Charles moved against England; but the fear and hysteria generated by the threat prompted Henry to seek an alliance with the other

The design of fortifications

During the 1530s Henry VIII initiated a castle-building campaign that was to place England in the midst of the great revolution in military architecture sweeping Europe. The previous hundred years had seen the basic principles of castle design challenged and overturned by the emergence of increasingly powerful artillery. Castles now had to withstand bombardment by guns, as well as to mount guns to fire back at attackers and, if coastal castles, to command the waters over which they presided. So castle walls had to be built lower and thicker to absorb the shock of bombardment and offer a wide terrace, or terreplein, on which guns could be mounted. These guns could either fire over the parapet of the wall, or be concealed and fire through embrasures cut into the parapet.

In late-fifteenth-century and early-sixteenth-century Europe, two approaches to fortification design emerged in the wake of the revolution in warfare brought about by the development and increasing power of gunpowder. In north Europe the tall, stone gun tower – of curved plan form, with thick tapering walls and mounting tiers of guns – seemed to be the solution. In Italy the geometric bastion – the central feature of a co-ordinated system of defence – was the preferred solution. Typically, a bastion projected beyond the walls it adjoined and mounted a large number of guns placed to fire both out towards the enemy and to fire along – and defend – the bases of the adjoining walls and neighbouring bastions. This use of mutually defensive fire became one of the characteristics of Renaissance artillery fortifications.

Leonardo da Vinci and Niccolò Machiavelli represent the southern European school of thought. They both favoured the new idea of low thick walls, while realizing that this system could lead to defensive weaknesses. Machiavelli's recommendation was the wide ditch that could be defended by caponiers – low, strong structures placed on the floor of the ditch, at right angles to and connected with the main walls of the fort, from which guns could be fired into attackers in the ditch. In 1502 Leonardo became engineer general to Cesare Borgia and pioneered a number of influential ideas. Leonardo made exposed surfaces curved, elliptical or backward-sloping to throw off enemy fire. He improved the design of gun embrasures – or casemates as they were called when fully enclosed – so that it would be more difficult for shot to enter, while vents would let out dense powder smoke. Leonardo, in his final fortification designs, brought his key ideas together to form a complete system of defence, including tiers of casemated gun positions firing one over the other. Many of these ideas were to appear in Henry VIII's gun-forts along the English coast.

During the 1520s in Italy the form and scientific advantages of the triangular or arrow-head shaped bastion, constructed of earth to better absorb the shock of bombardment and armed with artillery, were finally formulated. The triangular and well-armed bastion, projecting from curtain walls and supported and surrounded by other works, became the key element in a mutually supporting system of defence. This system meant that attacking troops could not reach the foot of bastions or curtain walls without suffering frightful losses. The triangular shape of the bastion, and the particular relationship between it and various related works, gave these Italian renaissance fortifications a very distinctive, geometrical, star-shaped form which, in essence, was dictated by the arcs of fire of the guns within the fortress.

Albrecht Dürer was a leading exponent of the northern European approach to artillery fortifications. He came up with the mighty stone-built gun tower, or *bastejas*, which would project from, and flank, a city wall. The tower, placed within the ditch, would have tapering sides and tiers of guns in casemates, with the lowest placed to fire at virtually grass-top level along the surface of the ditch. Dürer fitted his casemates with flues so that the gunners would not be hampered in their work by gunpowder smoke.

international pariahs, the Protestant powers. In particular, the Lutheran princes of Germany were approached – contact had been made as long ago as 1536 – and the result was a marriage alliance with Anne of Cleves in 1540. Although this was a disaster (the 'mare of Flanders' was quickly divorced), England's future direction had been decided.

When Charles and Francis returned to a state of war in 1542, the immediate crisis appeared to be at an end, and Henry courted imperial favour once more in the hope of reviving plans for the dismemberment of France. In 1543 he attacked Scotland, hoping to sever the 'Auld Alliance' and clear the way for higher priorities. Despite failing to achieve a decisive outcome, a continental campaign undertaken jointly with Charles was launched in 1544. Henry captured Boulogne, but Charles quickly came to terms with the French, leaving Henry totally isolated, and the cost of the expedition completely drained English resources. The tables were quickly turned, and in 1545 it was England that faced a devastating Franco-Scottish invasion.

Henry's desperate appeals for aid from the German Protestant princes fell on deaf ears, and he prepared to stand alone against enemies that threatened on at least three fronts. In the spring of 1545 England waited in daily expectation of invasion. But the country was prepared and steeled to resist the foe. Defensive armies were stationed in Kent, Essex, the West Country and along the Scottish border, and Boulogne was stoutly defended. And – most important – a new and powerful set of coastal fortifications had just been completed and the navy, also greatly strengthened, stood by in Portsmouth as the first line of defence.

The French invasion of 1545

On 3 January Francis I of France announced his intention to invade the British Isles in the summer in order to regain Boulogne and to liberate Henry VIII's subjects from the Protestant tyranny that had been imposed upon them. Francis's intentions are described in the contemporary memoirs of Martin de Bellay, 'a man of letters and a soldier', who wrote that after the failure to retake Boulogne by land attack, 'Francis… resolved on a counter stroke. He ordered a large and efficient fleet to be raised under the command of Claude d'Annebault, an experienced seamen and soldier, for the invasion of England.' This navy, according to de Bellay, consisted 'of 150 battleships, 60 decked pinnaces and 25 galleys from the Levant'.

Henry's new gun-forts along the south coast were to provide the backbone of the land defence against this invasion force, but the first – and main – bulwark against French aggression was to be Henry's new, apparently mighty, but completely untested navy. Over 12,000 English sailors were at sea in a mixture of ships in the spring of 1545 and Henry decided to exercise his new force in June by sending it on a training mission to Le Havre. This was meant to be a pre-emptive strike to wrong-foot the French, but things did not go well – the English ships were eventually chased out of the mouth of the Seine with no damage done to the French fleet. The English fleet made its way to Portsmouth where, by July, Henry had assembled a force of about 140 ships – forty of them large purpose-built warships, with the rest being requisitioned merchantmen.

On 15 July Henry moved to Portsmouth with his Privy Council to await the coming of the French, and on 18 July entertained foreign ambassadors aboard his pride and joy – his mighty warship, *Henry Grace-a-Dieu* – or more popularly the *Great Harry*. That evening the French fleet appeared off the Isle of Wight, anchoring for the night off Ryde. The next morning was windless, so Henry could do no more than draw up his ships outside Portsmouth harbour – his new floating gun platforms supported by his new stone gun towers standing along the shore line. As Henry dined with his Lord Admiral, Lord Lisle, aboard the *Great Harry*, news came that the French were attacking. While the fleet was cleared for action, Henry made for shore to establish himself in Southsea Castle – one of his newly completed gun-forts – where he could preside over the coming action.

The Battle of Portsmouth was a curious affair – an anti-climax after so many months of preparation – with the French losing their nerve and the English fleet failing to perform as well as Henry had anticipated. The French, having achieved the tricky task of assembling a large fleet off the English coast with no losses, now intended to destroy the English navy in its own waters. With that done, the French calculated that they could hold the Channel for a month while French land forces took a now isolated Boulogne.

The battle started when the French commander, Admiral d'Annebault, sent his force of twenty-five galleys against the English fleet. The attack was concentrated on the *Great Harry*, but no serious damage was done before the French squadron withdrew with English 'rowbarges' – a type of ad hoc galley – in pursuit. The wind now changed and the English fleet weighed anchor and started to sail out in pursuit of the galleys. It was now that the one event that makes the battle memorable took place. The majestic *Mary Rose* – the thirty-five-year-old veteran of numerous engagements and Henry's second largest warship – fired a broadside and then heeled over while making a turn to bring her other broadside into play. Before she could be righted the ship capsized, with dramatic speed and in full view of the king and his court standing in Southsea Castle. The general opinion, given soon after the tragedy, was that the ship was overloaded and the extra weight meant she leaned over more than was usual when making a tight turn so that water poured in through the gun ports. Within minutes, between 500 and 600 men and ninety-one much needed guns had sunk below the waves.

The English forces must have been stunned and demoralized, but the French did not attempt to capitalize on the situation. Rather than engaging the English fleet and instead of attempting to land and burn Portsmouth, the French commander slowly retreated to vent his wrath upon the Isle of Wight.

The island was attacked not simply because it was an easier target then Portsmouth. It also had the potential of acting as a springboard for an invasion of the mainland and – the French believed – could be held by them much as the English held Boulogne and Calais. D'Annebault calculated that, once taken, it would require 6,000 soldiers to hold the island with an additional 6,000 pioneers to construct fortifications. But the first task was to capture the island. It is now uncertain if the French were really committed to the idea of seizing the island and turning into a French fortress – a kind of Gibraltar off England's coast, which was only about 1,400 yards away at its nearest point, and within easy raiding distance of England's major naval dockyard at Portsmouth. It was a bold plan – probably too bold for d'Annebault – but he did order raids which, if all went well, could have resulted in long-term French occupation of the island.

Three raiding parties landed simultaneously on a front more than ten miles long – wisely, d'Annebault intended to use his superiority in numbers to divide the small number of militia on the island which would have to disperse if it was to respond to all three landings. The landing at Nettlestone Point, near Seaview, was successful. As de Bellay explains: 'The Seigneur Pierre Strosse was bidden to land below a little fort where the enemy had mounted some guns with which they assailed our galleys in flank and within which a number of Island infantry had retired. These, seeing the boldness of our men, abandoned the fort and fled southward to the shelter of a copse. Our men pursued and killed some of them, and burned surrounding habitations.'

At Bonchurch there was a similar story, with the militia being beaten off. But at Sandown the militia triumphed and drove the French back to their ships. De Bellay appears to refer to this unsuccessful action only in passing: 'In another place there landed two captains… who were both wounded in a fight with an English band that had assembled to oppose their landing.' A fourth landing – on a smaller scale and seemingly not part of d'Annebault's master plan – was also attempted. This took place at Whitecliffe Bay. De Bellay explains that a number of the 'fighting men' left on board the ships, seeing 'the countryside ablaze and the seaboard undefended, landed unobserved and without leave in a spot at a distance from their commander'. These freebooting raiders then 'scattered themselves over the country at will and with no plan of campaign'. When

Henry VIII's gun-forts

Provoked by his war with France, Henry was to build the most expensive and extensive scheme of coastal defences that England had ever seen. Most of the forts were built between 1539 and 1543 and all have a very strong family resemblance, drawing more on the north European gun-tower approach to artillery fortifications. Henry himself became passionately interested in fortress design, as he was to become in all manner of pioneering technology related to the prosecution of modern and scientific warfare. He must have picked up many current ideas during his expeditions into France and, after the Reformation of the 1530s, he had the money – confiscated from monasteries – to put these new ideas into practice.

Along the south coast, forts were built from Penzance to the Medway and Rochester with a number along the east coast – at Harwich for example and at Kingston-upon-Hull – and at Milford Haven on the Welsh coast. When possible, these forts were built on high ground and virtually all were to guard havens, ports, estuaries, inlets and bays that a French invasion might have used to disembark troops. Their purpose was not to deny the whole coast to invasion or raids, but to make it difficult for a major invasion force to be landed safely and speedily. And if the gun-forts could not prevent a landing, they were to disrupt and delay it until the local militias could be gathered – which would be done by a system of beacons and messengers – and massed to make a counter-attack.

Characteristically, these forts are centrally planned, compact in form, and feature a cylindrical central tower containing guns mounted in tiers of casemates and on the roof. The central gun tower is then protected by lower curved bastions mounting guns in casemates, firing through open embrasures or mounted on barbette platforms to fire over the top of the parapet. The forts – set in ditches – are all beautifully built of stone with thick walls, sloping parapets to deflect shots and chimney flues in casemates to remove gun smoke. They are both utilitarian and – with their fine, spare, decorative detailing – powerful and beautiful architectural creations. There is nothing else like them in Europe.

But they were not without functional faults, suggesting that their designer was unacquainted with the most up-to-date developments in fortress design, particularly in Italy. (While the king was probably involved in their design, he did employ a German military engineer, the German Stephen von Haschenperg, from 1539 until 1543 – when he was sacked for extravagance and general bad behaviour.) For example, the latest thinking preferred earth walls above stone for achieving strength, given their greater capacity to absorb the shock of shot. Also, Henry's roofs and upper gun platforms are generally not vaulted in masonry but made of timber and lead, and so vulnerable to plunging shot fired from mortars, and the curved form of the bastions meant that there was 'dead' ground around the bases of the forts that could not be swept by the fire of its guns.

However, despite his apparent shortcomings, von Haschenperg seems to have been responsible for the best and most geometrically coherent of Henry's forts. These include the three largest and strongest, built close to each other between 1539 and 1540 at Deal, Walmer and Sandown in Kent. The one at Deal – despite later alterations – remains a remarkable affair. It has a clover-leaf plan consisting of a central round tower adjoined by six smaller round bastions that rise above and within six larger semi-circular bastions, each linked by a short straight rampart. This fort had massive firepower, with locations for 145 guns on its three main levels firing through embrasures and from casemates in the bastions. In a new technological advance, guns were placed on wheeled carriages, allowing them to be loaded and moved with speed; heavy guns were placed on the roof to engage the enemy at long distance, with smaller guns for close-range work firing through the casemates. The preferred heavy gun was the culverin, firing a shot of around 18 pounds.

Von Haschenperg also probably designed the forts at Pendennis and St Mawes that adjoin each other to guard the approach to Falmouth harbour. St Mawes is a reduced version of Deal, with a tall central tower containing casemates presiding over three round bastions armed with guns firing through embrasures and through casemates. The bastions were furnished not just with generous casemates, supplied with flues to remove gun smoke, but also with lavatories so that gun crews did not have to leave their posts for long when nature called.

Opposite: *St Mawes Castle was built during the early 1540s to help protect Falmouth from French invasion.*
Below: *Deal castle – one of the largest and most impressive of Henry VIII's coastal defences. It could mount up to 145 guns.*

Warships

The fully sail-powered, heavily armed, wooden warship – in the form that was to dominate the seas until the 1840s – was conceived, in all its essentials, in the England of Henry VIII. It was to become the country's first and most effective bulwark against invasion in the centuries to come. English gunners fired faster, more accurately and more effectively than their enemies, and tactics had been developed to utilize the potential of a sailing ship's mobility. The objective now was to manoeuvre and to batter an enemy to destruction or to submission and not, as in traditional naval warfare, to come alongside an enemy ship so that soldiers could board and fight a version of a land battle while afloat.

On Henry's accession to the throne in 1509 the Royal Navy consisted of only seven ships. By 1512 it numbered nineteen, including the *Mary Rose* which, built in 1509–11, incorporated a number of new ideas such as heavy guns placed on lower gun decks and firing through gun ports. In the same year, the greatest of Henry's warships was laid down. It was a pioneering technical achievement that set a standard in the design of fighting ships and was to provide a model for years to come: the *Henry Grace-a-Dieu*.

This ship – popularly known as the *Great Harry* – was a wonder of the age. It was carvel-built (that is, without overlapping planks), had four masts and so could carry a vast spread of sail including 'topgallants' for additional speed, and displaced 1,500 tons. It contained seven or eight decks, several of which were gun decks, for the *Great Harry* is said to have carried around 185 guns. Placing the heaviest guns on the lower decks – firing in tiers through gun ports protected by hinged shutters – would keep a ship's centre of gravity low (which would help prevent it capsizing), while they would be in a good position to batter the hull of an enemy ship. The lighter guns placed on the upper decks were used to destroy enemy rigging and sailors.

The *Great Harry* was launched in 1514 and is reputed to have cost as much as £14,000 to construct. Her hitting power was truly formidable. If she fired a broadside, she would have thrown about 83,000 pounds of iron at the enemy in one mighty discharge. This was indeed a new and potent weapon: a ship designed to utilize the destructive potential of the new generation of powerful artillery, and 'armoured' – by means of thick baulks of timber laid inside her hull – to help protect her from the hitting power of similarly powerful sea monsters.

But Henry increased the potency of his navy not just by increasing the quality of his ships but also by increasing their number. Between 1509 and his death in 1547, 106 ships were added to the navy, virtually all of them intended specifically for battle around the English coast. They were an anti-invasion fleet that could also escort Henry's troops across the Channel and guard convoys taking provisions into Boulogne or Calais.

Henry's fleet deserved better results than it actually achieved. If it was never truly trounced by the French neither did it achieve a definitive victory. On the other hand, the French never managed to land a major invasion force on England's mainland, despite strenuous efforts in 1545, and this was largely thanks to the threatening presence of Henry's warships. The *Great Harry,* in particular, never fully realized its great potential. After the Battle of Portsmouth in 1545, it pursued its majestic, if ultimately futile, career beyond the reign of Henry only to fall on very hard times during the reign of Edward VI and then to burn – through an accident it is said – soon after Mary's accession to the throne in 1553. By then Henry's great creation was in decay. The Royal Navy was neglected and ships not maintained or replaced until the reign of Elizabeth when the navy – reconstituted as a fighting force – built most effectively upon the sound practices and principles established during Henry's reign. It was during the Spanish Armada battle of 1588 that, for the first time, the new tactics based on expert gunnery and manoeverability were tested, and proven, in a large-scale action.

An early nineteenth-century attempt to portray the pride of Henry VIII's navy – the Henry Grace-a-Dieu, *or* Great Harry, *launched in 1514. The ship displaced 1,500 tons and was alleged to have carried 185 guns – so it must have been far larger than this view implies.*

a body of the French reached the top of a hill, 'they were assailed by horse and foot so briskly that some were killed while others captured and the rest driven in disorder to the foot of the hill close to the shore.' According to de Bellay, the retreating raiders, reinforced by extra troops from the fleet, counter-attacked and forced the English to take refuge behind a stream where they destroyed a bridge to prevent the French crossing. This stand-off was terminated when d'Annebault, hearing of this uncoordinated action, at which no senior commander was present, ordered a retirement to the ships.

D'Annebault hoped that the sight of the island being sacked before his eyes would outrage Henry – still in Portsmouth – who would order his militia to mount a hasty counter-attack or his fleet to engage the French. If this happened, d'Annebault was confident that victory would be his. His fleet, stronger than that of the English, should triumph in combat while the superior numbers and training of his professional troops should lead to the speedy destruction of the local amateur militia forces and the occupation of the island. But Henry kept his temper and, rather than being drawn out, the English forces were ordered to retreat behind the River Yar and await reinforcements.

Artillery

From the fifteenth century, guns had been cast in bronze with cast iron used occasionally for some elements in some weapons. Cast iron was a better material for guns than cast bronze or brass, for it was stronger and could better withstand the pressure created by the explosion of the gunpowder propellant. And it was far cheaper than bronze. But manufacturing cast iron required very high temperatures, which could be achieved for small amounts of molten iron (for casting such small items as cannon balls) but were hard to reach and sustain when a large amount was required. Also, the molten iron might be flawed, for example by air bubbles – which could lead the weapon to burst without warning. However, by the early sixteenth century technical problems had been largely overcome and by the 1540s guns were cast in iron in England – particularly in the Weald of Kent and Sussex where the oak forests provided a ready supply of the vast amount of fuel required by the manufacturing process.

The ready availability of cast iron brought about a revolution in the design of guns, which were more powerful than their bronze-made equivalents and could now be manufactured in large numbers. Put simply, more guns were able to throw more weight of shot greater distances and with greater accuracy and power than ever before. This development was soon to transform the design of defences, the tactics of attack and – ultimately – to revolutionize warfare on both land and sea.

In the sixteenth century, artillery developed as two closely related but distinct families: the culverin and the cannon. The culverin family bore the characteristics of its bronze-gun ancestry. Culverins were made with barrels that were long, thin and small of calibre because they fired only a small charge of powder. But these characteristics produced remarkable results. The long barrel and small calibre made the culverin a high velocity weapon which could – if handled well – be very accurate and have a great range, up to 7,000 yards. But its shot – being relatively light at around 18 pounds – could not hit with great destructive force. The main advantage of these smaller guns was their relative lightness, which made them mobile and capable of being mounted on small craft as well as being moved easily around a fortress or battlefield.

The cannon family fully exploited the power of gunpowder. Cannon had large bores relative to their length, and so could contain large charges to fire heavy shot with great force at relatively close range – ideally of 200 yards or so. What they lost in range and accuracy, cannon gained in destructive effect. During the sixteenth and seventeenth centuries the cannon family was developed so that its massive punch was combined with the range and accuracy of the culverin family (which was to gradually become extinct during the eighteenth century).

The names and characteristics of the weapons in these two families is explained in W. Harrison's *An Historical description of the Iland of Britaine*, published in 1587. He lists the members of the Culverin family starting with the Culverin itself, which fired an 18-pound shot with a point blank range of 500 paces. Then there is the Demi-Culverin, firing a 9-pound shot with a range of 400 paces; the Saker, firing a 5-pound shot with a range of 360 paces; the Minion, firing a 4-pound shot with a range of 340 paces; the Falcon, firing a $2^1/_8$-pound shot with a range of 320 paces; the Falconet, firing a 2-pound shot with a range of 280 paces; and the Robinet, firing a 1-pound shot with a range of 280 paces. Harrison's cannon family includes the Basilisk and Cannon, both firing a 60-pound shot with a point blank range of 420 and 400 paces respectively, and the Demi-cannon, firing a 30-pound shot with a range of 400 paces.

In addition to these two families of ordnance there were also mortars (short-barrelled high-trajectory weapons for siege work), various 'Organ Guns' and 'Shrimps'. These were multiple guns comprising several small culverin-family types mounted on a single carriage. There were also small-calibre, quick-firing breech-loading swivel-guns which, getting off around nine shots a minute, were the machine-guns of their age.

This bronze culverin dating from 1542 was recovered from the wreck of the Mary Rose *in 1840. Culverins were made with barrels that were long, thin and small of calibre making it a high velocity weapon and – if handled well – very accurate.*

The type of ammunition fired by these weapons varied depending on the role it was to play. Solid round shot of stone but increasingly of cast iron was used to smash walls, timber ships and troops at long range. Hollow iron shells filled with gunpowder, and fused to explode and splinter some seconds after firing, were an innovation in the sixteenth century and generally fired by mortars. Grapeshot – a cluster of shot of about 1-inch diameter secured in a frame – was used to sweep the deck of an enemy ship or against infantry at close range (this ammunition was supplemented by case-shot or canister which was a case or can full of musket balls). Bar shot and chain shot – a pair of solid shot linked by a short iron bar or length of chain – was used to destroy a ship's sail and rigging.

This tactic worked. D'Annebault, clearly starting to feel uncomfortably exposed, decided not to continue his attack and started to search around for good reasons for quitting the island. As de Bellay explains, d'Annebault and his commanders agreed that the grand plan of taking and holding the island was too difficult a task, for the number of men it would require would not be forthcoming. And so the great opportunity within d'Annebault's grasp – an opportunity which if pursued successfully would have transformed England's relationship with France during the following centuries – was quietly abandoned.

To save face rather than to achieve any military purpose, d'Annebault decided to send some of his fleet on a raid along the Sussex coast while the abandonment of the Isle of Wight was organized. But even this did not go smoothly. The galleys wanted to take in water before sailing for Boulogne and, records de Bellay, the Chevalier d'Aux, 'a Provençal Captain of the Galleys raised in Normandy', went ashore on the island 'and climbed to the top of a hill to overlook them better'. There then followed a bloody and brutal little fight that, after more than 400 years, still has the power to shock. While on the hill d'Aux 'fell into an ambuscade of Englishmen who made him run so briskly that his men… were put to flight and deserted him. At this moment the Chevalier was struck in the knee by an arrow, which made him stumble and then on rising he was struck on the head by a bill… so severely that it beat his morion from his head and made him stumble when another blow dashed out his brains.'

While this ghastly scene was unfolding – the professional soldier pursued and hacked and beaten to death by a swarm of screaming peasants armed with cleavers – d'Aux's men continued their scamper to the shore. Here they took refuge in houses and formed a fighting line to protect the men bringing in water. Meanwhile the local barbarians were busily stripping the armour off d'Aux's butchered corpse. His death was, records de Bellay, 'a great loss to the king's service, for he was a right valiant and experienced gentleman'.

D'Annebault's raid along the Sussex coast was equally ill fortuned. On 25 July his ships appeared off Seaford and troops were sent ashore to burn the town and a mansion at Firle. But the local defence plan worked well. Beacons were lit to summon the Sussex and Kent militias while a force of around 300 local men attacked the French immediately. Chronicles state that 100 Frenchmen were killed but, by the time the militia reinforcements arrived, the raiders had made a hasty retreat. This raiding party returned to the Isle of Wight where it united with the main force which – by 28 July – had sailed out of English waters and was heading for home.

Henry VIII was delighted with the results of the action and spoke of his 'great joy that he had been able to measure his strength against that of our enemy'. This joy must have been increased when he heard that d'Annebault's forces, some of which had been disembarked at Boulogne, had failed to turn the tables against the English garrison.

A year later – in June 1546 – this war with France came to an end. Peace terms included the agreement that Boulogne was to be returned to France, but not until 1554 on the payment of two million crowns. Within a year of the peace Henry was dead, and with his death England was to move even further into the arms of the Protestant world, and direct confrontation with the rampant forces of the Habsburgs, the champions of Catholic Europe.

THE SPANISH THREAT

Mary Tudor became Queen of England in August 1553, and within a year had initiated and nurtured one of the most bloody invasions of the land in its history. This was not a military invasion as such, but its results were as tumultuous and as catastrophic as if a ruthless foreign force had landed. It was an invasion of the minds and souls of the English people, accompanied by a determination to turn them over to foreign domination and control.

Mary was a fanatical Catholic, and when she became queen it was her earnest desire to reverse her father's Reformation and bring England back into the Catholic world. But England, although only twenty years a Protestant country, did not welcome Mary's plans. This did not stop her crusade, and nor did the hostility felt by the English people for Spain – with its aim for domination in a Catholic world – prevent Mary from attempting to hand control of the English monarchy to Spain. She did this by agreeing in October 1553 to marry Prince Philip of Spain, son of the emperor Charles V. The English had been forced to accept a limited return to Catholicism but they could not tolerate being put under the heel of a Spaniard. Some powerful citizens, preferring the French to the Spanish, asked France to invade. Nothing came of this, but a rebellion broke out – led by Sir Thomas Wyatt – which aimed to stop the threatened Spanish occupation of England. The rebels, overcome by Mary's forces, were executed in hundreds.

The Spanish marriage turned out to be a political and personal disaster for Mary. Philip, who arrived in England in July 1554, found neither Mary nor the English to his liking. The English felt much the same about him and his arrogant courtiers, but Mary was distraught. After several phantom pregnancies no heir arrived, and Philip hardly helped matters by making himself as scarce as possible. After July 1557 he never returned to England again. But if the physical presence of Philip and his Spanish court in England was not as powerful as many had feared in 1553, the influence of Spanish ideas and conduct was horribly apparent. From November 1554 Mary – with the help of papal legate and former 'arch-traitor' Cardinal Reginald Pole – set about the violent imposition of Catholicism in England. The means she adopted, with hideous enthusiasm, were those of the Spanish Inquisition, with mass burnings of Protestants from 1555 and into 1558.

The so-called Armada Portrait *of Queen Elizabeth I, painted in 1588 by George Gower. It shows, at the top left, an English warship awaiting the advancing armada and, at the top right, the armada being destroyed by God through savage seas.*

The killing had to stop. Again France was approached for aid and in April 1557 Thomas Stafford landed with French troops at Scarborough in an attempt to raise the country against Mary. Nothing much was achieved and the invaders, including Stafford, were duly captured and executed. But in June 1557 France formally declared war on England and Mary's attack upon, and betrayal of, her subjects — coupled with her neglect of English fortifications and navy — were to have dismal consequences. In January 1558 Calais, the ancient English fortress port that had been the pride of previous monarchs for 210 years, was rapidly lost to French attack. The French did not attempt an invasion of England, although such an enterprise may well have succeeded given the demoralized and bitterly divided nature of English society.

Mary died in November 1558 — lamented by none, including her Spanish husband. Her legacy was dire. She had created an atmosphere of terror, intrigue and betrayal and, by attempting to make the king of Spain also the king of England, had encouraged among the English a great hatred and suspicion of Spain and of all Catholics. The consequences of these terrible years, their influence on English attitudes and behaviour, were to colour English history for generations to come.

The Spanish armada

During the early years of Elizabeth's reign, France was still regarded as the prime threat to national security, especially since the fall of Calais in 1558. The loss of England's last foothold on the opposite side of the Channel ceded a strategic naval advantage to the French, and for the first time since the raids of the Vikings the waters of the Channel and the North Sea truly were regarded as an unprotected hostile place from where invaders could appear. But from the mid-1580s Spain became the main invasion threat, and the joyous celebrations following the defeat of the Spanish Armada in 1588 showed clearly that Spain's attempt to add England to its portfolio of satellite states had been widely perceived as a very real and imminent danger.

The fear of France and then of Spain stimulated a reorganization of the navy at the start of Elizabeth's reign. The *Book of Sea Causes*, completed in March 1559, stated that the English naval capacity amounted to 22 sail, 45 convertible merchant ships and 20 supply ships, all of which required 10,600 sailors to man. It was recommended that the fleet should be increased by 50 per cent, and particular emphasis was given to medium-sized vessels (400–500 tons) that could be easily manoeuvred but retained heavy fire-power. The fleet was gradually expanded along these lines over the next few decades.

The revolt of the Calvinist states in the Netherlands was a cause of further concern for English security, and embroiled England in an overseas conflict that was to move inexorably towards confrontation with Habsburg Spain. English policy towards the Dutch was initially cool; at the inception of the revolt in 1566 the rebels were seen as a potential threat to English shipping. However, the destabilization of the region through Spain's heavy-handed and increasingly militaristic approach gave France the opportunity to make territorial gain; their intervention into Flanders raised the unpleasant prospect of the entire coastline opposite England falling under French control. In an attempt to prevent this happening, Elizabeth sanctioned an expedition of English troops into the Netherlands in 1572, with covert instructions to assist the Spanish generals if the French threat materialized.

However, Elizabeth's conventional anti-French, pro-Habsburg approach to foreign policy was quickly overtaken by external events, and England was dragged into a war with Spain through the combination of three main factors. Since England's break with Rome, religion had always played a major role in the formation of alliances; yet political realism had meant that England and the Habsburg rulers had kept on relatively peaceful, if somewhat frosty, terms, united by a common enmity towards France. Philip's accession to the Spanish throne two years after he married Queen Mary had challenged this pragmatic approach, as he was fanatically committed to the restoration of Catholicism throughout Europe. He was increasingly unable to accept a Protestant ruler of England, and actively supported plans to depose or assassinate Elizabeth in favour of her Catholic cousin, Mary Queen of Scots. Mary had been forced to abdicate in favour of her infant son (the future James I), and had sought sanctuary in England in 1568, only to be imprisoned. She remained a potent focus of Catholic ambition.

The personal enmity towards Elizabeth was given substance by Spain's growing military might across the Channel, which soon became the greatest threat to England's coastal security. The collapse of France into religious civil war necessitated its withdrawal from the Netherlands; and the English forces soon found themselves fighting alongside the Dutch rebels against the Spanish. From 1577 more and more pressure was brought to bear on Elizabeth to actively intervene on behalf of the rebels. The formation of the United

Provinces in 1579 provoked an even greater Spanish military response, and Philip threw vast resources behind an army of re-conquest led by the Duke of Parma. The assassination of the Dutch leader William of Orange in 1584 prompted desperate appeals to first France, and then England, for military support. In 1585 English troops, under the nominal leadership of the Earl of Leicester, were committed to fight against Spain on Dutch soil. This was an act of open aggression, yet the threat posed to both Elizabeth and England if the Netherlands were re-conquered was even more extreme and necessitated desperate measures.

As head of one of the few solvent states in Western Europe, Elizabeth was extremely concerned about the exhaustive costs of deploying English troops overseas in a war of attrition. Yet finance was an even greater problem for Philip, reliant as he was on New World revenue to bankroll his military schemes. Silver imported from his South American mines was used as collateral to secure loans from European finance houses, arranged at increasingly high rates of interest that Philip struggled to repay. Elizabeth's seizure of borrowed Spanish treasure bound for the Netherlands in 1569 caused a major diplomatic incident, and thereafter English privateering in the New World not only gained bullion for the English Crown but also seriously undermined Spanish ability to raise new loans. By attacking the treasure lanes, England was effectively limiting Spain's ability to wage war in Europe. In particular, Sir Francis Drake's raid on Panama in 1572–3 and subsequent voyage in 1577–80 damaged Spanish naval prestige while providing around £160,000 for the English treasury – the equivalent of a parliamentary subsidy. A more devastating direct attack on Spanish bases in the West Indies in 1585–6 not only saw Spanish ordnance fall into English hands, but also made it virtually impossible for Philip to secure new lines of credit.

The concentration of Spanish forces in the Netherlands may have been a cause for discomfort, but it was only after 1582 that Philip began to seriously consider plans to invade England. Any attempt required control of the Channel; the concentration of Habsburg naval power had already shifted from the Mediterranean to the Atlantic after the defeat of the Turks at the Battle of Lepanto in 1571, and was assisted by Philip's annexation of Portugal in 1580 which secured Atlantic bases on the Iberian peninsula. Finally, the annihilation of the French fleet by the Spanish Admiral the Marquess de Santa Cruz at Terceira in 1582 removed the last obstacle to Spanish plans for a direct attack on the English coast.

Philip had sought papal backing for the 'enterprise of England' as early as 1585, when initial plans for an invasion of England were masterminded by Santa Cruz. He presented a scheme to invade directly from Spain, shipping 85,000 troops in 200 flat-bottomed boats with an escort of 556 warships. However, the cost of such an exercise was prohibitive, and in 1586 the Spanish ambassador in Paris, Mendoza, proposed an alternative plan that would exploit England's vulnerable northern border. A small expedition would land in Scotland and march south, inciting Catholic risings against Elizabeth with the promise of the installation of Mary Queen of Scots as the new queen.

The plan was not adopted, as Philip favoured the use of the existing force in the Netherlands to batter England into submission, thus cutting off the supply of troops and money to his rebellious Dutch subjects. Additionally, Mary's execution in February 1587 wrecked Philip's plans to co-ordinate a popular rising from the English Catholics. Therefore Santa Cruz proposed an invasion fleet only slightly smaller than before, with a transport capacity for 60,000 troops, of which 30,000 were to be drawn from Parma's forces in the Netherlands. In December 1586 Pope Sixtus V had agreed to pay a million crowns towards the invasion; but only once Spanish troops actually landed in England. This was by no means guaranteed; a drawback in Santa Cruz's plan was that the Spanish forces were required to rendezvous at sea in unfamiliar and hostile waters, without a secure deep-water port in which to shelter the huge Spanish galleons. Similarly, Parma opposed any weakening of the Spanish position in the Netherlands, which he felt should be Spain's prime objective.

The power of maps

A potent weapon in the defence of Tudor England was the newfangled art of map-making. Accurate military mapping had started in England in the late 1530s. Henry VIII, threatened by French invasion, used the riches he had gleaned from the dissolution of the monasteries to employ expert – but very expensive – German cartographers. In line with progressive thinking, a survey of the threatened coastline was commissioned, to locate vulnerable spots where an enemy might land and to identify locations where forts should best be built and warning beacons sited.

The information contained by accurate maps gave Henry a greater power of control by providing direct and detailed information about large parts of the kingdom. Maps therefore allowed rulers to make, or at least be involved in, important decisions about anti-invasion plans.

Yet the new 'technology' was not without risks. Cartographers were very specialized craftsmen, and so important that they were courted by rival monarchs and were almost above the law. This made them potentially very dangerous, as they carried with them visual knowledge of a land. If a map-maker changed employment, he could do great damage to his former master by revealing the secrets of his country to an enemy. Accurate maps at this time were not only rare but also important top-secret state documents. They could be vital in defence against invasion, but could also be a virtual passport for an invader, showing likely landing places and identifying defences.

A detail of a map, produced for Henry VIII in 1538, shows the coast around Falmouth. This was an invasion hot-spot and, with the use of this map, likely landing sites could be identified and anti-invasion fortifications positioned for maximum effect. The newly-completed St Mawes and Pendennis castles are shown.

Tudor espionage and Mary Queen of Scots

As a leading Protestant power, England was from the 1540s vulnerable to the complex intrigues of Europe's Catholic states. Since 1538, when Pope Paul III excommunicated King Henry VIII, English Catholics had become – potentially – the enemy within. The arrival in England of Mary Queen of Scots in 1568 was a cause of great concern to the Government. As Elizabeth's natural successor, Mary quickly became the centre of Catholic schemes to place her on the throne, planned with the tacit approval of overseas powers. The threat prompted William Cecil, later Lord Burghley, to establish an intelligence network in a desperate attempt to keep one step ahead of the unseen enemy.

Cecil's embryonic secret service was entrusted to Sir Francis Walsingham, who developed a network of spies, informants, infiltrators and double-agents, and was dedicated to the task of finding incriminating evidence against Mary. His first step was to isolate her from her allies on the continent, who had been corresponding in cipher via letters passed by the French ambassador. Once she had been moved to Chartley in Staffordshire, Walsingham decided to establish a line of communication that only he could control. It is at this point that Gilbert Gifford became instrumental to his plans; his interception of Gifford's letters provides a rare insight into the shadowy world of Tudor espionage.

Gifford had first come to Walsingham's attention in the early 1580s via intercepted letters to his kinsmen, a prominent Catholic family in Staffordshire; and it is likely that he had been feeding information to Walsingham while resident at the Catholic college at Rheims. In 1585 Gifford was able to win the trust of Thomas Morgan, Mary's agent and chief correspondent in France, and in December agreed to return to England on Morgan's behalf in an attempt to re-establish links with Mary via the ambassador. However, Gifford was 'arrested' on his arrival at Rye and brought to Walsingham's agent and decipherer Thomas Phelippes, where he was entertained as a foreigner under the pseudonym 'Nicholas Cornelius'.

Walsingham, Phelippes and Gifford then set up a simple yet effective line of communication to Mary from her agents abroad. Beer was to be delivered to Mary's household at Chartley from Burton; but the casks would contain letters to Mary from her friends hidden in a box inserted via the bunghole. Gifford's role was to collect the letters from the French embassy, pass them to Phelippes who would attempt to crack the code (the skill of 'deciphering') and then pass them back to Gifford, who would deliver them to the brewer – 'the honest man'. Showing the hallmark of a true spymaster, Walsingham then arranged for another agent, Paulet, to recheck the letters after Gifford had handed them back to ensure no additional material had been added. This was a sensible precaution; Gifford admitted to Morgan in 1586 that he was in league with Walsingham, but with the intention of serving the Catholic cause, and appeared to have been passing English secrets to the exiles in France.

However, Walsingham's plan was a success, and by August 1586 he had obtained sufficient details to unmask the Babington conspiracy (so called after Anthony Babington, one of the instigators), which centred on an invasion financed by Spain coupled with the assassination of Elizabeth. Mary's involvement in the affair was undeniable, and she was duly executed on 18 February 1587.

Officially, Gifford was declared to be one of the conspirators, and he fled to France on the pretence that he was in danger from the English authorities. Unfortunately his erstwhile friends on the continent had discovered his double role and, branded a traitor, he was thrown into a French jail with his life in jeopardy. Nevertheless, Gifford appears to have continued practising espionage on Walsingham's behalf from his cell – prisons were a remarkably good place to make contacts with enemies of the state – but despite promises of aid and a pension in England when free, Gifford never regained his liberty and died in 1590.

A page of ciphers used by Sir Francis Walsingham and his team of spies in 1587 to send coded messages intended to entrap Mary Queen of Scots in acts of treason against Elizabeth. The symbol – or cipher – for Gilbert Gifford is shown next to his name (bottom right).

In the year of Mary's death, Walsingham also recorded some ideas on 'a plot for intelligence out of Spain' – in effect, the model for a modern intelligence collection plan. It included 'special operations', a disinformation section and the promotion of economic warfare. A key component of Walsingham's espionage system was England's ambassadors resident in the countries posing the greatest threats. These men were to make use of 'diplomatic immunity' to gather information from local sources and secretly send it home. The main problem with this regular abuse of hospitality was that England hosted foreign embassies who were all playing a similar game.

The reliability of these 'official' secret agents could be somewhat dubious. Sir Edward Stafford, English ambassador to Paris when fears of invasion were at their height in the 1580s, unquestionably provided Walsingham with useful intelligence on Spanish plans; the only drawback was that Stafford seems to have been passing English secrets the other way as well. Stafford's claim that this was a pretext to win the enemy's confidence did not wholly convince Walsingham, who used him to unwittingly carry false information to the agents of the King of Spain. Overall, there is no doubt that Walsingham saved Elizabeth from assassination, and his work to delay the sailing of the Armada and to discover its strength and plans made a significant contribution to its defeat.

In the event, the news that the bases in the West Indies required urgent refortification and supply of guns and shot after Drake's raids diverted necessary equipment away from the immediate theatre of war. Drake then conducted an offensive raid into Cadiz harbour in the spring of 1587, where a large section of the Spanish armada was assembling. This episode severely limited the scale and probable success of the invasion attempt, as (according to Drake's report) thirty-seven ships were burnt or destroyed – including twenty-three warships and Santa Cruz's flagship – along with valuable containers for food and water supplies. Replacement barrels made from green wood were eventually used, with the result that a sizeable proportion of the provisions had rotted by the time the fleet had reached the Channel.

Peace negotiations had been attempted at various points since 1585, but increased in frequency throughout 1587 and 1588; yet it is clear that Spain viewed the talks as a means to gain more time to continue preparations. England similarly garnered information on the progress of the Spanish invasion plans from a network of spies and informants, and also used the time to make contingency plans against the doomsday scenario of a Spanish army managing to land in England. Various groups of key maritime counties were placed under the command of Lord-Lieutenants, responsible for organizing the defence of each area. In February 1588 Elizabeth's council formed a special sub-committee with responsibility for overall home defence, which calculated the total cost to be in the region of £250,000. Sir Francis Walsingham estimated that a maximum of 26,000 foot soldiers could be raised to repel an initial land-based attack, with another 24,000 reserved for the protection of the Queen, who famously and defiantly told her troops assembled at Tilbury of the 'foul scorn' she felt for 'Parma or Spain, or any prince of Europe [who] should dare to invade the borders of my realm'.

While the numbers involved would appear to be impressive, it was largely a paper force, never put to the test and totally without experience – a complete contrast to the battle-hardened soldiers under the command of the Duke of Parma across the Channel. A heavy burden was therefore placed on the English navy to prevent the armada from making its rendezvous with Parma's troops and escorting them across the Channel. Despite Drake's raid in 1587, the armada was able to reach sufficient strength under the command of the Duke of Medina-Sidonia (Santa Cruz had died in February 1588) – a soldier who by his own admission was inexperienced in naval affairs. By May 1588, 128 ships had been assembled, containing 20 galleons, 4 galleases and 4 large and heavily armed merchant ships, supported by a further 40 armed merchantmen; most of these were larger than England's biggest vessels and consequently less manoeuvrable and more vulnerable to a fast-moving attacker. A contemporary list details the grand scale of the operation: 8,350 sailors and 2,080 galley slaves; 19,290 soldiers; 2,630 large guns to fire 123,790 cannonballs. Although the tonnage was about the same as the defending English fleet, and Parma's army in the Netherlands had been reduced to only 19,000 (as opposed to the original 30,000), the venture still posed a formidable threat to England.

The armada set sail from Lisbon on 20 May, arriving at Corunna for repairs before making its way towards the Channel in the second week of July. The English navy, consisting of 197 vessels, had been split, with the bulk under the command of Lord Howard of Effingham – with Drake as his second-in-command – stationed at Plymouth in readiness for an pre-emptive attack on the armada before it reached the Channel. The remainder of the English naval force was held in readiness off the Downs under the command of Lord Henry Seymour. However, Effingham had been prevented from launching his raid by unfavourable winds, which swept the armada into English waters on 19 July. With England's doom at hand, initial resistance was offered on 21 July. Effingham's fleet of smaller, faster and more manoeuvrable vessels was able to gain the tactical initiative by working its way windward of the larger galleons of the Spaniards and harassing them with long-range fire. This fire inflicted heavy casualties on the packed decks of the Spanish ships but only seriously damaged one

A letter from Sir Francis Drake to Queen Elizabeth I announces the defeat of the Spanish Armada.

galleon – the *San Salvador* – which was abandoned after suffering a massive explosion and later captured.

The Spaniards maintained a tight crescent formation as they sailed through the Channel and for the next three days the English fleet shadowed them, firing broadsides and keeping out of grappling range to avoid ship-to-ship fighting, the tactic preferred by the much larger galleons packed with troops. A general engagement was fought off Portland Bill, with several of the biggest Spanish warships rendered ineffective, and more damage was inflicted off the Isle of Wight on 25 July. Yet with both sides running low on ammunition, the armada managed to battle its way to Calais by 27 July, where it waited to meet Parma's army. Despite its losses and its failure to destroy any English ships, the armada had – by fighting its way to its rendezvous point – gained a tactical victory.

At this stage of the campaign, England's fate still hung very much in the balance. Despite its losses, the armada was still capable of fulfilling its prime objective by acting as an escort for the flotilla of flat-bottomed boats upon which the bulk of the invasion army would embark. Rejoined by Seymour's squadron, Effingham decided that the only way to prevent a landing in England was to upset the Spanish embarkation preparations; in any case, English supplies were running low and a blockade could not be maintained for long. With time on the Spaniards' side, it was decided to send fire-ships into the harbour at Calais in the hope of causing as much damage as possible while forcing the armada to sail out, thus giving the English fleet a chance to re-engage. On the night of 28 July, eight sizeable ships were fully rigged, coated with pitch and armed with guns loaded and primed. The ships were then set ablaze just before midnight and placed on a direct course for the armada.

Although Medina-Sidonia had made preparations for just such an attack, his protective screen of small boats was hopelessly inadequate for the task of grappling much larger vessels and dragging them aside. Two fire-ships were deflected, but the remaining six – billowing flames and with their heated cannon firing-off – had the desired effect. In panic, the captains of the armada cut their anchor ropes and fled, dispersing without formation into the clutches of the waiting English navy off Gravelines. Throughout the following day, the Spanish fleet – dispersed so its ships could not offer each other mutual protection – was driven along the Channel and into unknown waters, where many were holed, driven ashore or ran aground in the shallows. Without ammunition, supplies or any safe port in which to make repairs or regroup, Medina-Sidonia was forced to abandon the venture. He was left with no option but to make a hazardous voyage home around the coasts of Scotland and Ireland, where many more vessels were lost by being blown on to hostile and rocky shores or engulfed by huge seas. By the time the armada straggled home, forty-four great ships had been lost, with the majority of the remainder in no further state to sail, and around 15,000 men had perished.

The English were unable to exploit their victory off Gravelines, as they too had run out of shot. With Seymour left behind to make sure Parma did not embark his land troops, a small squadron pursued the armada as it made its way north, ensuring that no landing was effected in Scotland.

The greatest menace for over 500 years had been vanquished but, in 1588, this victory appeared only temporary.

Opposite top: The armada is attacked off Gravelines by English ships. This Dutch print, dating from the seventeenth century, shows the mêlée to be more confused and close-range than it was and exaggerates the number of Spanish ships sunk during combat.

Opposite bottom: A cartoon-like contemporary English map shows the early advance of the armada along the Channel. On the left, the action off Portland Bill is depicted while, on the right, the armada – in its defensive crescent formation – makes for Calais with the English ships in close pursuit.

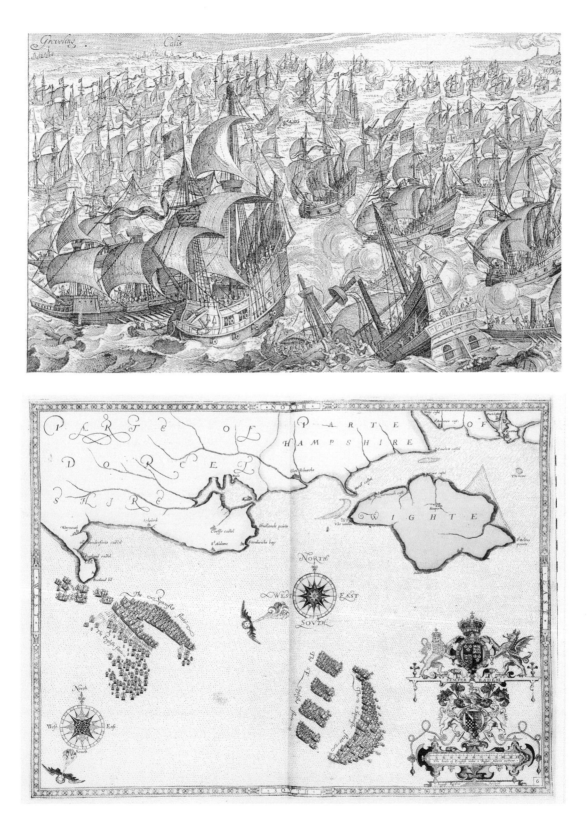

The molestation of Mousehole

The Spaniards came back in 1595. They still wanted to humiliate and even conquer England and in 1590, when Spain occupied Blavet in Brittany, Spain secured an excellent base from which to harry the south-west of England. So the quiet fishing village of Mousehole, not far from Land's End in Cornwall, became an unlikely theatre of war.

A Spanish raiding party appeared off Mousehole at sunrise on the morning of Wednesday 23 July 1595. It consisted of four galleys – ships powered by banks of oars as well as by sails. They were fast and capable of manoeuvring close in-shore and so ideal vessels for a quick raid along a rocky shoreline. As well as sailors and galley slaves, the small fleet carried 200–400 veteran troops with a number of experienced officers including Captain Richard Burley, a Dorset recusant who was, no doubt, there as translator and adviser. The commander of the Spanish expedition was Don Carlos de Amezola. He wrote a detailed account of the raid, as did a contemporary English chronicler, Richard Carew. Together these accounts – both in their similarities and in their differences– tell a fascinating and revealing tale.

The raid had several specific aims. Amezola states that one was to harry passing English shipping with the hope of regaining Spanish treasure and cargo ships captured by the English off Pernambuco, Brazil. In addition the Spanish hoped the action would delay Sir Francis Drake's impending expedition against Panama. More generally, the raid was intended to do the King of Spain's enemies some harm – to 'spoil the weak places of the realm' as prisoners taken during the raid were told. There was also a bigger – if somewhat tentative – aim: to seize and hold a base in enemy territory which could be used as a launch pad for raids and act as a powerful bargaining tool in any subsequent negotiations.

The seizure of a part of England had tempted the Spaniards since the 1580s. Cornwall was particularly attractive since it was virtually surrounded by sea and could, the Spanish fancied, be seized and held with relative ease. Also the Spaniards believed that many of the inhabitants of Cornwall would be delighted to be liberated from the Protestant faith and could be quickly and happily returned to their old Catholic ways. The Spaniards knew that Cornwall had risen in revolt 50 years earlier to resist the imposition of the new Anglican book of Common Prayer and as late as 1604, in a report made to the Crown, Spanish analysts remained in support of the view of 'certain Englishmen' that a third of the country was still Catholic.

This mini-crusade at Mousehole started on a rocky beach a few hundred yards to the west of the town's harbour. Here, records Amezola, 'with great dispatch the infantry were put ashore' and quickly climbed a nearby hill in order to gain a commanding view of the country. The lead party was under the command of Don Leon Dezpeleta while Sergeant-Major Juan de Arnica was 'the first to go ashore in that kingdom'. The total force landed, according to Amezola, was 400 men including troops bearing firearms – harquebusiers – and pikemen. Carew records that 200 Spaniards took part in the landing.

The inhabitants spotted the Spaniards before they landed, but there was no resistance to the landing. What could a handful of fishermen do against a large body of well-armed professional soldiers?

Having secured Mousehole, the Spaniards – behaving just as Spaniards were supposed to behave – marched in military order arrogantly around the town. Meanwhile the galleys came in close to land, with their bows pointing inshore. The guns, located in the bows, were then fired and a bombardment of the defenceless town commenced. The reason for this violence is unclear but it seems to have been a means of achieving the traditional aim of channel raiders: to terrify the population and devastate the town. As Amezola put it, 'the shot struck the houses and at the sight of this the inhabitants fled, so that our men had the opportunity to set fire to the town, which must have more than two hundred houses.'

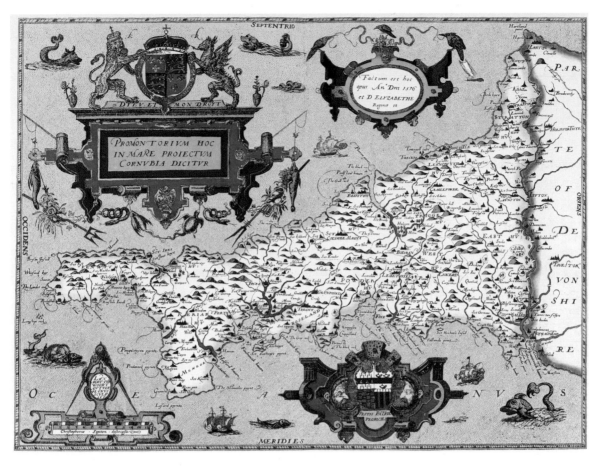

An Elizabethan map of Cornwall shows its exposed and island-like shape that made it a tempting prospect for invaders who could use the moat-like River Tamar to defend their conquest from English counter-attack.

But, it seems, at least one man did not flee. He was the local squire, Jenkin Keigwin, and he lived in the best house in town, a substantial stone-built mansion. Keigwin may have put up a fight against the marauding groups of Spaniards torching the town. If so, he was successful in the defence of his property because his was the only house to survive the Spanish incendiaries and stands to this day. But he died in the process – legend says hit by a shot which has been preserved in the house ever since. The shot reveals something about the way in which Keigwin died. It is made of cast-iron, weighs about 3 pounds and has a 3-inch diameter. If it is authentic – and it is certainly the type of shot the Spaniards would have used – then it would have been fired from a small culverin-type gun called a Minion or a Falcon. But even these small guns weighed around half a ton and were too heavy to be landed hastily. So if Keigwin was killed by this shot then it came from a gun mounted on a galley and fired from some distance away. Given the inaccuracy of such weapons, this could not have been an aimed shot but a chance hit scored during the general bombardment. Perhaps it was out of respect for Keigwin's dogged defence of his house that ended in his almost accidental death that the Spaniards spared a building that they clearly had it in their power to destroy.

That the Spaniards killed Keigwin, either accidentally or on purpose, there can be little doubt. The burial register for the parish church at nearby Paul survives, and in it is an entry recording that 'Jenkin Keiguin of

The sixteenth-century Mousehole home of Jenkin Keigwin as it was in the late nineteenth century. It was the only house of substance to survive the Spanish attack on the town and Keigwin died in the process of saving it.

Mouwsholl being kild by the Spaniards was buried the July 24 1595'. This was the day after his death, while the Spanish were still in possession of the town. Three other victims of the Spaniards are named in the register: John Pearce, also buried on the 24th; Jacobus de Newlen 'occisus fuit per inimicos et sepulto est 26th die Juli' (killed by enemies and buried here on the 26th July); and Teck Cornall, who suffered a 'similar' fate and was also buried on the 26th.

But why did Jenkin Keigwin fight so hard to defend his house? There is a clue to this question surviving inside the building. The house has now been much altered but enough survives to show that it must have been an elegant and fashionable home in the 1590s. There are the remains of a barrel-vaulted room on the first floor and one ambitious stone fire surround – and it is on this fire surround that the clue can be found. On the right-hand corner is a strange carved motif, which appears to show a barrel set within a pointed frame. It is a rebus – an enigmatic visual pun upon a word or name. The barrel, or keg, is set within a pointed arch or window. And thus the name is expressed: keg and window or Keigwin. The rebus was a piece of wit that appealed greatly to the late medieval and Tudor mind and this is clearly an ancestral home – a signed piece clearly worth fighting for, even dying for.

While Mousehole was being bombarded and Keigwin was fighting for his home, a second party of Spaniards had struck inland. This group, the vanguard of the raid, consisted of the toughest and roughest elements of the expedition. As Carew put it, this party was made up 'of their basest people'. When they reached the parish church at Paul, half a mile inland, they promptly started to sack it. It was a bloody and savage business. Amezola described what happened: 'in the surrounding hamlets we burned a mosque, with a solid tower, in which a lot of people had taken shelter'. As well as these people there was also in the church what Amezola describes as 'a horse carved in wood and greatly embellished, serving as an idol, worshipped by the people'.

The description of the church as a mosque is revealing. The Spanish invaders saw the Protestant English as heathens – like the Muslims whom the Spaniards had battled for centuries – and this church was a church no longer in Spanish eyes because it had been desecrated by fifty years of Protestant worship. This was a Holy War, with all the savagery, bigotry, fanaticism and misunderstanding that disfigure such enterprises. The wooden horse was probably no more than a hobby-horse, which was used as an innocent prop in religious festivals, or during village fairs.

But the church was not completely destroyed. The timber roof was burnt off but the tower and the columns in the nave survived, and it must be assumed that the people taking shelter in the church were spared because, according to the parish register, there was no mass burial. However, in his account of the raid Amezola claims that fifty English were killed with others carried away as prisoners. There may have been more than four deaths with, for varied reasons, burials taking place later in more distant parishes. But it is hard to believe that fifty or so people could have died or disappeared without their fate being mentioned in contemporary records.

After attacking Mousehole, the galleys sailed around the headland into Mount's Bay. They now, it seemed, had Newlyn and Penzance at their mercy. But the local militia – by now fully alerted and mustered – decided to make a stand. When Spanish troops came ashore, landing on the broad beach, they faced a body of armed militia gathered by the local grandee Sir Francis Godolphin, who was Deputy Lieutenant of Cornwall and responsible for its defence. The Spanish stated that the English numbered 1,200, but half that number is probably nearer the mark with the odds about two to one against the Spaniards. The militia attacked with some spirit across the sands and the Spaniards appeared to be in trouble. But then the Spanish soldiers displayed their professionalism. They maintained their discipline, kept close formation and started to march around the militia – outflanking them, cutting them off from the safety of the land and threatening to encircle them. At the same time the artillery in the galleys started to throw shot into the militia formations and Spanish musketeers attacked their flank. These were classic military tactics: bombardment to disorder the enemy ranks coupled with aggressive envelopment.

The part-time soldiers could not take it and Godolphin ordered a retreat to Penzance that quickly turned into a rout despite the fact that no casualties had been suffered. The Spaniards then advanced on Penzance; Godolphin attempted to rally his troops but they again fled. The town was then set ablaze.

Curiously, St Mary's Church in Penzance was – unlike the church at Paul – spared from destruction. It seems that Burley, the English Catholic guiding the Spaniards, pleaded for St Mary because it was 'a place in which mass had once been said'. But this was also true of Paul church. Perhaps it was the dedication to St Mary, the most Catholic of figures, that saved it. But the Spaniards would not celebrate mass in the church – it had been defiled by years of Protestant worship. Instead Brother Domingo Martinez celebrated mass – a Victory Mass on St Dominic's Day – on an open-air field altar within sight of the enemy.

The raid was over, and as Godolphin made a cautious return to Penzance – now accompanied by numerous reinforcements – the Spaniards boarded their galleys and slowly pulled out to sea.

The raid had major repercussions in England. All knew that Spanish invasion was still a possibility and what really worried the Government was that this action was not just a raid but a reconnaissance in force for a full-scale Spanish invasion. If this was the case then the raiders of Mousehole had certainly found not just a weak link in the English defences, but a gaping great hole. One embarrassing fact revealed by the raid was that the battery mounted on St Michael's Mount – the fortified rocky island that commands St Michael's Bay – was unable to engage the enemy because the gunners had little powder and were on strike in protest against low wages.

The Spanish triumph at Mousehole and the bay shamed and greatly alarmed the English authorities. How, after years of anti-invasion preparation and training of local militia, could the Spanish land, do so much damage, and get away with no casualties? The Government appears to have got into something of a panic, and soon after the Mousehole incident Queen Elizabeth told her leading captains, Drake and Hawkins, to be back in England in time for an anticipated Spanish invasion attempt next summer. Elizabeth's intelligence service was good, for the Spaniards did indeed try for Ireland in October 1596 but were beaten back by the weather.

However, the immediate response to the fiasco was to blame the natives. Godolphin upbraided the people of Mousehole for their lack of vigilance. Sir Nicholas Clifford, head of the relieving force that arrived too late to engage the Spaniards, stated that 'Penzance, had the people stood with Godolphin … had been saved, but the common sort utterly forsook him.' Hannibal Vyvyan, Governor of nearby St Mawes Castle, wrote of the 'Cornishmen's infamous cowardice', while Richard Carew – still smarting about the 'disgrace of these people' when writing six years after the raid – did concede that they were 'very meanly weaponed' with no idea what to do when the Spaniards landed for they were 'a people unprepared against accidents through our long-continued peace'.

Unlike Penzance and Newlyn, Mousehole never really recovered from the raid. After 1595 nothing more is heard of its chapel, fairs, markets or status as a borough. It was – and remains – a sad and diminished victim of an invasion that is still mourned in Mousehole to this day.

CHAPTER FIVE

THE DUTCH WAR

In March 1603 one of the great and traditional highways of invasion into England was closed. With the accession of King James VI of Scotland to the English throne as James I, the border with Scotland was, it seemed, finally secured. Now if an enemy came, he could attack only from the open sea – and James also secured the seas around Britain. In the summer of 1604 peace was made with Spain after nearly twenty years of warfare.

The new reign had certainly started well. But peace can have a pernicious effect. The navy was neglected, ports and royal dockyards went into decline, and James – who had an intense horror of warfare and firearms – let the militia movement decay. So when the king died in March 1625, Britain was not only once again at war with Spain (a consequence of a grossly mismanaged attempt to unite the Spanish and British monarchies through marriage) but also in a much weaker military state than when peace had been made twenty years earlier.

However, the real threat to Britain in the early seventeenth century came not from Spain but from the new Protestant power and trade rival: Holland. Before this rivalry could come to a head, England was plunged into the turmoil of the Civil War. Nearly a decade of warfare meant that by the early 1650s England had one of the most experienced – and arguably the best – armies and navies in the world. This was manifest when, during the years of the Commonwealth, English arms triumphed over all who tried to oppose the will of the new Republican government.

The Dutch, when hostilities broke out with England in 1652, met their match in the person of the Commonwealth Admiral Robert Blake. A series of naval engagements culminated in July 1653 with the resounding English victory in the First Battle of Texel when at least fourteen Dutch ships were lost and 4,000 Dutchmen – including their great Admiral Trompe – were killed. The England of the Commonwealth was triumphant on the seas, pursued an almost imperial policy in America and the West Indies and was able in October 1655 to view with disdain a Spanish declaration of war. When the restoration of the Stuart dynasty took place in 1660 England had enjoyed a decade of world power and prestige. The violence and disruption of the civil war were already a distant memory, and an empire of great potential wealth was being built up.

Samuel Pepys, a witness and reporter of the chaotic and desperate response in London to the Dutch raid of 1667 along the River Medway. 'All our hearts ake,' groaned Pepys on 12 June, 'I do fear so much that the whole kingdom is undone … God knows what disorders we may fall into.'

But before the new decade was half over, the country – fatally and speedily weakened by the corruption and incompetence of the new Stuart court – found itself at war once again with an old foe. And this time England was terrifyingly ill-equipped for a war that was to cause one of the greatest panics in the nation's history.

War with the Dutch was inevitable – the result of a power struggle between two competing nations for influence and trade thousands of miles away. War, when it threatened, was a popular prospect in England. As Samuel Pepys observed in his diary for 1664, most of the court, including the Duke of York, was 'mad for a Dutch war', and the City shared the same view.

On 22 February 1665 England declared war on Holland and the prospects seemed good when the English won the opening engagement – the Battle of Lowestoft – on 3 June. But things soon started to go wrong for the English. By 11 December Pepys felt obliged to observe in his diary that all 'goes very ill, by reason of lack of money'.

In February the next year, England declared war against France – an action that could only undermine its efforts against the Dutch, as was revealed in mid-June 1666 when the Dutch won the bloody Four Days Battle. In early August the English raided Holland and, having destroyed a large fleet of merchant ships, landed

Aphra Behn – femme fatale

A striking manifestation of national decline brought by the Restoration was the English espionage service, which had been the most efficient in Europe during the Tudor period and the Commonwealth of the 1650s. Spending was cut back and so, with resources in a state of collapse, the service fell into chaos. An insight into the ramshackle espionage service during the reign of Charles II is offered by Aphra Behn's brief and inglorious career as a special agent.

Behn, the first woman to earn her living as a professional writer in England, was approached by Charles II's spymaster, Lord Arlington, to undertake a mission to Antwerp. She was to spy on William Scot, a Republican soldier in the pay of the Dutch and in league with other English exiles. Theoretically, Scot had been working for Arlington, but had betrayed two English agents to the Dutch and could no longer be relied upon. Amid fears of further Dutch hostility, Arlington was desperate for accurate information.

The sting lay in the fact that Behn had been romantically involved with Scot, and was to employ her feminine wiles to re-establish contact with him, discover the extent of his knowledge of Dutch affairs and attempt to win him back to the Royalist cause. For the purposes of correspondence, Behn was given the codename 'Astrea' and Scot was to be referred to as 'Celadon'.

Behn travelled to Antwerp in 1666 and established contact with Scot. The mission was not a great success. She began to run out of money, revealed much of her mission to other agents, and was unable to persuade Scot to meet her in Antwerp more than three times. Even then, Scot's 'intelligence' hardly warranted such a grand description, and probably added little to the information that Arlington's other agents were supplying. Nevertheless, Behn was able to pass news that the Dutch planned to attack England with a proposed landing at Harwich and a blockade of the Thames. However, the English authorities appear to have lost confidence in her and – with an inefficiency typical of the Stuart secret service – what useful information Behn did gather was not properly followed up.

Behn's mission was soon terminated. She returned home to a debtors' prison because her adventures abroad had exhausted her slender resources. Decently, Arlington bought her liberty. A worse fate awaited Scot; his life as a double agent was exposed to the Dutch and he simply 'disappeared'. And the next year – 1667 – the Dutch did attack the region of the Thames Estuary and Harwich. But Behn's warning had been in vain.

and burnt a small undefended town called Schelling. This raid, which inflicted an estimated £1 million worth of damage, infuriated the Dutch who saw the Great Fire of London of the following month as divine retribution.

The financial scandals that dogged Charles II, his court and Government weakened the navy at this most crucial time. Underfunded, the navy lacked material and men and in consequence its morale plummeted. Pepys noted in his diary of 23 September 1666 that the Dutch war had cost in two years £3.2 million, of which 'above £900,000' was still owed. Typical of things to come had been the mass walk-out of rope makers in the summer of 1665 when, in Portsmouth, dockyard workers were not paid their wages. Sailors were treated equally badly. This loss of resolve due to corruption, incompetence and gross financial mismanagement during a period of war was to have catastrophic consequences. In Holland things were very different. A well-conceived plan of attack was worked out. The Dutch wanted to end the crippling war but reckoned that the best terms would come after a significant victory. A tax was raised to finance the fitting out of a strong fleet and a search started for English deserters or for Cromwellian refugees – die-hard English Republicans – who knew the waters of the Thames.

The first Dutch move was a minor diversionary raid in April to the Firth of Forth. Nothing much developed from this action, but it did draw English attention away from the Dutch forces being gathered near the island of Texel. Tension mounted as reports started to reach England of this strong force that was clearly waiting for the signal to invade – but when and where? The best guess, based on intelligence reports, was the area of the Thames Estuary or the Medway. On 4 June the Dutch fleet, under the command of Admiral Michiel de Ruyter with Cornelis de Witt representing the Dutch Government, sailed for England, and three days later anchored between Harwich and the Thames Estuary. The news caused great alarm in London. Pepys records chaos in the Navy Office when it was learned that eighty Dutch ships were off Harwich. Lord Oxford was dispatched to raise the Essex militias and a bridge of barges thrown across the Hope Reach (the stretch of water where the Thames makes a turn below Gravesend before turning east past Canvey Island). Despite these efforts the English were, at this moment, virtually helpless.

One Dutch squadron sailed towards Sheerness, the key to both the Thames Estuary and to the River Medway, Chatham and Rochester. In command of English warships at Sheerness and in the Medway was Sir Edward Spragge. In June 1667 he had only a meagre force which included just one frigate, the *Unity*, and one large man-of-war, the *Monmouth*. Spragge chose to place the *Monmouth* in a protected anchorage rather than send it against the enemy – not a bold move but probably the wisest.

The Dutch squadron under Van Ghent sailed on an incoming tide round Garrison Point towards Sheerness. The English frigate *Unity* got in one broadside and then retreated up the Medway along with the smaller English ships – so much for the contribution made by English naval power. It was now up to the fort at Sheerness to prevent the Dutch sailing up the Medway and burning the assembled shipping. Everything depended on it putting up a stout defence but, when the Dutch attacked at five in the afternoon of 10 June, the English suffered a catastrophe. The first shots fired from the sixteen guns mounted in the fort threw them from their carriages – the wood had rotted through lack of maintenance. Seven were quickly brought back into action and, according to one man present, the Dutch were at first loath to press the attack home after the first few shots hit them. But resistance quickly crumbled. The fort failed to protect the gunners from Dutch shot and morale broke. All but seven men fled when they learned that Dutch troops had landed only a mile away and were preparing a land attack.

With the fort lost, the Isle of Sheppey and its principal town, Queensborough, were at the mercy of the Dutch. To their credit the Dutch resisted the temptation to take revenge for the brutal burning of Schelling the previous year. The Dutch then took Sheerness town along with a magazine full of naval stores.

On 10 June rumour of disaster reached the City. Pepys wrote in his diary: 'News brought us that the Dutch are come as high as the Nore; and more pressing orders for fire-ships… we all down to Deptford… and set men to work; but Lord, to see how backwardly things move at this pinch.'

In the early hours of 11 June the Duke of Albemarle arrived at Chatham to take charge of its defence. He discovered a state of near panic. As he later reported to Parliament: 'I found scarce 12 of 800 men which were then in the king's pay in his majesty's yards, and these so distracted with fear that I could have little or no service from them… I found no ammunition there but what was in the *Monmouth*, so that I presently sent to Gravesend for the artillery train to be sent to me.'

Meanwhile the Dutch were preparing their next move. Having secured Sheerness, they could now move against the shipping in the Medway and against the dockyard at Chatham. The Medway – narrow in places and full of treacherous sand-banks and shallows – was a difficult river for an invader to navigate, but the prizes it offered were too tempting to resist. The chief hope of keeping the Dutch out of the river rested on the chain. It stretched from Hoo Ness to Gillingham and was 350 yards long with links 6½ inches in circumference.

long been recognized as a vital but potentially v
at Landguard since 1544 – indeed there was unt
1667 Landguard Fort was the scene of the bigge

In late June the Dutch ships cruised off the e
Great Yarmouth in turn. The freedom with whic
of the Royal Navy.

On 28 June Admiral de Ruyter's fleet, anchor
sent from Holland with an experienced troop cor
the Dutch government: 'An exceptional service
to the enemy if the army and landing forces cou
attack by ships on one side and the army on the
of.' This action was agreed and by 30 June the D
north of Harwich. By ten in the evening, sevent
ships based in Harwich contemplated attack bu
deterrents.

On 2 July the Dutch attacked. The landing
north from Landguard Fort to the River Debde
for a ship-borne assault – protected on each flan
landed in shallow-draught sailing vessels – gallio
joined the attacking force. The *London Gazett*
and one Dutch estimate spoke of 3,800, but the

The assault force was under the comma
Commonwealth soldier. The force was landed
shot was fired in opposition as the Dutch mari
formed themselves in parade ground order on
with muskets, divided into 36-man platoons.
commanded by Colonel Francis Palm and twe
Hoorn and Dolman landed and their men line

The Dutch force was then split into three
600 men spread out around the beachhead to
mustering to the north. Roads leading to the
guns the Dutch had landed. The River Del
beachhead, was lined with men. A further 60
and to secure the landing craft and embarka
party to take the fort. The aim of the attack
enter the harbour and capture Harwich.

The bulk of the Dutch fleet was anchored o
attack on the fort. One squadron – comprisin
to force the harbour entrance and bombard t
war under Vice-Admiral Cornelis Evertsen, t
fort with rolling clouds of gunsmoke and shot.
(around 200 yards), at which their heaviest
But these squadrons were thwarted by the sh

The English view of the Dutch attack along the River Medway. On the right foreground is Rochester Castle and Cathedral. Beyond, looking east towards the sea, is Chatham and Upnor Castle under attack while English ships burn. In the far distance is Sheerness, also in flames, with Dutch squadrons riding in the estuary.

Pulleys at either end, housed in cranc-houses, kept the chain taut about 9 feet below the surface. This meant that shallow-draught ships, such as fire-ships, could cross. On 11 June, with frantic haste, Peter Pett – the master shipwright at Chatham – had ordered a floating stage to be towed into position near the centre of the chain to raise it higher in the water. Later on the night of the 11th, Albemarle had ordered Pett and other dockyard officials to sink three ships as near the chain as possible to provide a further obstacle should the Dutch break it.

Undaunted, the Dutch decided to attack. At 6 a.m. on 12 June they set sail from Sheerness in line-astern. This formation, forced on them by the shallows, was extremely risky because it meant that only a few ships at a time could bring their guns to bear on a land target. Against an organized and resolute defending force, this strung-out attack could have ended in disaster. But the English failed utterly to make the most of their chance. In fact, they failed to attack at all. Instead, when the Dutch reached the chain it was they who attacked. First the Dutch captured the English frigate, the *Unity*, guarding the Gillingham end of the chain and then two Dutch shallow-draught fire-ships attempted to break the chain and eventually succeeded. One of these then placed itself next to the English ship the *Matthias*, which caught fire and eventually exploded. The English ship protecting the Essex end of the chain was then attacked. It sunk the first fire-ship sent against it but was set on fire and surrendered. The Dutch then sailed up the Medway a little beyond the chain and captured and burnt the grounded *Sancta Maria* and bombarded and took the batteries at either end of the now useless chain. During

this ferocious morning's work, the Dutc
prisoners without loss to themselves – bu

The pride of the Royal Navy – the *Ro*
had been ordered to go aboard to defen
which had sunk the Dutch flagship durir
a shot being fired. As Pepys recorded te
with a boat of nine men, who found no

These events produced huge dismay a
– the *Loyal London*, the *Royal Oak* and t
in their hulls to prevent the Dutch takin;
smaller craft were set adrift or scuttlec
batteries to cover the river approach.

Alarm and dismay at Chatham was
be an invasion proper and that the Dut
in his diary on 12 June: 'And so home,
have broke the chain and burned our sl
so much that the whole kingdom is und
To bed with a heavy heart… full of fea
touch of real terror about it. Clearly l
could mean the end of England.

The final major defence against Dut
ships were moored – was Upnor Cast
defences against the Spaniards, but i
And, more to the point, this English g
waited at their posts and at 2 p.m. on
was the first real resistance the Dutch
forward in a longboat to set an examj
damaged the half sunk *Loyal London*,

But the Dutch did not press home tl
defensive bombardment, and did no
Upnor had held: the Dutch adventur
Sheerness. As the Dutch fleet and th
replaced by a sense of deep shame. Na
it happen again? The answer was: it cot

Landguard Fort

After their success in the Medway the
and disorganized English. Raids on Pc
to the fleet from Holland. Even a ful
was considered. But in the end the pc
first had to take Landguard Fort.

Landguard Fort stands on the Esse
into the sea and overlooking the mout

small party – 'the seven men of Moidart' – only just evading English naval patrols. Charles landed in the Outer Hebrides where he was strongly advised to turn back; but he pressed on regardless and reached the Highlands in July 1745.

When he raised the Jacobite standard at Glenfinnan on 19 August, Charles could not have expected the initial level of support that flocked to his banner on a surge of nationalist and anti-Hanoverian feeling. The expedition soon became a full-scale rebellion as the Stuart forces were left unchallenged to march inexorably from Glenfinnan to Edinburgh. By the time Charles entered the capitol he was at the head of a substantial army.

Opposition was finally mounted under the command of Sir John Cope, who landed his forces and marched towards Edinburgh. Charles met him at Prestonpans, and after a fifteen-minute battle Cope and the English troops were put to flight. The victorious Jacobite army then continued to march south, raising the stakes by turning the venture into an invasion of England. They won another skirmish at Carlisle, and pressed on through the winter, past Newcastle to Manchester, and finally to Derby.

It was at this point that the expedition ground to a halt. Charles had managed to sustain the invasion with his assurances that overseas aid would appear once the border was crossed, winning over Highlanders who (more realistically) thought that Scotland was prize enough. The French forces never materialized, although an attempt to ferry troops across the Channel was thwarted only by the vigilance of the English navy. Support was similarly lacking within England, and the Highland chiefs decided to cut their losses and return home. As in 1715 the decision to retreat sealed the fate of the rebellion.

A massive English force was mobilized under the Duke of Cumberland, and chased the hungry and increasingly ragged Jacobites back into Scotland and north to Inverness. On 16 April 1746 the Scots were brought to battle at Culloden. Vastly outnumbered and outgunned, the Jacobites were massacred; when the shattered remnants of the army reassembled at Ruthven a few days later, only 1,500 troops appeared. Facing starvation, the army disbanded and English reprisals began.

After its victory in 1746 the English Government resolved to hold the Highlands like a conquered enemy territory. To do this, it extended the system of military roads that had been cut through the Highlands by General Wade from 1725 in the wake of the 1719 Spanish invasion. These roads – 250 miles of which had been well and speedily built by 1737 and supplied with a series of often spectacular bridges – were to allow English troops to move quickly from strong point to strong point and to sweep the Highlands for rebels. The Government also strengthened, rebuilt and added to the thirty forts that Wade had constructed and which had, generally, proved inadequate during the 1745 uprising.

At the centre of this improved system of Highland defences was the new Fort George which – massive in scale and placed on a strategically vital spit of land projecting into Moray Firth – is one of the great artillery fortifications of Europe. Started in 1746 under the control of the military engineer William Skinner, with William and later Robert Adam working as designers and building contractors and completed in 1769, the fort was to be the key to the Highlands. It was to act as a central depot and strong point in times of trouble and was to prevent Jacobite and French invasion fleets entering the Moray Firth on their way to Inverness, 9 miles to the east of the fort.

Opposite: A mid-eighteenth-century plan of Fort George on the Moray Firth. On the east side of the fort (top of picture) is a sloping glacis and a triangular ravelin detached in front of the main gate of the fort and standing in the wide defensive ditch. To the west of the ravelin are two arrow-shaped bastions connected by a curtain wall. Additional bastions mount guns that command the waters of the Firth.

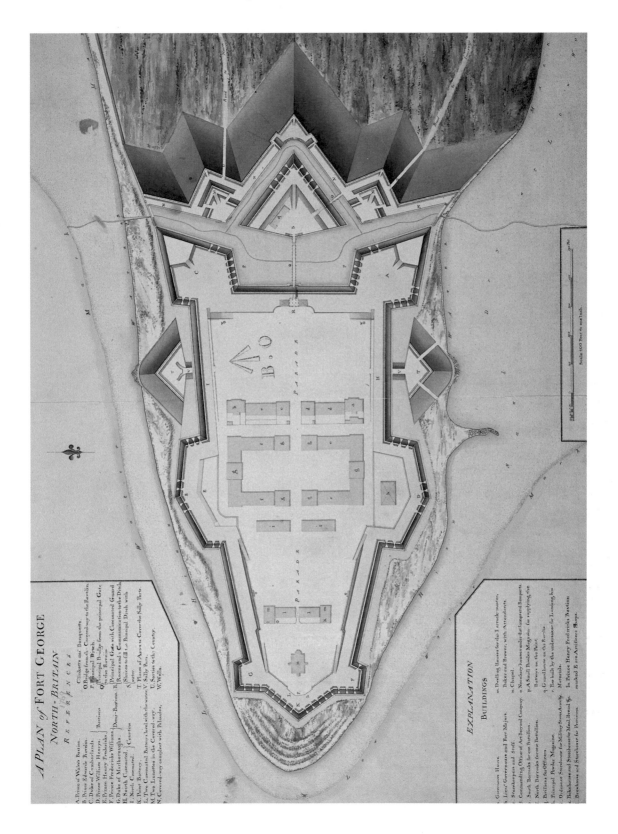

An aerial view of Fort George as it is today. Placed in a strategically vital spit of land and massive in scale, it is one of the great military fortifications of Europe.

The design of the fort represents state-of-the-art mid-eighteenth-century fortification. Cannon mounted on a series of large bastions command the waters of the Firth while the fort was protected from land assault by a series of defensive works placed with scientific precision. These included a glacis (a sloping and exposed flat area of ground in front of the works which would be swept by fire), a ravelin (a heavily armed mini-fort placed in front of the main works), ditches, bastions, and a curtain wall bursting with cannon. All these works were calculated to offer defence in depth: attackers would not only come under fire from many directions, but the deeper they infiltrated into the fortifications the more intense would be the fire unleashed upon them.

Fort George was never tested by enemy attack. When the invader next came, it was to a part of nearby coast that was not so well prepared.

CHAPTER SEVEN

AN AMERICAN INVASION

The defeat of the Stuarts in 1746 put an end to French invasion threats – but only for ten years. By 1755 British and French troops were fighting in India and North America, and France reached the conclusion that conflict in these distant theatres of war could be decided to French advantage by action in Europe. If Britain once again felt threatened by invasion, ships and troops would be kept at home rather than being sent to reinforce Britain's beleaguered colonies. So in 1756 the Marshal of France, the Duc de Belleisle, evolved a bold, indeed almost suicidal, plan for three simultaneous landings in Scotland and Ireland as well as in England itself. But, despite French military and naval successes in the Mediterranean, its warships were unable to give the Royal Navy the slip and so could not dominate the Channel long enough to escort the invasion barges gathered between Dunkirk and Cherbourg.

However, the French did not give up and in 1759, as British arms achieved success after success in India and North America, they became increasingly determined to compensate for losses abroad by the delivery of a devastating attack on Britain itself. France attempted to include Russia, Sweden and Holland in the invasion plan that envisaged the landing of 20,000 men at Glasgow, with Edinburgh as the primary diversionary target and another 20,000 landing in Essex, with London as the main objective. The French plans were well known in Britain; the militia was mobilized and British warships haunted the French coastline making sure that no fleet of any size put to sea and even bombarded Le Havre where a large amount of shipping – including invasion barges – was destroyed. French hopes were finally dashed in November 1759 by the crushing British naval victory off Quiberon Bay. Christmas 1759 was a season of real cheer in Britain with much to celebrate – Clive's continuing triumphs over France in India, the end of French ambitions in Canada with Wolfe's victory at Quebec, and now Admiral Hawke's victory at Quiberon Bay – an action celebrated by a pantomime in London, which launched the patriotic chorus: 'Hearts of oak are our ships, Hearts of oak are our men, We always are ready, steady, boys, steady, We'll fight and we'll conquer again and again.'

Britain's successes served only to inflame yet further French aggression. In 1762 invasion was threatened again – this time in collaboration with Spain – in an attempt to stop Britain in its triumphant tracks. But before fresh hostilities broke out in the Channel the Seven Years' War came to an end, in February 1763, greatly to Britain's advantage. This further intensified France's desire to invade and humiliate Britain, and invasion plans

This Exact representation of that Instrument of French refinement in Assassination, the GUILLOTINE is submitted to the Gentlemen of the Phalanx, & other well-wishers to the King & Constitution of Great-Britain,

by their devoted Servants at Command
The Assassins of the King of France.

Whither—O whither shall my Blood ascend for Justice?—my Throne is seized on by my Murderers my Brothers are driven into exile;—my unhappy Wife & innocent Infants are shut up in the horrors of a Dungeon,—while Robbers & Assassins are sheathing their Daggers in the bowels of my Country!—what will become of thee?—Ah! ruined, desolated Country, dearest object of my recent where misery was to me the sharpest pang in death;—the?—O Britons! vice-gerents of eternal Justice, arbiters of the world, I look down from that height of power to which you are raised, & behold me here, ignored of Life, & of Kingdom, see where I lie, full low, festering in my own Blood! which flies to your august tribunal for Justice. By your affection for your own Wives & Children—rescue mine—by your love for your Country, by the blessings of Life, & Liberty, which you possess; by the virtues which adorn the British Crown—by all that is Sacred & all that is dear to you—revenge the blood of a Monarch most undeservedly butchered,—and rescue the Kingdom of France from being the prey of Violence, Usurpation & Cruelty.

Pub.d Feb.16.th 1793 by H.Humphrey No.18. old Bond Street

The Blood of the Murdered crying for Vengeance.

J.G.y des.t et sec.t pro Bono publico.

Above: *Joseph Priestley – scientist, cleric and author of pro-French radical pamphlets – was typical of the type of independent political thinker that the government sought to silence through its strengthened sedition and treason laws. Priestley was eventually hounded from the country and settled in America.*

Opposite: *A cartoon by James Gillray puts the conventional Government view that the French Revolution was a brutal affair that threatened the security of Britain. In fact, during the early years of the revolution its ideals of freedom, equality and fraternity were welcomed by many in Britain and even after the executions of 1792 and '93 many still looked to France for inspiration and liberty.*

Overleaf: *James Gillray's print of 1796 - entitled* The Promised Horrors of French Invasion *– shows French troops parading along St James's Street while St James's Palace burns, White's club is raided and various members of the Government and ruling elite are scourged, murdered or carried through the street in pieces. Gillray may have intended this to be an ironic and satiric view, but this print also reinforces the Francophobia being stoked up by the Government.*

Paine's ideas were echoed by other radical figures, notably Joseph Priestley, a Unitarian preacher, scientist and, more dangerously, a writer of anti-establishment texts. Priestley had already attacked the Government's repressive policies in America and the authority of the established church, and was regarded with suspicion by the Government. When in 1791 he wrote a pamphlet defending the French Revolution and calling for changes to the monarchy in England, this was the last straw for the authorities and in particular for George III. A mob – probably put together and led by Government agents and reactionary sympathizers – sacked Priestley's house in Birmingham, destroying not only most of his papers and books but also his laboratory. A shattered man, Priestley eventually fled to America, where he was to die in 1804.

The year after Priestley published his pamphlet, the authorities were preparing to suppress revolutionary thoughts and actions. British and Prussian troops were barracked around London and in May 1792 a Royal

Proclamation was issued against 'divers wicked and seditious writings'. But later that year, the increasing violence in France – especially the 'September Massacre' – started to cool popular support in Britain for the Revolution. It was now that the authorities used the horrors of the Revolution to flame national francophobia. Invasion by a fanatical French army intent on spreading the Revolution was feared by the British Government and the aristocracy and by the beginning of 1793 – following the execution of the French king in January – the country was generally behind Prime Minister William Pitt's decision to confront the new French Government. This led to its declaration of war against Britain, Holland and Spain in February and March 1793. The popular terror of the extremes of the French Revolution is well expressed in James Gillray's print of 1796 (see pages 92-3): entitled the *Promised Horrors of French Invasion*, it shows French troops goosestepping along St James's Street, London while various prominent persons are publicly scourged or dangled, in parts, from gibbets.

When war broke out with France, those British sympathetic to the cause of the French Revolution were perceived by the British authorities as a potential fifth column. Many radicals, including Thomas Hardy, the founder of the London Corresponding Society, and Thomas Holcroft, a friend Blake and of Tom Paine, were arrested in 1794 for 'High Treason'. Sedition trials became a commonplace and the type of evidence that was used – based on eavesdropping by government agents, hearsay and vindictive denunciation – created an atmosphere of suspicion, intrigue and fear. Punishments were potentially ferocious but in practice in Britain were confined to short periods of imprisonment and fines. Juries were very reluctant to condemn people to death or transportation for simply voicing their opinions.

The Government's sustained efforts to control popular opinion in Britain only increased the divisions in society that the legislation was intended to remove. When the king opened Parliament in October 1795 the crowd, according to Francis Place who was a member of the committee of the London Corresponding Society, 'hissed and groaned' and called out 'no Pitt, no war, peace, peace, bread, bread'. The Government used this disturbance as an excuse to increase its campaign against radicals. The suspension in 1794 of the Act of Habeas Corpus, a move which gave the Government power to arrest and detain without trial, was reinforced in 1795 by two Acts against 'treasonable and seditious practices' and 'seditious meetings and assemblies', and by the 'Seditious Meetings Act' of 1799. These laws marked the end of open and organized radicalism in England. In 1798 the entire committee of the London Corresponding Society was arrested while the society itself was in 1799 declared an illegal organization.

The Government's greatest test came in 1797, when elements of the Royal Navy mutinied. The navy was the steadfast bulwark against invasion and foreign aggression, but now the loyalty of this national institution and saviour was in question. The cause of the unrest was not – initially or primarily – revolutionary sentiment on the part of the mutineers but grievances about bad food, poor medical conditions, lack of shore leave and erratic pay. As the world order appeared to be dramatically and rapidly changing around them some sailors wanted their wooden world put to rights as well. The mutiny broke out in the Channel Fleet at its moorings at Spithead, Portsmouth in April 1797 and then spread in May to the fleet anchored at the Nore. The Admiralty and the Government were deeply shocked – as was the whole nation – by this apparent collapse of resolve and discipline within Britain's main defence against French invasion.

Government action, although initially tardy, was effective. The more reasonable demands of the Portsmouth mutineers were conceded, discipline was re-established, and there were no severe punishments. The Nore mutineers – whose aims were more political – were suppressed more fiercely and their leader, Richard Parker, executed.

The mutiny had been dealt with, but had the spirit of the Royal Navy been broken and its power as a fighting force crippled at the very moment when it was needed most? The answer to this alarming question came quickly for only a few months later the North Sea fleet won a major victory at Camperdown (see page 99).

The French invasions of Ireland

In November 1795 the Directory came to power in France, bringing a new stability. The internal and external crises that had threatened to destroy the Revolution were past and France could now concentrate on the overthrow of its most determined enemy: Britain. The spirit of the Revolution was still burning bright in France, and the country remained committed to spreading the ideals of the revolution – equality and freedom – through a world still largely dominated by oppressive monarchies. It was intent on wars of liberation not conquest and no one, perhaps, craved the sort of freedom offered by the Revolution more than did the Society of United Irishmen.

The society had been formed in the early 1790s with the aim of obtaining better representation for Irishmen – Protestant and Roman Catholic alike – in an Irish Parliament dominated by Anglo-Irish landlords, and protecting and promoting Ireland's trade and manufacturing interests that were being controlled and exploited by mainland Britain. At first the United Irishmen were committed to reform rather than revolution, but violence and intransigence were starting to dominate relationships within Ireland. In September 1795 clashes between Catholics and Protestants led to the foundation of the breakaway Protestant Orange Order, while the Catholic Defenders remained linked to the largely Protestant United Irishmen. Martial law was declared in Ulster in early 1796 and it was rapidly becoming clear to the United Irishmen that the British Government would never bow to legal, constitutional pressure. The Society would have to fight if it wished to gain political and economic independence for Ireland – and the natural ally in this struggle was Revolutionary France.

Early in 1796 one of the founders of the United Irishmen – Theobald Wolfe Tone – made his way from exile in the United States to Paris to gain French aid in the liberation of his country from British oppression. Tone was a remarkable character, a Protestant who initially sought 'a union of Irishmen of every religious persuasion in order to obtain a complete reform of the legislature, founded on the principles of civil, political and religious liberty' but who had gradually and reluctantly been forced to embrace violence. By 1796 Tone accepted that only through military action could the United Irishmen 'subvert the tyranny of an execrable government, to break the connection with England, the never-failing source of all our political evils, and to assert the independence of my country'.

Under the name of Citizen Smith, Tone arrived in Paris with no connections and little French, and set about the difficult task of gaining a French army for the invasion of the British Isles. He floundered for a few months but then met the young and dynamic General Louis Lazare Hoche, then the most admired and successful soldier in the French Republic. To a degree, Tone's aims coincided with Hoche's vision for a liberated Europe and things moved forward rapidly – especially when Tone was joined in Paris by two other leading United Irishmen and patriots, Lord Edward Fitzgerald and Arthur O'Connor. By the autumn of 1796 Hoche had obtained the support of the Directory and a plan was hatched – and an incredible plan it was too. Ireland was to be invaded by wave upon wave of French regular troops supported by a horde of conscripted convicts. The first wave – 6,000 strong – was to land in Galway, as were the next two waves, with the final wave of 20,000 men landing in Connaught. These French troops were to be supported by the United Irishmen and thousands of Irish who – Tone and his colleagues promised Hoche – would rise up as one man against the English the moment the French arrived. This great invasion force was to be transported and guarded by the might of the recently combined French, Dutch and Spanish fleets which, for once, meant that the Royal Navy would be outnumbered in its home waters.

Hoche's flight of imagination soared yet higher. To divert British help from its embattled troops in Ireland, Hoche planned diversionary raids on the British mainland itself. The first raid – led by General Quantin out of Dunkirk – was to attack Newcastle where the 'Legion Franche' would burn the docks and shipping and destroy local coalmines. The second raiding party was to land at Bristol – the second city of Britain – which was to be sacked. The secondary invasion location was Wales, with the final target being Liverpool. This raid was to be undertaken by the 'Legion Noire' which, like the 'Legion Franche', was to be composed largely of convicts (see page 103). So the invasion of Ireland was to be the key component in a massive, co-ordinated and mutually interdependent plan of attack upon Britain. To a large degree, each element of the attack depended on the success of the other elements. It was a bold but potentially highly problematic plan – not least because it assumed great military actions would be achieved by the poorest quality troops imaginable.

Disregarding the obvious weaknesses of the plan, Tone remained optimistic and enthusiastic and even weathered the initial – and rather ominous – setbacks. First, the force destined for the invasion of Ireland was radically reduced in size, with the first wave numbering around 15,000 but with no further waves organized. Then, in November, the raid against Newcastle turned out to be a fiasco, with the French troops mutinying while at sea and forcing an ignominious return to port and the cancellation of the attack.

Despite the dramatic failure of this diversionary action, the Irish adventure was still on. By late 1796 the landing site had been chosen – Bantry Bay instead of Galway Bay as originally proposed. Bantry Bay was a haven only two days' sail from the invasion port of Brest and close to Cork, the major port and city of west Ireland, which it was estimated the French could capture in a few days. So, even given the problems that were starting to beset the scheme, Tone really still had every reason to remain confident. The fleet carrying the invasion force was impressive: forty-seven vessels including nineteen powerful ships-of-the-line. The French troops were regulars and of the highest quality, and General Hoche himself was in command. In contrast, the number of regular British troops in Ireland was small – around 12,000 – and most of these were of poor quality. And, most reassuring of all, Tone was convinced that there would be a spontaneous national uprising against the British the moment the French landed. With luck, all would go well and Ireland would be freed. But, as events were to prove, luck was the one thing that Tone conspicuously lacked.

Things started to go badly wrong even as the French invasion force left Brest on 15 December 1796 under the command of Admiral Morand de Galles. Due to confusion, a British blockading force and perhaps treachery, the fleet split up on leaving port and never fully united again. One of the ships that never rejoined the main body of the fleet was the *Fraternité*. This vessel was not only de Galles's flagship but it also carried Hoche. The failure of the ship to rejoin the gradually reassembled fleet, or even to make its own way to Bantry Bay, remains one of the great mysteries of the adventure. Was the captain of the *Fraternité* in the pay of Britain and determined to compromise the invasion by removing its commanders? Did Hoche want to dissociate himself from what he had come to believe was an inevitable failure? Weather conditions were atrocious but this did not prevent smaller ships from struggling into Bantry Bay. Whatever the reason, the lack of strong and positive leadership in the bay was to have catastrophic consequences for the French and Irish cause.

By 21 December the first portion of the scattered and storm-battered French fleet arrived off Bantry Bay. These included the eighty-gun *Indomptable* that carried Tone, travelling to Ireland under the alias of Adjutant-General Smith. But the weather was so violent that a landing was not possible. As Tone noted in his diary: 'There cannot be imagined a situation more provokingly tantalising … we were near enough to toss a biscuit ashore … in all my life rage never entered so deeply into my heart.' This state of affairs continued over the following days. Tone begged the military and naval seconds-in-command – Grouchy and Bouvet – to be more

Opposite: *Theobald Wolfe Tone – an initially moderate Protestant reformer who was eventually forced to embrace violent revolution as the only means of achieving Ireland's freedom from English rule. A leading members of the Society of United Irishmen, he led a French invasion force to Ireland in December 1796.*

daring and risk a landing no matter the dangers of the weather. On 24 December Grouchy decided to make an attempt to land an advance guard of 6,400 men and four pieces of artillery. Tone was jubilant, but the next day new winds whipped up even higher waves and the landing was called off. That night Admiral Bouvet cut his anchor ropes and made a dash for the open sea and on 26 December the naval third-in-command, Commodore Bedout, decided to withdraw. There was nothing that the heartbroken Tone could do but ponder what might have been. As he confided to his journal, 'had we been able to land the first day and march directly to Cork, we should have infallibly carried by coup de main… My prospects at this hour are as gloomy as possible. I see nothing before me but the ruin of the expedition, the slavery of my country and my own destruction…'

Three days after Tone and the French ships left the bay a second force of French ships straggled in. These were portions of the scattered fleet that had weathered the storm at sea, reassembled and now arrived at an empty bay. Eventually a sizable squadron lay at anchor in the bay with around 4,000 troops on board, but landing again proved impossible. One ship, *La Surveillante*, which limped into the bay on 31 December was so badly storm-damaged that she was scuttled. After a few bewildering days this belated and demoralized invasion force left the bay on 6 January – just as the weather changed from storms to calm – and made its way back to Brest.

Britain had been saved – despite the spectacular non-appearance of the Royal Navy that William Pitt had reassured Parliament in October 1796 was 'the national defence of this kingdom in case of invasion'. There is little doubt that if the French had got ashore, Cork would have fallen within days and it is possible – as even the British authorities accepted – that Dublin would have been occupied in a week. As Tone correctly observed, Britain had 'not had such an escape since the Spanish Armada, and that expedition, like ours, was defeated by the weather; the elements fight against us'.

Tone and Hoche planned a second invasion of Ireland, during the summer of 1797. This time the entire Dutch army of 15,000 men – which had been under the control of the French Revolutionary Government since May 1795 – was to be hurled at an unspecified target in the British Isles. Tone bobbed around on a Dutch warship anchored off the Texel while the Dutch and French commanders talked grandly of landing first at King's Lynn or Harwich before making for Ireland. Meanwhile the British fleet blockading the Dutch port gradually increased in number and the invasion army – having eaten all its supplies – was disembarked. Wolfe Tone, again facing the ruin of a promising invasion plan, set off to enlist Hoche's aid in speeding the fleet to sea. But Hoche – the great advocate for the invasion of England – had died in September. The invasion plan was not abandoned, but without Hoche's leadership and political support it failed to take a powerful or coherent form. In October the Dutch invasion fleet eventually sailed for England but was met and soundly defeated off Camperdown on the Dutch coast by a British fleet under the command of the veteran Admiral Duncan. The invasion of the British Isles collapsed, but the threat was far from removed.

The invasion of Killala

The Bantry Bay adventure, although abortive in the short term, did succeed in helping to set in motion a chain of events in Ireland that were to have major, if tragic, consequences for the people of the country. The United Irishmen, naturally disappointed by the failure at Bantry Bay, believed the French would try again – as

Opposite: *General Louis Lazare Hoche was the most successful soldier in the early years of revolutionary France and the champion of proposals to invade England, Ireland and Wales. His premature and unexpected death in September 1797 made way for the rise of Napoleon Bonaparte.*

indeed they did. But before they returned, a patriotic uprising, stimulated by the evidence of French support offered by the Bantry Bay expedition, had taken place in the spring and early summer of 1798. But the uprising was a national calamity. It resulted in massacre, appalling violence and cruelty on the part of both patriots and loyalists and finally ended in brutal suppression by the British authorities. So the French return in late summer was an appallingly ill-timed if swashbuckling affair.

On 22 August 1798 1,100 French soldiers under the command of General Jean Humbert landed near Killala, Co. Mayo, in an Ireland still traumatized by the recent bloody events and aftermath of the uprising. In these dreadful circumstances the raid was initially surprisingly successful. Humbert, optimistic in his expectations of local support and French reinforcements, aggressively swept aside local loyalist resistance and marched triumphantly inland to take the town of Ballina. To Humbert's dismay, local support was decidedly half-hearted but he picked up some recruits and, in high spirits, marched on Castlebar. Awaiting him was a British force composed largely of Irish militia with some Scottish and English Fencibles (volunteer forces) and regulars in support. The British force was outmanoeuvred by Humbert who, despite being deserted by most of his Irish volunteers, routed the British at the point of the bayonet.

After the battle Humbert, joined by significant numbers of the defeated Irish militia, marched on. But, despite his victory, volunteers still failed to flock to Humbert's banner. This was a bad sign for the French, confirming the demoralized and terrified nature of the country. On the other hand, vast numbers of British soldiers were gathering around the small Franco-Irish force which clearly had nowhere to go and nothing to achieve since igniting a new insurrection was clearly out of the question. On 8 September Humbert's wandering force came up against a vast royal force at Ballinamuck, Co. Leitrim. A short exchange of fire took place to satisfy honour and then Humbert surrendered. He and his men were granted honourable terms – indeed, the French officers were fêted when they entered Dublin.

But a very different fate awaited the Irishmen that the French had enticed into their service. As the French surrendered, the Irish fled with the British in hot pursuit. Many were slaughtered on the spot while others, who were taken prisoner, were hanged from trees – the fruits of failed revolution were ghastly indeed. But the killing did not stop at Ballinamuck. When loyalist forces retook Killala more executions took place. And as this was happening Humbert and his men were making a joyful and ceremonial exit from Dublin, singing revolutionary songs and cosily stowed on British ships en route to France. The last important victim of this ghastly misadventure was not taken until two weeks after the recapture of Killala. Wolf Tone, making his way to Ireland to join Humbert, was captured at sea by a British warship. For his treason Tone faced certain death – the only question was how. He pleaded for military execution, which was denied him and so, to escape the ignominy of a traitor's death, Tone committed suicide. He died on 19 November 1798 – and with him died all hope of Irish independence. Less than two years later William Pitt, deeply alarmed by the events of 1798, persuaded the Irish Parliament – which represented at least limited independence from Britain – to vote for its own dissolution. In January 1801 the Act of Union with Great Britain made Ireland formally subordinate to Westminster.

CHAPTER NINE

FISHGUARD: THE LAST INVASION OF BRITAIN

The utter failure of Bantry Bay in January 1797 did not stop the related 'diversionary' raid against Wales. The French force arrived at Fishguard, in west Wales, the following month, in what was to be the last invasion of Britain. Doomed before it even started, the adventure on Welsh soil lasted a mere three days and ended in embarrassment for French and British alike.

Not planned as an invasion of conquest, it was to be more than just a hit and run raid. The orders – compiled by General Hoche – identified three principal objects: to raise an insurrection in the country; to interrupt and embarrass the commerce of the enemy; and to prepare and facilitate the way for a larger invasion force by distracting the attention of the British Government. But, most important, this raid was not intended to harm the ordinary British people. Rather it was to be meant to be the first step in liberating the oppressed of the country from the domination of the English ruling class, to set alight the flame of revolution.

Quite why the French Directory believed that the British proletariat – and the Welsh in particular – would rise up in violent rebellion is hard to understand. The ideals of the revolution were championed by many in Britain (see page 89) but virtually all its supporters – Welsh as well as English – would have been horrified by the notion of change achieved at home through violence. Changes were needed but through reform, argument and agitation, not through a bloodbath. Also, despite the Welsh Dissenters' differences with the established church, they were hardly likely to prefer the policies of the atheistic French Revolutionary Government.

The initial plan of attack was to take and sack Bristol and then sail to Cardiff, march across Wales gathering local support, and finally to attack Chester and Liverpool. The French force of 1,400 was led by Colonel William Tate, a seventy-year-old Irish-American veteran of the War of Independence. The troops under Tate's command were an extraordinary body that, in its very nature, seemed to contradict the declared aim of the expedition to win the hearts and minds of the British people. The force was named the Legion Noire – the Black Legion – because of the colour of its coats, but it could well have been named after the character of its legionnaires. General Hoche, who raised the force, described it as composed largely of 'men from all the prisons

The 1,400 members of the French Legion Noire surrender to British militia at Fishguard in the west of Wales in February 1797. The French incursion – which lasted a mere three days and ended as a fiasco – was the last full-scale invasion of Britain.

in my district … with picked convicts from the galleys, still wearing their irons'. As well as 800 or so convicts – granted freedom only for the duration of the campaign – there were 600 regular troops. These (who presumably continued to wear their standard blue uniforms) were supplied from a number of regiments and it must be assumed that officers regarded the request for men as an opportunity to get rid of troublemakers.

However, the background of some of Tate's officers suggests that the force might have been at least a little more professional and competent that its origin suggests. Many of the officers were émigrés who had military experience – for example Jacques Philippe Le Brun, Tate's second in command, was the former Baron de Rochmare – while others were motivated and spirited adventurers like the Irish officers, among whom was Lieutenant Barry St Leger.

The fleet carrying this unlikely invasion force sailed from Brest on the evening of 18 February. It consisted of only four ships and was under the command of Commodore Jean Joseph Castagnier. By the 22nd, it was anchored to the north-west of Fishguard, screened from the town by the Pen Anglas headland. Castagnier now sent his smallest ship to discover if the invasion force was likely to meet any significant opposition if it landed at Fishguard harbour. To be on the safe side, the French reconnaissance ship flew the Union Flag but – to the great surprise and dismay of its crew – the gunners in the fort fired at it. As it happened, the shot was a blank, probably because the fort had only three cannonballs in its magazine, but the French were thrown into some confusion by this unexpected resistance. Clearly – at the very least – their true identity was known.

To decide their next move, Tate and Castagnier questioned a local seaman they had captured to see if they could discover the strength of the forces defending Fishguard. Their captive – obviously a wily fellow – doubled the number of men he knew to be in Fishguard. He said there were 500, well armed and trained. In fact there were four companies of the Fishguard Fencibles – a militia regiment consisting of amateur part-time soldiers – numbering 285 men and officers in the immediate area, but only about half the force was actually in Fishguard. Castagnier and Tate had another source of local information with them – a member of the Black Legion called James Bowen, a native of Fishguard. Bowen, who had been a servant at Trehowel farm on the Pencaer Peninsula, had been arrested as a horse thief and transported. But he had managed to escape, found his way into the Legion, and was now acting as an adviser.

The prisoner's information, combined with the alert action of the fort, persuaded the French commanders to avoid a direct assault. Instead the little fleet sailed west to make a landing against a steep and rocky cliff face, Carreg Wasted Point, well away from the guns of the port. It was a difficult, dangerous landing, but by the early morning of 23 February the Black Legion had firmly established itself on the windy cliff-top. Then the French fleet sailed away – an action that was part of Hoche's plan and had been agreed by Tate. But if Hoche believed that abandonment would put the legion on its mettle he was wrong. From the moment the ships left, and the legion was isolated on potentially unfriendly shores, morale and discipline started to plummet.

Tate himself, like the majority of his men, was in mental turmoil. For him this should have been a dream come true. For years the veteran soldier had honed a fanatical hatred of Britain, and had agitated energetically in France for direct military action against his foe – and he was at last in a position to hurt his enemy. But his nerve suddenly failed him. As Tate later said, referring to himself in the third person in best military manner: 'He had often been in battle over his shoes in blood, but he had never felt such a sensation when he put his foot on British ground – that his heart failed him in a way he could not describe.'

Initially at least, Tate tried to act in a correct military manner. He sent a patrol of twenty-five grenadiers – the first men ashore and in theory the most efficient of the invasion force's fighting men – in search of the enemy and of a suitable location for headquarters. In command was Lieutenant St Leger. The party made straight for Trehowel Farm – which suggests that Bowen was acting as guide. The grenadiers burst into the farm and were greeted with a vision: a sumptuous wedding banquet. The tenant farmer, John Mortimer, was to have been married that day, but had fled. All military duties forgotten, the starving invaders fell on the food and drink.

But what were the British forces doing? By the time the fort had fired its blank at the probing French ship, news had arrived in Fishguard that the ships anchored behind the Pen Anglas headland were French. The commander of the Fishguard Fencibles, Lieutenant Colonel Thomas Knox, rushed to his command post in Fishguard Fort. Despite his rather grand rank, Knox was – like his men – an amateur soldier and held his command purely because his father, the Under Secretary of State for America during the War of Independence, had raised the regiment in 1793 and financed its running ever since. Knox saw no sign of the French in the harbour or in the bay or on Goodwick Sands, a natural landing place just to the west of Fishguard and beyond the range of the fort's guns.

Knox set out to find them and, crossing Goodwick Sands, met seventy of his Fencibles – the first to answer the summons to action. Knox halted their hasty and unplanned advance, wanting to organize his men and discover the number and location of the enemy before attacking. With the Fencibles was a regular officer called Nesbitt; Knox sent him forward with a small party of scouts to gather information, while he led his soldiers back to the fort to await developments.

rewarding work, since most were well stocked with wine that had been recently gathered from the wreck of a Portuguese merchant ship.

One party of dispirited French foragers made for the small medieval church at Llanwnda. They set fire to it, probably using the Bible as kindling, for it survives in a scorched and battered condition, and stole the communion plate. The tower and most of the nave survived the fire and the chalice was later recovered, but this was hardly the way to win the hearts and minds of the Welsh or to encourage them to join the revolution and rise up against their English oppressors.

But worse was to happen. Another party of French went to Caerlem Farm. As they approached, a maid, Mary Williams, tried to escape. The soldiers shot her in the leg, presumably to stop her flight, and then raped her. This was at about the same time that St Leger and his grenadiers were proudly raising the tricolour over a liberated Wales. Mary Williams survived and the Government subsequently awarded her an annual pension of £40 for her ordeal. Not all of the French caperings were so tragic. A drunken French soldier was plundering a house at Brestgarn when a longcase clock in the dining room prepared to strike. The working of its mechanism sounded like a musket being cocked, and made the stupefied Frenchman fire and flee. The clock remains in the farmhouse – complete with a bullet hole roughly at heart height. Drunk or not, the Frenchman seems to have been a good shot.

But not all the confrontations that day between the French and the British were bloodless. A party of British sailors from St David's advanced along a lane below Carn Gelli, and came face to face with five French foragers. Shots were exchanged and when the smoke cleared one Frenchman lay dead and another two, and one sailor, were wounded. The rest of the French had fled. This brief skirmish was the only real fire-fight of the invasion.

Colonel Tate is said to have witnessed this encounter from a vantage point on the top of Carn Gelli, known to this day as Tate's seat. It further demoralized him. If a bunch of civilians – the sailors did not wear uniform – could do this to his men, what would happen when they came up against the British army? And, as far as Tate could tell, the British regulars were now arriving. While on top of Carn Gelli Tate saw, to the east on the hill above Fishguard, figures gathering. They were dressed in red with black hats and white trousers and were carrying muskets. As far as he could tell these were the regular British troops he feared. In fact they were Welsh women dressed in their traditional red capes, white dresses and tall black hats and carrying sticks. It is one of the myths of the Fishguard invasion that Tate's spirit was finally broken when he mistook local women for massed ranks of British regular soldiers. But if the women did gather above Fishguard to look towards the French positions – which is highly likely – then Tate's mistake is quite understandable. At the distance that separates Carn Gelli from Fishguard it is possible to distinguish forms and colours but not – even through a telescope – to see any clearly distinguishing details.

Another myth surrounds the activities of one of these local women – Jemima Nicholas, the town cobbler and something of an Amazon. At some point during this day or the next she is said to have gone out to the Pencaer Peninsula and single-handedly captured twelve Frenchmen. If this is the case, they must surely have been drunk or more than willing to call it a day. Whatever the truth, Jemima was hailed as a local heroine, dubbed Jemima Fawr (the Great Jemima) and rewarded with a Government pension of £50 per year. In all, during this troubled day about five Frenchmen and two Welsh were killed in petty or drunken squabbles. No recruits had been made and no transport acquired. By the evening of the 23rd Tate had decided enough was

Opposite: *The* Royal Oak *in Fishguard. This was the British headquarters during the invasion and where the terms of French surrender were drafted. The nine-pounder cannon in the foreground was in Fishguard fort at the time of the invasion.*

enough. His men were drunk and disorderly, he had seen them beaten by what he took to be local farmers and he believed he saw regular British troops gathering for the kill. He felt low-spirited and abandoned. The only real question was how the business could be brought to an end with safety and some dignity.

At nine in the evening of the 23rd, Tate's second in command, Le Brun, walked into Fishguard and was conducted to Cawdor's headquarters at the Royal Oak. Le Brun carried a letter from Tate offering a conditional surrender which, Tate hoped, would include the force being returned to Brest in British transports. The French envoys were detained and Cawdor wrote a note to Tate, demanding the unconditional surrender of his whole force. Early the next morning, Tate agreed to the British demand.

The invasion was over. Although the physical damage and the loss of life had been minimal, the consequences of this adventure were immense, both for the country and for the people who took part. On the national level the affair not only caused much fear and panic but provoked an immediate financial crisis. On 24 February, when news of the invasion had first reached the City, there was an unprecedented withdrawal from the Bank of England; and the next day, stock slumped. On the 26th – after a meeting between the king and the Privy Council – the Bank of England suspended cash payments. Tate may have been a bungler but, even as he was held a prisoner in Wales, the reverberations of his wayward adventure seemed set to bring riots in London and even to bring down the Government. The solution, the bank and Government hoped, was to continue transactions by issuing paper money. Bank notes had long been in use but these had value because they could be exchanged on demand for cash – for silver or gold. This was not the case with the £1 and £2 notes then issued by the Bank of England. After a few days things calmed down. The City merchants accepted the notes and thus – with the face value of the notes validated through use – the City breathed again and trade continued.

As for the Black Legion, the men were delighted to surrender and by the end of 1797 most had been returned to France. In contrast, the future facing the senior and non-French officers of the legion immediately after capture looked decidedly less rosy. The Irishmen were in danger of facing trial and execution for treason, while Tate was almost unhinged by worry and fear. However, it was soon decided by the British authorities that no one would be executed – a move that would only provoke retaliation against British and Royalist prisoners in France. All officers were to be treated as prisoners of war, and in November they were repatriated to France as part of an exchange for captured British officers. All, that is, except St Leger. He had already gone, having escaped from confinement in Porchester Castle.

As for General Hoche, the mastermind behind the invasion, he had been posted to Holland before Tate left Brest and so was, in effect, removed from military control of the invasion he had launched. Then, in September, he suddenly died – of consumption, it was said, but there were rumours of assassination. Whatever the cause, the way was open for the rise of Hoche's foremost rival: General Napoleon Bonaparte. In late 1797 Bonaparte – fresh from his triumphs in Italy – seems to have shared Hoche's enthusiasm for the invasion of Britain. He wrote to the French Directory that France 'must destroy the English monarchy, or expect itself to be destroyed by these intriguing and enterprising islanders … Let us concentrate all our efforts on the navy and annihilate England. That done, Europe is at our feet.' In November Bonaparte told the Directory that he had given all necessary orders to move 'our columns to the ocean' and that 56,000 men were already assembled for the invasion of England.

CHAPTER TEN

FANTASTIC FORTIFICATIONS

The failure of the French invasions of Ireland and Wales in 1796 and 1797 – and Admiral Nelson's destruction of the French fleet in Aboukir Bay in August 1798 – appeared to relieve Britain from the immediate threat of invasion. Volunteer and militia battalions were still drilled and ancient coastal fortresses were gradually brought up to date, but far less urgently. The relaxed approach appeared to have been justified in March 1802 when, with the Treaty of Amiens, France – now run as a dictatorship with First Consul General Napoleon Bonaparte as the autocratic head of state – made peace with Great Britain. But the peace was uneasy with both sides, intensely suspicious of each other, failing to honour the terms of the treaty that included the restitution of conquered territory. Things came to a head in May 1803 when Britain, which had refused to evacuate Malta as agreed and had unsuccessfully demanded the French evacuation of Holland, declared a new war against France.

But the France that Britain confronted in May 1803 was not the same old enemy of fourteen months earlier. France was a more powerful and, for Britain, a more sinister enemy than ever before. Bonaparte, created Consul for Life in August 1802, had a tighter grip on the country, his military machine was better organized and his aggressive energies and confidence had reached new heights. In May 1804 Bonaparte's power was put on an even firmer footing when the senate conferred upon him the title Emperor Napoleon I.

The consequences of these great and rapid changes in France were, for Britain, tumultuous. The fear of invasion returned – and with a vengeance. The new Emperor was infuriated by the way reactionary Britain had managed, through a mixture of bribes, diplomatic cunning and unlikely military prowess, to block the development of his grand strategy for Europe and for the east. This would have to stop and – as far as Napoleon was concerned – would only end when Britain had been crushed economically and militarily. Invasion was the answer and, for Napoleon, did not seem to be a great problem. As he put it in 1803: 'The Channel is but a ditch and anyone can cross it who has the courage. Let us be masters of the Straits for six hours and we shall be masters of the world.'

And Napoleon seemed determined to demonstrate the truth of this assertion. In 1803 he amassed on the cliffs around Calais and Boulogne an Army of England 130,000 strong and a flotilla of 2,000 boats to carry the host across the Straits of Dover. The presence of this army put huge political pressure on the British Government to reach terms with the Emperor but, as Napoleon implied fifteen years later when a prisoner on St Helena, this army was more than just a bargaining tool: 'The invasion of England was always regarded

as practicable. Once the descent had been effected, London must infallibly have been taken… It would certainly have succeeded with 160,000 men, provided that they could have presented themselves before London five days after their landing.'

Events unfolding across the Channel in 1803 meant that it was, clearly, now time for Britain to defend itself in earnest – but what was the best method? The Royal Navy, pursuing the policy that the best defence is offensive, blockaded French ports to disrupt trade and to stop an invasion fleet from sailing, and hunted the French coastal waters and the high seas for French shipping. The volunteer militias, around 150,000 strong in 1800, were trained to new heights of efficiency and re-equipped. But it was generally believed in Britain that this was not enough to resist invasion or destructive raids from the newly strengthened and more determined France. A new generation of fixed defences was needed. But what form should these take and where should they be built? During the anxious and urgent debates that took place in 1803 and early 1804, certain points emerged and were agreed. Works should be concentrated on those parts of the English coast most accessible to a French invasion fleet.

Defensive preparations had, effectively, got under way in the early 1790s when the Government's Board of Ordnance started work on the production of a detailed 1-inch-to-1-mile map of Kent for use by defending forces. This map was published in 1801 as the first part of the Ordnance Survey of Britain. It was opposite the area shown on this first OS map that Napoleon was massing his Army of England. This area of Kent was also vulnerable because, as the British also calculated, the French would be forced to sail to England by the most direct route – from Calais, Boulogne or Dunkirk – because of the destructive power of the ever loitering Royal Navy. If the French attempted a longer route to attack a more distant part of the British coast, its invasion fleet would be longer at sea and thus vulnerable for a longer period to the terrifying power of the Royal Navy. So, when all things were considered, the British Government and its military advisers took the only logical step and decided to concentrate anti-invasion defences along the south-east and east coasts with particularly vulnerable landing sites and ports being given extra protection. The obvious starting point for this building campaign was to strengthen existing fortifications in the ports within the invasion zone – notably in and around Dover – and then to add new works to these key locations as required. But what about the rest of the coast? Should a series of strong points be constructed, or should there be a linear defence that formed a continuous coastal crust but – being extended – could not offer great strength at any single point?

The answer came from a junior Royal Engineers officer, Captain William Ford. In 1794 Ford had been present at an action at Martella in Corsica when a French garrison, lodged in a squat, round, thick-walled gun tower, had held out against – indeed badly damaged – a number of attacking Royal Navy warships. The strength of the structure, and the damage it had inflicted on British warships, gave Ford an idea. He suggested the construction of a chain of similar towers, positioned to give each other mutual support, along the threatened parts of the English coast and around other important locations in Britain vulnerable to French raids. Ford made his proposal in 1803 yet – despite the desperate nature of the French threat – there was no immediate response.

Ford had submitted his proposal to his senior officer, Brigadier General William Twiss (the commanding engineer of the southern district), who evaluated the proposal, approved it and passed it on to the Commander in Chief of the British army, the Duke of York. The Duke approved the proposal in April 1804, as did the First Lord of the Admiralty, and again nothing happened. It was not until October 1804 – over a year after the

Opposite: *Napoleon Bonaparte in his coronation robes after being crowned Emperor in 1804. His new absolute power, his military genius and his determination to crush British opposition to his will made the new Emperor a very formidable enemy.*

Above: *The Army of England is reviewed by Napoleon at Boulogne on 15 August 1804. This army of 130,000 men – whose tents stretched as far as Calais and were visible from the cliffs at Dover - was ready and more than willing to spring at a moment's notice upon 'perfidious Albion'.*

scheme was first proposed and while Britain trembled in expectation of imminent invasion – that Prime Minister William Pitt (recently returned to power) finally approved the building of Ford's Martello towers.

Twiss was dispatched to survey the coast between Beachy Head and Dover to select sites and negotiate with the various landowners, but still nothing was started. In November 1804 Twiss had to report to the Board of Ordnance that 'from the lateness of the season, and the few materials collected… it will not be proper to begin them until Spring'.

Cost was clearly a major cause of delay: each tower, it was estimated by Twiss, would cost £2,000 and consume 450,000 bricks. In fact each was to cost nearer £3,000, while one document in the Public Record Office suggests that towers cost £5,000 each exclusive of the expense of the ditch. The last tower built on the south coast – at Seaford and larger than usual – cost £18,000. To put this cost in context, for this money at the time it would have been possible to build about fifty cottages, or a small village. The towers were built under the control of Lieutenant General R. Morse of the Royal Engineers, the Inspector General of Fortifications, with construction in the hands of independent local builders.

Top: *A Martello tower at Bantry Bay in Ireland. Built in the spring of 1805, the Irish towers predate the construction of the slightly larger English equivalents. Constructed of massively strong masonry, the tower mounted a long-range 24-pounder cannon on its roof.*

Above: *This early nineteenth-century view of a group of Martello towers emphasises the defensive and offensive power of this system of coastal fortification. Each tower can offer its neighbours supporting fire, while together the 24-pounder cannons mounted on the roof of each tower could cover the surrounding sea with a devastating fire.*

At last, in the spring 1805, the building of the south coast Martello towers began. This was nearly two years after Ford had first suggested them and about one year after Martello towers – of smaller size and simpler than those proposed for England's coast – had been built at vulnerable points around Ireland's coast such as on Bere Island, Bantry Bay, where the French had attempted a landing in December 1796. By the end of the summer of 1805 England's south coast was a shambles of belatedly started and half-built forts, barracks and towers. If the French had landed then – as well they might – these works would have done little or nothing to stop them. Despite the close and menacing presence of the French, there was a curious atmosphere of apathy in England.

Trafalgar and the wooden wall

The Battle of Trafalgar was in fact won even before the first cannon was fired. The true victory over the French invasion plans lay with the 'unobtrusive heroes' of the Royal Navy who patiently watched over the ports scattered along the enemy coastline, twenty-four hours a day, 365 days a year, effectively preventing the French and Spanish from putting an invasion fleet to sea.

Blockading was the Admiralty's first line of defence. Admiral Cornwallis had perhaps the most difficult job in co-ordinating fleets off Brest, in the Bay of Biscay and the western approaches to the Channel. Nelson, meanwhile, guarded ports in the Mediterranean, where he stayed for over two years without leaving his flagship. For the most part these voyages, with no destination and no end in sight, must have been a loathsomely tedious and humdrum experience. The British instinct was to fight, and yet the French could not be lured out of port.

Life on board a ship of the line was hard. Between 600 and 800 men – and sometimes more – were crammed on to the decks of a ship no more than 200 feet long, living from day to day in the greatest privation. The crews included miscreants handed over by local magistrates, and those press-ganged into service. Order was maintained with strict discipline – lashings were liberally administered for drunkenness, fighting or general disobedience. However, all the time they were cruising the coastline, these unlikely crews were gaining practical experience. Napoleon believed that his fleet would be conserved in port while the British wore themselves out at sea, but this policy meant that his men could not be trained in gunnery or seamanship and had little or no experience in open waters.

Opposite: The Battle of Trafalgar, October 1805, as portrayed in the early nineteenth century by Clarkson William Stansfield. In the centre is Nelson's flagship, Victory, *surrounded by wrecked and dis-masted enemy vessels. The extremely close-quarter action is probably no exaggeration.*

Yet such was the British awe of Napoleon that rumours abounded of 'secret weapons', and many along England's south coast lived in daily fear of Napoleon and his troops emerging from a Channel tunnel (a French mining engineer, Mathieu, had in 1802 submitted a plan for a tunnel to Bonaparte), or descending upon them in vast balloons. Few, however, seemed to realize that one technology had advanced to such an extent, and was so nearly within Napoleon's grasp, that the whole balance of naval superiority could quite easily have shifted in his favour. An American engineer working in Paris, Robert Fulton, achieved very real success with his first steam engine during the summer of 1803. As the movements and speed of sailing ships were entirely at the mercy of the weather, a few steam-driven tugboats, used to pull the French fleet out of harbour when the weather was too calm for the British fleet to have given chase, could have led to a successful invasion. In 1804 Napoleon ordered a special commission to study the results of Fulton's work. His response to their conclusions was enigmatic: 'I have just read the report on the project of Citizen Fulton, the engineer, which you have sent me, I might add, much too late, since it is one that may one day change the face of the world.'

Despite his close personal control over his navy, much has been made of the fact that Napoleon was first and foremost a soldier, with little love or understanding of the sea. Nothing appears to illustrate this more clearly than his final audacious plan to overcome Britain, and the orders he gave that would ultimately lead to the Battle of Trafalgar. The essence of his plan was that Admiral Ganteaume and his fleet would escape from Brest, Villeneuve and his fleet would evade Nelson and sail from Toulon, both would liberate other French and Spanish fleets and then rendezvous in Martinique in the West Indies. The enormous fleet secretly assembled there would return to Ushant, take the English by surprise and then sail up the Channel. For many reasons this plan failed. British intelligence was good, and the blockade was even better: Ganteaume could not run the gauntlet of the English forces at Brest without causing a battle, which was against Napoleon's orders. Thus he did not put out to sea and the invasion was doomed from the very beginning.

Villeneuve meanwhile did escape from Toulon, where Nelson followed him to the West Indies. Hearing of Nelson's imminent arrival, he chose to return to Europe rather than fight him there, which would have weakened the fleet for the second part of the plan. On the journey back, Villeneuve knew the British were waiting for him, and with many men suffering seasickness in the stormy weather he turned his weakened fleet south to Cadiz. The British fleet stationed there allowed him into harbour, and slowly, over the next six weeks, more ships assembled to keep him there.

The conclusive battle off the Cape of Trafalgar on the Spanish coast took place on 21 October 1805. Villeneuve and his men, and a reluctant Spanish fleet, outnumbered the British so the French had a chance. In the bloody engagement over 450 British sailors died, and more than ten times that number on the other side. The combined fleet was, as the British planned, 'annihilated', but the greatest loss was Nelson, for whom the hardened sailors 'wept like wenches'.

After Trafalgar, Napoleon realized he could not easily achieve the naval superiority he wanted, and postponed his invasion plans indefinitely. In time, his defeat would lead to a unique period in naval history, when the Royal Navy was so prestigious that sea-warfare practically ceased. Most of Britain's rivals on the seas had been Napoleon's allies, and so when he fell, he took them with him. The brave men in the British fleet not only averted imminent invasion, but also provided a more secure future for their island base for many years to come.

In 1796, when the plan to raise a volunteer army was getting under way, the Government was concerned that the public was not scared enough. A portfolio now held in the British Library reveals the extent to which the Government was committed to a war of propaganda. The folio contains hundreds of pamphlets and broadsheets – most published in 1803 and 1804 – aimed at alerting the public to the perils of the moment. Many are satirical and most mock Bonaparte and the French in one way or another, but the underlying message is deadly serious. The enemy *is* coming: be prepared.

A more tangible expression of the Government's concern was the construction, from 1804, of an alternative 'capital' for use if the French managed to invest or capture London. Located at Weedon Bec in Northamptonshire, the new capital was placed as far from the sea as it is possible to get in Britain. With incredible speed, barracks, magazines, store-houses and a royal pavilion – where the Royal Family could be lodged – arose beside a spur of the Grand Union canal. It was military planning and engineering on a massive scale demonstrating that, if the test came and the French invaded, then Britain was determined to fight to the finish.

But the test did not come. Instead, in October 1805, the invasion threat was removed – at least in the medium term – by Nelson's victory at Trafalgar. But Napoleon's smashing victory in December at Austerlitz proved that he remained the great land power in Europe so that, as far as Britain could then see, invasion by the French remained a very real possibility.

The Martello tower building programme continued at a fairly leisurely pace – no doubt as a result of Trafalgar and due to the death in January 1806 of William Pitt, who had proved himself a great champion of fixed fortifications. By the end of the summer of 1806 only six of the towers were complete and it was more than two years before all seventy-four of the south coast towers – including larger redoubts at Eastbourne and Dymchurch and stretching from Seaford in the west to Folkestone in the east – were completed.

Although Napoleon retained an Army of England and occasionally threatened invasion during the half decade after Trafalgar, the real likelihood of French invasion was over by 1808. But it was at exactly this time that the Government started the second phase of its Martello tower-building campaign. From 1808 to 1812 twenty-nine towers were built along the east coast, from St Osyth in Essex north to Aldeburgh in Suffolk, to command some of the loneliest coast and inlets in England. The terminal date of 1812 for the building campaign is significant, for it was in that year that Napoleon, following his catastrophic defeat in Russia, was finally robbed of the power to invade Britain.

In total 103 towers were built between 1805 and 1812. Each tower was to be set roughly 600 yards apart (although occasionally closer when defending key targets and more distant when on rocky terrain) and each was to mount at least one 24-pounder gun. Operating together, and supported by intermediate batteries and field works, the towers could deny a large area of coast to the enemy or, at least, make a landing very costly indeed. French ships attempting to land troops in an area commanded by towers 600 yards apart could have come under fire from the long-range 24-pounders – effective up to a mile or so – of around fifteen towers.

Martello towers were of massive masonry construction with walls around 13 feet thick at the base on the seaward – enemy – side and rising to a height of 34 feet. They were scientifically designed, being of irregular elliptical or ovoid form externally but with round rooms internally so that the towers presented extra thick and more acutely curved faces towards the sea to withstand and deflect enemy shot. Each tower is three storeys high with a massive, centrally positioned internal curved pier of brick and stone to support a vaulted upper floor. This strong masonry-vault made the interior of the tower proof against falling shell and shot and provided a strong supporting platform for the 24-pounder cannon mounted on top of the tower. The floor below the gun deck provided living and eating accommodation for the garrison of twenty-four men and one officer.

The ground floor – windowless and secure – acted as a magazine for gunpowder and a storage room. Entry to the tower was via a drawbridge, across a defensive ditch, into the first floor, with the staircase to the roof and to the ground floor set within the thickness of the wall.

Not one Martello tower fired a shot in anger at a foreign invader. This led them to be regarded, after the end of the Napoleonic War, as great and expensive follies. But the fact that these towers were never used is, perhaps, their greatest tribute. The invasion threat was much diminished by the time the building campaign got into full swing but no one could be sure this was the case until 1812, when Martello tower construction ceased. The French showed respect for the Martello. They contemplated this chain of strong, squat, well-armed little towers with trepidation and nicknamed them 'bulldogs'. At the very least Martello towers acted as a great deterrent to anyone considering an action against the south and east coast of England. The best defence is that which deters the enemy from attempting any attack at all.

The Martello tower system of defence protected nearly 200 miles of the coast but, as was clear to the British planners, some parts of this potential invasion zone were particularly vulnerable and would need significant additional protection. Most vulnerable were those areas that offered the French a potentially easy and quick disembarkation. The British were of course right to fear a speedy attack for – as Napoleon admitted later – if he could have landed and sped his forces to London within five days then Britain would have fallen. So the British plan was – at its most simple – to cause the French delay while volunteer and regular army units were gathered and united to form a mobile reserve capable of mounting a counter-attack. The chain of Martello towers was the first land-based line of defence – delaying and disrupting a landing – but it was clear that, for a quick thrust to London, a French force sailing at speed from the Calais area only had three landing sites to choose from. So it was essential that the defences of these locations be strengthened – again to delay if not to utterly confound a French landing. Of the three areas, two were ports which, if captured, would offer the opportunity for a speedy disembarkation and build-up of weapons and supplies: these were Chatham/Medway and Dover. The third location was the flat and inviting – at least for an invader – expanses of the Romney Marsh between Hythe and Rye.

The Thames Estuary and the Medway were already heavily defended in 1803, largely as a result of the Dutch attack of 1667. Consequently, no Martello towers were built there but the strength of the Chatham Lines, defending the Royal Naval Dockyard from land attack, was greatly increased by the massive expansion of Fort Amhurst. Dover was strengthened by a radical upgrading of the ancient castle that was rapidly transformed – starting in 1798 under the control of General Twiss – into a modern artillery fort. More significant was the fortification of the Western Heights that adjoin the castle hill. It was recognized that the fatal weakness of Dover's traditional fortifications was that they were organized to repulse an attack from the sea but offered little serious defence against an attack from inland utilizing modern, powerful long-range artillery. If the French landed an assault force a mile or so down the coast then attacked Dover from the rear, the port and town would be at their mercy. And the weakest link was the Western Heights that overlook the castle and so could provide an excellent location from which French guns could pound the castle to rubble. The neat answer was to turn the town's weakest point into its strongest citadel.

The fortifications that eventually spread along and around the summit of the heights were to include batteries firing out to sea to increase the town's offensive firepower, barracks linked to the harbour by a spectacular triple helix staircase known as the Grand Shaft and a powerful self-contained fort called the Drop Redoubt. This element, the strongest of the new works, was intended to defend the town from land attack and to deny the Western Heights to enemy occupation. The works started in 1804 and, when complete in 1815, they formed – and remain – the most spectacular example of Napoleonic period fortifications in Britain. The

Above: *The Drop Redoubt on the Western Heights at Dover was built to defend the town and port from land attack. Built between 1804–15, the redoubt represents the cutting edge of military design and construction. It is now an abandoned and haunted place.*

Drop Redoubt and the Grand Shaft show how architectural beauty can be achieved through a concern for utility and through the ruthless expression of function. They both have a sublime scale and are expressions of a marvellous marriage between pure, engineered, construction and elegant Regency architectural detailing. Twiss, Ford and their fellow military engineers who created these masterworks are the unsung – indeed virtually unknown – architectural heroes of the war years.

The Drop Redoubt represents the cutting edge of military design and construction in the first decades of the nineteenth century. It was designed to act independently of the other fortifications on the Western Heights and to be a place of immense strength. It was to be capable of powerful long-range offensive fire directed towards an enemy advancing from inland, while devastating defensive fire could also be poured on an enemy that approached to within musket-shot of its walls. To achieve this long- and close-range fire-power the redoubt was armed, according to an Armaments Return of 1805, with thirteen 24-pounder cannon, with an effective range of about a mile, and two 24-pounder carronades – weapons like huge shotguns – that could scatter their charges with deadly effect up to 1,150 yards. As with most artillery fortifications since the early sixteenth century the walls of the redoubt were made thick and formed with earth revetted (that is, faced) with brick so that they could best withstand the impact of shot. The redoubt – an irregular pentagon in plan – also kept a very low profile to present a difficult target for enemy gunners. Wide, deep ditches provided protection from direct assault. The structures within the redoubt – the row of casemates with their vaults of parabolic form and the mighty brick and earthbuilt magazine – are examples of immensely strong and beautiful construction.

Designed to withstand the heaviest French bombardment, the Drop Redoubt has not been able to withstand decades of neglect and persistent vandalism. It is now an abandoned, sad and haunted place.

Above: *The top entry to the Grand Shaft at Dover. The three staircases allowed troops to move – at speed and in bulk – up and down the 140-feet deep shaft that connected the port with the barracks and defences on the Western Heights.*

Immediately to the south of the Drop Redoubt ranges of barracks were built in 1804 (and sadly demolished in 1965) to house 1,300 men. This was the garrison that was to man the fortifications on the Western Heights and defend advanced works around the port. The problem was how to connect the new barracks on the heights with the harbour so men could move quickly between the two. To Twiss the answer was obvious: a shaft. The shaft was to be 26 feet in diameter and 140 feet deep; with three intertwining spiral staircases, it would ensure that troops, moving three abreast on each staircase, could descend or ascend in bulk and at speed.

The design of the Grand Shaft – completed by December 1807 – is bold, simple but ingenious and extremely functional. The shaft contains two vertical cylinders, the inner one pierced with a series of round headed windows taking light from the central light-well. Between these two concentric cylinders are the three winding staircases, each formed with stone treads supported on brick arches. The three staircases discharge onto a small top-lit court that is connected to the quay by a 180-foot-long tunnel. The Grand Shaft is a unique piece of military engineering that has a strange, sculptural – abstract – beauty that transcends its purely utilitarian purpose.

The last of the major defensive works was the construction of the Royal Military Canal. The idea behind it – conceived in late 1804 at the time the scheme to build the Martello towers got the go-ahead – was straightforward. The Romney Marsh – with wide flat beaches and near both the French coast and vital military locations in south England – was a likely location for invasion. One way of removing the problem was to flood it – a very radical solution since the marsh provided a home and livelihood for many. A less radical solution was to separate the marsh from the mainland by a wide defensive ditch or canal along the edge of the highland – the old shoreline in Anglo-Saxon times – to the north of the marsh. This canal, 28 miles long, was to run from Shorncliffe, in the east, to Appledore and then, utilizing parts of the rivers Brede and Rother, to Rye in the west.

This is the idea that occurred to Lieutenant-Colonel John Brown, a Royal Engineer, who submitted his plan in September 1804 to his military superior, General Sir David Dundas, Commander of land forces of the Southern District. Within the month William Pitt approved the scheme and ordered that work should start immediately. Brown was appointed military director and Sir John Rennie, the designer of Waterloo and London bridges, was appointed consulting engineer and work started on 30 October 1804. The canal was to be made 62 feet wide at the surface and 9 feet deep, although in execution the canal is, in some sections, little more than half the projected width. The spoil from excavation placed to the north of the canal was to form a 35-foot-wide parapet with a firing platform to provide musketry positions, and a 30-foot-wide road that could be used to move troops and guns at speed. In addition, the eastern portion of the canal was dug as a series of angled sections so that cannon, placed at strategic locations, could fire along its length to destroy boats attempting to cross – these enfilading cannon were to ensure that there was no stretch of water uncovered by fire.

Final completion of the canal was not until the spring of 1809 when it was extended from Winchelsea to Cliff End to cut off the Pett Levels. Defensive cannon were not put in position until 1812, when the threat of French invasion was effectively over. The final cost of the canal was a staggering £234,310.

The Royal Military Canal is – in its scale and speed of construction – one of the most incredible feats of military engineering ever undertaken in Britain but, as a defensive work, it has always been controversial. If the French had managed to cross the 20 or so miles of the Channel they would surely have leaped this 60-foot-wide ditch with ease or, if that proved too costly, they could have outflanked it.

But the canal was a key element in William Pitt's defensive strategy for the south coast because it was part of a system of defence in depth, with delay as the primary aim. The Martello towers were the first line of defence, with those at Rye and Dymchurch (including an extra strong redoubt) intended to prevent the French from outflanking the canal or from destroying the sluices that kept its water level high. When these towers had done their work – delaying and damaging the French – then it would have been the turn of the canal to cause further delay and casualties. And the canal – although it lacks the width of the Danube or Rhine – could have proved an unexpectedly tough nut to crack in direct assault, for a water-crossing made in the face of enemy fire is always a difficult proposition. Every hour gained by the defenders could mean the difference between defeat and victory for Britain. If the British could win time to gather an army to launch a counter-attack against the invasion beaches before the French had built up their forces or penetrated deep inland, then the island could be saved.

If the canal's military virtues were not much appreciated by Englishmen at the time, the Germans in 1940 viewed it very differently. The Romney Marsh beaches were seen as excellent landing sites but the Royal Military Canal was recognized as a deadly anti-tank ditch. In the Operation Sealion invasion plan (see page 158) the German high command allocated the 7th Parachute Regiment the specific key task of taking the canal in the Hythe region and securing the bridges across it.

CHAPTER ELEVEN

THE NINETEENTH-CENTURY ARMS RACE

The Napoleonic war launched a technological revolution in the weapons and material of warfare. Arms had been needed not only in vast quantity but also to a higher quality. So the techniques of highly engineered mass-production – pioneered during the Industrial Revolution of the late eighteenth century – were allied to arms manufacture. For example, the process of cast-iron production was improved, as was the method of precision boring a cast-iron cannon to ensure that it fired shot with the maximum power and accuracy. Also, the war concentrated the minds of arms manufactures and inventors so a range of new and improved weapons appeared which had a profound influence on the way anti-invasion fortifications would be defended – and how they would be attacked.

This development in weaponry was expressed most dramatically, and significantly, in the rapid evolution after 1800 of the British infantry firearm. The standard weapon was the muzzle-loading smoothbore flintlock, known universally as the Brown Bess. The pattern in use had been introduced in 1730, when the size and design of muskets had first been standardized, and had been modified in the 1770s. The musket fired a large, soft lead ball weighing roughly one ounce and of .5 calibre. The ball was not accurately made and would fit relatively loosely in the barrel, so when fired it would ricochet up the barrel and spin out of a true line. This meant the musket was desperately inaccurate beyond 50 to 70 yards, while the ball's loose fit in the barrel also meant that much of the energy of the exploding gunpowder charge in the barrel escaped around the ball rather than propelling it forward with maximum force. Consequently, as well as being inaccurate, the musket was a low-velocity weapon with a maximum range little beyond 200 yards.

Loading the musket was a time-consuming business. The ball and gunpowder charge were wrapped in greased cartridge paper and, when loading, the end of the cartridge was bitten off and then the gunpowder emptied down the muzzle of the barrel followed by the ball with the paper rammed in last to act as wadding. This lengthy loading process meant that only two or three aimed shots could be fired every minute. The firing mechanism was also problematic. The hammer held a piece of flint which, when the trigger was pulled, fell on a metal plate to make a spark that ignited fine-grain gunpowder in the firing pan. That, in turn, ignited the main

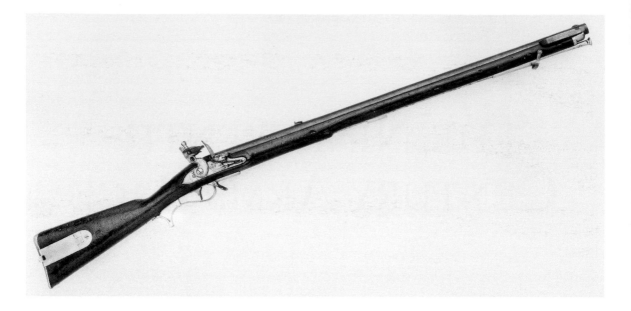

Above: *The Baker Rifle was made in London from around 1800 and issued to specialist rifle regiments. Although still incorporating the old-fashioned flintlock firing mechanism, the Baker Rifle helped to revolutionise the battlefield because it had a rifled barrel which could fire balls with greatly increased accuracy and range.*

charge in the barrel. The appreciable delay between pulling the trigger and the ignition of the main charge did nothing to help the accuracy of the weapon. Worse still, the flintlock was virtually unusable in the rain and was very unreliable even in good weather conditions when the flint could fail to spark or the priming charge would merely 'flash in the pan' and fail to ignite the main charge. This meant that around 40 per cent of all shots were misfires.

The limitations of this standard infantry weapon dictated basic military tactics. It meant that troops had to operate in massed, co-ordinated volley-firing formations fighting in close proximity to the enemy, since nearly half of every volley would consist of misfires, while the shots that did go off would be highly inaccurate and carry for a very limited distance. In the late eighteenth century there was a technological development that was to form a key element in the transformation of the infantry weapon into a more accurate, long-range weapon. This development first manifested itself in Britain in 1800 in the Whitechapel factory of Ezekiel Baker. He produced muzzle-loading flintlocks, but with a spectacular difference. The barrel was not smoothbore but rifled – that is, made with a spiralling groove cut inside so that, when fired, the tight-fitting ball would spin to achieve far greater accuracy and range. This was a highly significant innovation that helped to reconfigure the battlefield: rifle-armed marksmen and light infantry could operate independently as skirmishers, to harass enemy formations with accurate, long-range rifle fire. Despite its increased range and accuracy, the Baker Rifle was still slow to load (slower than the smoothbore since it took longer to hammer the lead ball down the grooved barrel) and was still subject to misfires. Another innovation soon took place that was, eventually, to revolutionize the way in which the main charge of the weapon was ignited.

In 1805 the Reverend John Forsythe realized the fact that fulminate of mercury explodes on impact could be put to practical use in the discharge of firearms. The result was the replacement of the flint and flash pan with the percussion cap. This is a copper-made container filled with fulminate of mercury and placed over a hollow

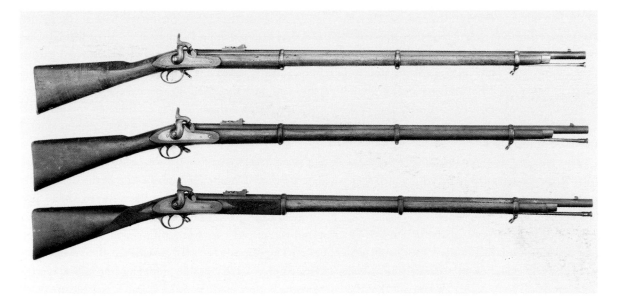

Above: *The Enfield Rifle was not only the first percussion rifle purpose-made for the British army – it was adopted in 1853 – but also the first precision-made mass-produced object of any kind. It was a superb weapon – accurate and reliable – but quickly overtaken by rapid advances in weapon technology.*

nipple. When the trigger is pulled, the hammer hits the cap; this explodes, sending a spark down the hollow nipple to ignite the main charge in the barrel. This percussion system was far more reliable than the flintlock and also increased firing rates, but it was not utilized in military weapons in Britain until 1839.

The infantry firearm was not the only dramatic development during the first decades of the nineteenth century. For example, tugs powered by coal-fired steam engines were considered by the French in 1803 as a means of transporting invasion barges across the Channel, and aerial warfare – in the form of hot air balloons – was contemplated by both the French and the British. In the Public Record Office is a letter of about 1803 outlining a plan to discharge balloons, 18 feet in diameter, carrying 20 pounds each of explosives, against the French invasion flotilla. The balloons were to be launched from about 200 ships, arranged ten wide and twenty deep, which the writer estimates to be capable of discharging 'one thousand balloons at the same moment to be done by signal; they may be arranged within three miles of the Harbour of Boulogne – within sight and yet out of range of either shot or shell'.

The Battle of Waterloo and the end of the war with France in 1815 slowed down the technological development of armaments and fortifications. But this was to be only a temporary state of affairs. By the 1850s Britain was alarmed by the military strength, the apparent imperial ambitions and the aggressive stance of Second Empire France ruled by Emperor Napoleon III. France and Britain had been allies during the Crimean War of 1854–6 but by the end of the decade French invasion was once again haunting the imagination of some British politicians. The most alarmist of these politicians happened to be the Prime Minister – Lord Palmerston – who came to power in 1855.

Palmerston either completely misinterpreted the empty blustering of the weak and vulnerable French emperor as a real threat to the security of Britain, or created a fear of French invasion in a bid to unify a country troubled by social divisions and still haunted by the spectre of revolution raised by the Chartist demonstrations of the late 1840s. Whatever the reason, when the French started to strengthen their naval base at Cherbourg and to experiment in the construction of fast, well-armed, iron-clad warships, Palmerston declared that invasion was imminent. If the French came under steam power then they could outmanoeuvre the sail-powered British fleet, take a major harbour to speed the landing of reinforcements, scatter the small number of British regulars based in England and then march on London. New ships and new fortifications seemed the obvious answer. A Royal Commission 'To Consider the Defences of the United Kingdom' was established in 1859 and Palmerston promoted the construction after 1860 of a vastly expensive network of massive fortifications around the coast of Britain.

This programme of fort-building coincided with significant developments in the weaponry with which those forts would be defended – and with which they could be attacked. Despite the introduction of the Baker Rifle in 1800, the standard infantry weapon remained the smoothbore, percussion-cap musket. But in 1853 – just before the Crimean War broke out – the .577 calibre Enfield Rifle was introduced. This was not only the first percussion rifle purpose-made for the British army, but was also the first precision-made mass-produced object of any kind. Its various components were not crafted laboriously by hand as with the Brown Bess, but were made quickly and very accurately by machine and were fully interchangeable so that repair could be speedy. This precision engineering also meant that the barrel was a perfect circle with its rifling accurately made so that it provided a very snug berth for the bullet. And the bullet itself had changed to present a dramatic improvement over the kind of round slug jammed into the muzzle of the Baker Rifle. A French soldier – a Captain Minié – had come up with a projectile that became known as the minie ball. It was cone-shaped to improve its ballistic quality but, more important, it could be dropped easily into the rifled barrel, yet on firing the bullet would engage with the rifled grooves and be spun to gain greater range and accuracy. This was achieved by a simple idea. A wooden or baked clay plug was fitted into the base of the bullet which, when the charge exploded, was driven into the soft lead bullet which expanded into the grooves as it travelled up the barrel.

The percussion-cap Enfield Rifle could be loaded and fired more quickly than the flintlock musket, was accurate at a range of 500 yards and was highly reliable, with only 0.5 per cent misfires. It transformed the battlefield and provoked changes in other aspects of warfare. Close-action engagements became deadly indeed with, for the first time, infantry armed with rifles capable of laying down a longer-range and more accurate fire than could be achieved by smoothbore artillery. Designers of fortifications and manufacturers of artillery had to respond to the new challenge – and quickly.

New technology and new challenges brought about a revolution in artillery design and manufacture during the 1850s. For over 300 years the vast majority of artillery pieces had been smoothbore muzzle-loaders. But in 1854 William Armstrong, a Tyneside hydraulic engineer, began to develop a breech-loading gun with a rifled barrel. The object was to increase accuracy, range and rate of fire. Armstrong also came up with a novel form of construction. Instead of making the gun entirely out of cast iron, in the usual manner, he shrunk a wrought-iron sleeve over the breech area of a cast-iron barrel. This construction method utilized the superior tensile strength of wrought iron to produce a reinforced barrel that was far tougher than a cast-iron equivalent and so could fire a larger charge.

The rifling system Armstrong devised was curious. The barrel had a large number of shallow grooves scored on its inner surface which engaged with the soft coating on the elongated shell, giving the shell an axial spin as it travelled up the barrel. Armstrong's advanced and inventive design proved to be somewhat ahead of the technology of the time. The breech-loading mechanism lacked strength so the gun could take only a relatively small gunpowder charge and failed to fully realize the potential of the reinforced barrel construction. This meant that the Armstrong gun – although accurate over a long range – lacked the hitting power of the largest

A 16-pounder cannon of around 1860 shows the influence of Armstrong's innovation. The barrel is rifled and its breech is reinforced with a wrought-iron sleeve, but Armstrong's breech-loading system has been abandoned; this gun was loaded in the old-fashioned way, through the muzzle.

conventional smoothbore muzzle-loaders. In 1860, despite this problem, the Royal Navy accepted Armstrong guns of different calibres but decided to use them in combination with heavy-calibre smoothbore muzzle-loaders. These would be used to smash the armour plating on enemy ships, while the Armstrongs were to be used at longer ranges against wooden ships and for the bombardment of land targets.

This triumph of tradition over innovation had a curious influence on the design of artillery during the following decades. Essentially the design became retrograde, with breech-loading being dropped in favour of a return to muzzle-loading, although a number of Armstrong's innovations – notably the shrunk, wrought-iron barrel sleeve – became a standard feature of the new muzzle-loaders. Armstrong's arguments for the advantages of rifling were also gradually accepted and increasingly old smoothbore cannon were turned into rifled muzzle-loaders by the insertion in their bore of a rifled liner. Shells were fitted with small lugs that were engaged with the spiral groove in the barrel when loaded from the muzzle and so were given a spin when travelling up the barrel after firing. Despite the failure of Armstrong's breech-loading system, his ideas about rifling and cannon construction were incorporated into artillery production to create a massively more powerful – if still slow to load – range of artillery. The making of ordnance now became an utterly scientific business with up-to-date mathematical and engineering techniques applied to the design of guns, shells and different types of propellant. By the 1880s steel had replaced wrought iron as the material of choice – largely due to the pioneering work of Sir Henry Bessemer and Alfred Krupp – and the age of heavy and massively powerful artillery dawned.

The creation of the new and more powerful Royal Navy that Palmerston craved was stimulated by the appearance in 1858 of the pioneering French ironclad and partly steam-powered warship *La Gloire*. Britain responded by building an even more powerful modern warship, HMS *Warrior*, which survives in Portsmouth Royal Naval Dockyard. It was Britain's first iron-hulled and partly steam-powered warship and the strength of its construction, combined with high speed and massive firepower, made HMS *Warrior*, when launched in 1860, the most powerful warship in the world. And its sole job was to patrol the Channel waters to prevent French invasion.

The hull is constructed around an immensely strong wrought-iron frame. The central portion of the hull – called the Citadel and containing the main armament of the ship – is a multi-skinned, composite construction. The outer skin of the hull is made of iron plates ⁵/₈-inch thick, backed by 18 inches of solid teak to absorb the shock of cannonball strikes, and with an inner skin of 4¹/₂-inch-thick wrought-iron plates to add extra strength and to stop wooden splinters flying around inside when the ship was under attack. All of this was a response to the rapidly increasing power and accuracy of guns used in forts and on enemy ships. Speed was achieved by the combination of sail and steam power that gave the ship a maximum speed of 14 knots – well over twice the average speed achieved by conventional sail-powered, wooden-walled warships.

The armament was not vast in quantity but the guns were huge and packed a phenomenal punch. There were twenty-six muzzle-loading smoothbore cannon, each firing a 68-pound shot, and ten Armstrong rifled breech-loaders. These fired shot weighing a massive 110 pounds.

HMS *Warrior* certainly looked like the most powerful weapon on earth. Charles Dickens described the ship as a 'black vicious ugly customer… whale-like in size, and with as terrible a row of incisor teeth as ever closed on a French frigate'. Napoleon III observed gloomily that, when at sea, *Warrior* looked like a black snake among the rabbits. The ship never fired a shot in anger – and that was the proof of its great initial success. The ship – and the technological and industrial might of Britain that it expressed – was simply too powerful for any other ship, or any other nation, to think of challenging. *Warrior* was the ultimate deterrent.

The technology of armaments and military design evolved rapidly during the 1860s – largely as the result of the American Civil War of 1861–5, which proved to be an immensely influential testing ground for new technologies and techniques of war. One consequence was the squat, unwieldy but immensely powerful steam-powered ironclad and iron-hulled warship – or Monitor – armed with turret-mounted guns. By 1866 the Royal Navy had ordered its first ocean-going ironclad with turret-mounted guns and in the early 1870s sail was finally abandoned in favour of fully steam-powered warships.

By 1871 HMS *Warrior* was redundant and was withdrawn as a first-line warship. It had been in service only ten years.

The 1859 Royal Commission recommended the protection of Britain's main dockyards with new fortifications on both the sea side and the landward approaches. The recipients of these new works included Portsmouth, Saltash, Plymouth, Milford Haven, Sheerness and Chatham. The total cost was estimated at £11,850,000, a vast sum equal to about £520 million now. The project was hotly debated in Parliament during the summer of 1860, some cuts were made and in July a Bill for the construction of the defences was approved. During the following years some of the proposed forts were abandoned and others truncated, but by 1867 seventy-six forts and batteries had been completed or were in the process of construction. This was the largest fortification-building programme that any British government had ever undertaken in peacetime.

The new generation of anti-invasion forts produced under Palmerston's patronage are an extraordinary mixture of the traditional and the revolutionary inspired, as with the design of warships, by the events of the American Civil War. Traditional is the basic form including deep earth-made and low-profiled ramparts, wide ditches, bastions, caponiers and casemates. Revolutionary are the materials of construction. To give the traditional

HMS Warrior – *launched in 1860 – was better armed, armoured and faster than any comparable ship. She was the terror of her age, the ultimate maritime weapon of the mid-Victorian world, and her sole job was to guard the Channel against invaders.*

forms additional strength to withstand the impact of new powerful artillery, iron and mass-concrete were used along with earth, brick and granite.

Fort Nelson, one of a series of massive artillery forts built on Portdown Hill above Portsmouth to protect the dockyard and city from land attack, is typical of the more traditional type of Palmerston-era fortifications. Built between 1862 and 1871, it consists of thick, low, earth built and brick-clad ramparts surrounding a huge parade ground (below which is a large subterranean powder magazine), protected by wide deep ditches strengthened with caponiers. Guns were mounted to fire over the ramparts, through embrasures and from casemates. A visually more dramatic example of a similar type is Fort Brockhurst, which was completed in 1863, and features a large circular 'keep' with projecting bastion-like caponiers and set in a wide water-filled moat. Hurst Castle, facing the western end of the Isle of Wight, is an extreme example of the battery solution. It incorporates a 1540s gun tower that is flanked by a majestic single-storey sweep of sixty-one granite-built and wrought-iron shielded casemates. Fort Hurst is the largest casemated fort ever built in Britain and is a magnificent and commanding structure. It never saw a shot fired in anger – not even during the Second World War.

More unusual still is Spitbank sea fort, built off the bed of the Solent itself and intended to prevent the French navy from getting close enough to bombard shipping anchored in Portsmouth dockyard. Started in 1861 to the designs of Captain E Steward of the Royal Engineers, Spitbank Fort is circular in form, has grit-stone and granite foundations which were laid by divers, and a thick masonry wall which is a composite construction of granite, limestone and sandstone walls with an inner core of concrete blocks. This lower structure supports the gun floor. This is constructed in two halves. The half facing out to sea has armour-plated walls formed by layers of wrought iron and teak while the half facing inland is of brick and granite construction. The casemates behind these outer walls, vaulted and incorporating brick, concrete and iron beams, were to contain nine massive

Above: *Hurst Castle – built during the 1860s to guard the western sea approach to Portsmouth and incorporating a gun tower of the 1540s – possesses the largest range of casemates in any British fort. Single storey, built of granite and reinforced by wrought iron shields, the curving range of casemates forms one of the most majestic sights in British military architecture.* **Opposite:** *The keep at Fort Brockhurst. Built in the 1860s as part of Lord Palmerston's campaign to protect British ports from invasion, Fort Brockhurst forms part of the land defences of Portsmouth.*

10-inch or 12½-inch rifled muzzle-loading guns facing out to sea and six 7-inch guns facing towards land. Work on the fort stopped in the spring of 1862 so that lessons learned by studying the results of actions in the early phase of the American Civil War could be applied. Works were not started again until March 1867 and finally completed in 1869.

At the time that Palmerston's forts were being completed in the early 1870s the infantry weapon changed again. During the 1860s the Enfield muzzle-loader had been adapted by fitting a breech-loading mechanism and was called the Snider rifle. This weapon was clearly a compromise and it did not compare with the fine, bolt-action single-shot cartridge-firing Chassepot rifle that the French army had adopted in 1867, or with the slightly earlier and similar Prussian Dreyse 'needle-gun'. But the Snider did introduce one new idea into the British army. It fired a cartridge designed by a Colonel Boxer which for the first time included shot, powder and primer and which was simply inserted in the breech and fired. But this hybrid was not long in service. In 1871 the British Army adopted the Martini Henry Rifle. This was an entirely different class of weapon. It was loaded at the breech and fired a Boxer-designed .45 calibre bullet with a .577 calibre base. The bottle-shaped rolled brass cartridge was extremely powerful for it contained a gunpowder charge that was relatively large for the size of the bullet fired.

The main object of the Martini Henry was increased reliability and rapidity of fire – but in both these aims it fell far short of what was possible in the 1870s. Multi-shot repeating rifles were available from the mid-1860s – notably the Henry, and the Winchester from the early 1870s – and their systems could have been adapted for military use. But the military authorities ignored the potential of these weapons because they believed infantry armed with a magazine rifle would fire off their ammunition too fast, wasting money and making it necessary to adapt equipment to enable men to carry more ammunition. As for reliability, the Martini Henry could be a man-killer – but with the victim being the shooter, not the target. When the gun was hot the brass cartridge expanded in the breech and the extractor, rather than pulling it out, just pulled off the rim of the cartridge making its removal very difficult – not a pleasant predicament when being charged by a Zulu impi.

The British Army did not get a magazine rifle until the early 1890s when the bolt-action Lee-Metford was introduced, to be quickly superseded in 1895 by the Lee-Enfield with a ten-round magazine. The Lee-Enfield, firing cartridges filled with more powerful cordite instead of gunpowder, was, with its reliability, rapid fire potential, long range and accuracy, to become arguably the greatest infantry weapon of all time. It was a tremendous advance over the smoothbore muzzle-loader that was in general use little more than fifty years earlier. The development of the personal weapon used by an infantryman during the nineteenth century reveals the immense technological advances that took place in the field of warfare during the century – advances that influenced the way in which objectives were attacked and the way in which defences were designed and built. The new type of magazine rifle, together with mobile machine-guns that came into general use in the 1880s, were to redefine offensive and defensive warfare in the twentieth century.

The Franco-Prussian War of 1870 put an end in Britain to fears of French invasion. Naturally at first British public opinion supported Prussia as it trounced Britain's traditional – and recently predatory – enemy. Thomas Carlyle, when he compared 'noble, patient, deep, pious and solid Germany' with vainglorious France probably represented a common British view in the early months of the war. But as the Prussians pursued an embattled France with a stern ruthlessness and bombarded Paris, British opinion turned. Soon Prussia was seen as a military state committed to savage wars of conquest. By the mid-1870s ruthless, ambitious and efficient Germany – the new empire and power in Europe – was becoming Britain's main potential enemy. But before the focus finally changed to this new challenger, and possible invader, there was one final shiver about the invasion threat posed by two old enemies: France and Russia.

In the mid 1880s there was a sudden panic that France and Russia, operating together with a combined fleet, could sweep past the Royal Navy and strike with terrifying ease and speed at the very heart of the British Empire: London. The capital's defences were outmoded – most dating from the late seventeenth century and the Napoleonic war – while the regular army was small and mostly policing the far-flung British Empire. This 'bolt from the blue' attack on London could, it was feared, be delivered successfully by an enemy force of 100,000 men or less. A flurry of learned and sensational articles and anxious debates in Parliament stirred up public and political concern. Typical was a little book, published anonymously in 1885, entitled *The Siege of London*. It envisaged a French invasion that culminated in a tremendous battle in Hyde Park, the capitulation of London and the eventual loss of India, the Cape, Gibraltar and Ireland.

The consequence of this new fear of France was an increase in the size and improvement in the training and equipment of Britain's militia and volunteer forces and in the construction, to the south-east of London, of a ring of fortified mobilization centres. These were partly inspired by Lieutenant General Shaw Kennedy's proposal of 1859 for a ring of 300 forts around London and Major William Palliser's 1871 paper on 'The use of earth fortresses for the defence of London and as prevention against invasion'. Good and typical surviving examples of mobilization centres are Box Hill Fort and Henley Grove Fort near Guildford. These were to act as fortified supply depots and as rallying points around which local volunteers would muster and from which they would draw arms and ammunition.

The fear of French invasion was finally, and formally, laid to rest in 1904 with the signing of the Entente Cordiale between France and Great Britain. But by that time Britain's fear of France had been firmly replaced by the fear of invasion by the new enemy: Germany.

PART THREE
TOTAL WAR

CHAPTER TWELVE
IMPERIAL EXPANSION: THE NEW ENEMY

In 1800 German-speaking Europe was a fragmented conglomeration of over 300 kingdoms, electorates, principalities, grand duchies and bishoprics. Within a century a united Imperial Germany had emerged as a European superpower that represented a potential threat to Britain and its empire. Imperial Germany, created and steered by the 'Iron Chancellor', Otto von Bismarck, overwhelmed France in 1870, while the British looked on in awe at the rapid defeat of their traditional foe. This was the time of Pax Britannica and 'splendid' political isolation, but policies that had served Britain well for 100 years would be defunct by 1900. By then France had emerged as an ally while Germany, in its aggressive quest for empire and world influence, became the new potential invader of Britain's shores.

Kaiser William II, Queen Victoria's eldest grandson, inherited the German Empire in 1888. The Kaiser was judged by his mother to be 'as blind and green, wrong-headed and violent on politics as can be'. His uncle 'Bertie', later Edward VII, described him succinctly as 'the most brilliant failure in history'. William II considered himself a supreme ruler, signing the Munich city visitors' book with the words 'Suprema lex regis volutas est' (the King's will is the highest law). He despised his parliament (the Reichstag), and ousted Bismarck within two years of ascending the throne, replacing him with a succession of weaker men who effectively diluted the Chancellor's powers in favour of the Crown.

The Wilhelmine era was characterized by the vision of 'Weltmacht' or 'world power', which sprang from the rapid population growth, economic expansion and industrialization of the German Empire. Greater strength brought greater ambition – other European powers were scrambling for colonies across the globe, and Germany wished to compete. It was not just a matter of prestige and prosperity, described by one of its architects as 'irresistible as a law of nature'. The German economy would atrophy if it did not acquire colonies that could provide raw materials and markets for its finished products.

Key to this policy was a strong naval fleet, but at the time William II came to the throne the German navy was held in such low esteem that the few available ships were presided over by army generals, and the majority of Germans believed that 'every man and every penny' should be conserved for land battles. Thus, when William installed Alfred von Tirpitz as Navy Minister and proceeded to sweep away all previous German naval strategy, European heads turned.

In retrospect, the first clatter of pebbles heralding the landslide of distrust between Britain and Germany can be traced back to the German Naval Laws of 1898 and 1900. In order to build battleships, Tirpitz had to persuade the Reichstag to provide cash for a venture that reversed traditional defence policy. In order to justify his demands Tirpitz designated a new German enemy: Britain. A memorandum produced just nine days after he assumed office clearly illustrates this point:

> For Germany, the most dangerous naval enemy at the present time is England… Our fleet must be constructed so that it can unfold its greatest military potential between Heligoland and the Thames… The military situation against England demands battleships in as great a number as possible… A German fleet… built against England [requires]: 1 fleet flagship, 2 squadrons of eight battleships each, 2 reserve battleships for a total of 19 battleships…

William approved Tirpitz's memorandum, which was quickly drafted into a bill. The Kaiser prepared the way for the Navy Bill by informing the Reichstag that 'the development of our battle fleet has not kept up with the tasks which Germany is confronted and 'Our fleet is not strong enough to secure our home ports and waters in the event of hostilities', adding however that 'We are not thinking of competing with the great sea powers… a policy of adventure is far from our minds.' The Bill became law in March 1898.

In 1900, Tirpitz returned to the Reichstag with a bill aimed to catapult Germany into the rank of second naval power in the world: 'To protect Germany's sea trade and colonies in the existing circumstances, there is only one means: Germany must have a battle fleet so strong that even for the adversary with the greatest seapower, a war against it would involve such dangers as to imperil his own position in the world.' Tirpitz's timing was impeccable. Britain was embroiled in a bitter and bloody war with the Boers in South Africa – a people with whom the Germans considered themselves racially and culturally akin. Sympathy naturally lay with the 'plucky little Boers' and anti-British feelings were running high. Tirpitz manipulated a public sense of crisis and frustration to sweep his Second Navy Bill into law, and the German battle fleet swiftly doubled from nineteen ships to thirty-eight.

Three more Navy Laws followed in 1906, 1908 and 1912. Each one was passed on waves of anti-European, and specifically anti-British, feeling. In 1906 and 1911 Britain had supported France against Germany in confrontations over occupation of Morocco. In 1908 the Kaiser increased the German naval fleet by convincing the Reichstag that his uncle, King Edward VII, was cunningly weaving a political 'web of encirclement' around the Reich.

However, without easy access to the North Sea, Germany's expanded naval power would be hamstrung. The construction of the Kiel Canal, connecting Kiel-Holterau with the North Sea at Brunsbuetell, was therefore of supreme importance. The canal began life as a private commercial venture but it quickly became clear that the German navy would benefit greatly from access to the North Sea and the Baltic without having to sail around Denmark. The canal took eight long years to construct, and the Kaiser himself laid the final stone in the summer of 1895.

Opposite: *A German cartoon of June 1909 which fears the deadly consequences of the great naval race between England and Germany. The road of gun barrels comes to a sudden end, suggesting that the careering Dreadnoughts have a bleak and dangerous future.*

Britain could not help but react with alarm to this and other building programmes such as the Berlin–Baghdad railway, which presented a threat to British colonies in Asia, and an increasingly erratic and aggressive German foreign policy. The first casualty was Britain's foreign policy of 'Splendid Isolation' from other European powers, which had served her since Trafalgar. In December 1895, Europe was electrified by reports of a bungled arms raid perpetrated in an attempt to overthrow the Transvaal Government, which was linked to the British military. On the continent, support for the Boers ran so high that in March 1896 Chamberlain, then Foreign Minister, told a conference that 'the shadow of war did darken the horizon', the reason being 'the isolation of the United Kingdom'. Despite Prime Minister Lord Salisbury's opinion that 'isolation is much less dangerous than the danger of being dragged into wars which do not concern us', Chamberlain began doggedly to pursue an Anglo-German alliance, failing on three separate occasions to wring commitment from the German government before talks finally broke down in 1901.

Britain then looked elsewhere to replace the assistance Chamberlain had sought from the Kaiser. This was found in an alliance with Japan in 1902 to protect mutual interests in the Far East. Two further agreements with France and Russia were signed in 1904 and 1907 respectively. Both the French and the Russian 'Ententes' were presented as harmless colonial agreements devoid of military commitment, and elicited a muted response from Germany, summarized by Chancellor Bernhard von Bulow: 'We need not be alarmed by ententes in regard to matters which do not directly concern us. We cannot live on the enmities of other nations.'

The vague instinct in Britain that Germany must not achieve hegemony on the continent also found substance in the rebuilding and restructuring of the Royal Navy. Despite worldwide acceptance of its superiority, the Royal Navy of the late nineteenth century was outdated and disorganized, drowning in tradition and thoroughly unready for war. The remedy for all its ills was found in the shape of John Arbuthnot (Jacky) Fisher who as early as 1901 had identified Germany as the new enemy when he wrote 'we must reconsider our standard of naval strength in view of the immense development of the German navy'. Fisher became First Sea Lord in 1904 and immediately set about revolutionizing the fleet with a swathe of controversial reforms. His priorities were clear. If war came he wanted the British fleet to 'hit first, hit hard and keep on hitting'. He was constantly stimulated by innovation, and perhaps his greatest achievement was the design and construction of HMS *Dreadnought* – the world's first all-big-gun battleship. The premise was simple: 'The fast ship with the heavier guns and deliberate fire should absolutely knock out a vessel of equal speed with many lighter guns.' The result would be 'HELL!'

Fisher convened a Committee on Designs to work out details and produce drawings for the prototype, which took seven weeks in January and February 1905. There was no precedent for this work, yet the committee successfully planned and went on to construct a 17,000-ton gargantuan, carrying 5,000 tons of armour and featuring ten 12-inch guns that were capable of firing 6,800 pounds of shell simultaneously – the equivalent to two or three of the most modern battleships. The designers took enormous risks. The limitations of standard steam engines had led to previous ships being nicknamed 'monsters with short legs', but *Dreadnought* was to be powered by turbine engines, which were still at the forefront of technology. The experiment was successful and the ship was to consistently achieve speeds around five knots faster than her predecessors. Furthermore she was built for only £181,000 more than pre-Dreadnought ships, and in record time. The launching of the ship in 1906 made headlines across the world and the German Admiralty paid close attention to her progress. In the Kaiser's opinion she constituted the 'armament of the future'.

Not everybody in Britain was euphoric about Jacky Fisher's success. Naturally, in producing a ship that instantly rendered all previous designs obsolete, he had condemned not only enemy ships, but also the entire British fleet at a stroke. Chancellor Lloyd George considered the Dreadnoughts 'a piece of wanton and profligate ostentation… We did not require them… Nobody was building them and if anyone had started

HMS Dreadnought *returning to Portsmouth in 1907. When launched in 1906 the the heavily armed, strongly armoured and fast Dreadnought outclassed all existing battleships and transformed the future of naval warfare.*

building them, we, with our greater shipbuilding resources, could have built them faster than any country in the world.' The implication was that the naval arms race, which was of so much greater importance to Britain than mainland Europe, would now start again on a level playing field. However, this was not quite accurate in one crucial instance. German ships were inferior to their British pre-Dreadnought counterparts – limited in size and tonnage by the depth of the Kiel Canal. Tirpitz was forced by British innovation to take the difficult decision to spend a great deal of time and money to build not only bigger ships, but also to enlarge the canal to accommodate them. Fisher later exulted in the fact that Germany had been 'paralysed by the Dreadnought which had halted all German construction for a year and converted the Kiel Canal into a useless ditch'. Based on a calculation of the time it would take to widen the canal, Fisher also speculated that 'the Battle of Armageddon' between Britain and Germany would break out in October 1914 – the Kaiser probably choosing to launch hostilities on a weekend with a bank holiday. Work on the canal was completed in July 1914 and the First World War broke out on a bank holiday weekend the following August.

Germany began to build Dreadnoughts, and with such efficiency that in 1909 Britain found itself in the grip of a full-blown navy scare. Since 1905 Britain had been governed by a Liberal cabinet that was committed to cutting the defence budget in order to fund social reform. As a result of its reductions in July 1908 Britain had twelve Dreadnoughts as opposed to sixteen built, building or authorized by Parliament. Meanwhile, within two years, beginning in the summer of 1907, Germany had laid down or ordered nine Dreadnoughts. If both building programmes met projected targets, then in 1912 Germany would possess thirteen Dreadnoughts to Britain's sixteen, which was not considered by the Admiralty to be an adequate margin to ensure naval supremacy. To compound the crisis, ominous reports began to filter back to the British government of secret German building programmes – of guns and other components stacking up in Germany shipyards, and of keels being laid down months prior to the dates scheduled by German naval law. Assuming that the reports were true, and if maximum capacity of German shipyards was being utilized, then the unthinkable would occur: the Royal Navy would be outnumbered. In time, the grounds for the scare proved to be false, as despite confirmation of some illegal shipbuilding activity, the delivery date of the German Dreadnoughts was not brought forward. But the press hysteria surrounding the issue forced Jacky Fisher, who felt that his position had been eroded, to retire from the Admiralty shortly afterwards.

The press hysteria in 1909 was just one outlet for the vulnerability Britain felt when confronted with her political isolation in late-nineteenth-century Europe. It did however, prove to be an effective medium for an alternative outpouring of emotion – a new genre of polemical spy stories and invasion thrillers whose authors came to be known as the 'paper warriors'. The first of these stories, *The Battle of Dorking: Reminiscences of a Volunteer*, appeared in 1871, the year in which Germans gathered at Versailles for the inauguration of the first Reich, following their victories in the Franco-Prussian war. On 3 January 1871 a military correspondent for *The Times* reported that the invasion of England was 'a rather favourite topic of conversation' with German officers stationed in France.

The Battle of Dorking, written by George Chesney from a background of military experience, appeared in May and tells the story of a successful German invasion of England. At a time in which the British press was reporting reasons why British defence forces were 'not sufficiently large or sufficiently organized to make invasion virtually impossible', the tale is naturally cautionary, painting a picture of a nation in which 'the rich were idle and luxurious; the poor grudged the cost of defence'. The narrator bemoans the fact that 'There, across the narrow Straits, was the writing on the wall; but we would not choose to read it.'

The story was originally printed in *Blackwood's Edinburgh Magazine*, but the publishers struck gold when they hit upon the idea of producing sixpenny copies, which began to sell at the rate of 80,000 copies per month. Between May and October of 1871, Chesney's tale reached out to every echelon of British society. This political awakening continued to manifest itself in a steady stream of literature based on the imminence of foreign invasion. In 1882 a scheme to build a 20-mile railway tunnel from Calais to Dover was proposed in Parliament and, amidst public uproar, a constant stream of penny novels poured off the presses, with titles such as *England in Danger*, *The Seizure of the Channel Tunnel*, *Battle of the Channel Tunnel* and *How John Bull Lost London*.

The best of the invasion genre was Erskine Childers's novel *The Riddle of the Sands*, published in 1903. In this, two young Englishmen stumble across a secret German invasion plot and become embroiled in 'an experimental rehearsal of a great scene, to be enacted, perhaps in the near future – a scene when multitudes of sea-going lighters, carrying full loads of soldiers, not half-loads of coal, should issue simultaneously, in seven ordered fleets, from seven shallow outlets, and, under escort of the Imperial Navy, traverse the North Sea and throw themselves bodily upon English shores'. One of the Englishmen demonstrates a certain respect for Germany: 'Here's this huge empire, stretching half over Central Europe – an empire growing like wildfire, I believe, in people, wealth, and everything. They've licked the French and the Austrians and are the greatest military power in Europe...'

Few other British writers echoed Childers's basic respect for Germany and its intentions. In 1909 Chancellor Bethmann-Hollweg commented on an atmosphere between England and Germany that was 'chilly with distrust'. Attempts to limit the arms race had failed, with Britain preferring to pursue a costly and wasteful policy rather than commit to a position of neutrality if Germany became involved in a war. In time, the millions of pounds expended in achieving naval superiority bought reassurance, and temporarily improved relations between the two nations, but across Europe a dangerous trend had been initiated. Weapons were accumulating in the armouries of states harbouring bitter grudges, and the balance of power became ever more delicate as tensions grew. In 1914, as Winston Churchill observed, 'the vials of wrath were full'.

CHAPTER THIRTEEN

NEW TECHNOLOGY: THE AIRSHIP

The twentieth century saw the rapid introduction and development of a technology that was to transform warfare, and have a profound influence on both how Britain was attacked and how it was defended. The enemy was now to invade from a new dimension – the air – and for the first time the civilian population of Britain, and not just its soldiers, would be in the front line. The seriousness of this new threat was recognized immediately. When Blériot flew the Channel in 1909 there was a near hysterical reaction from the British press. In the *Daily Mail*, H. G. Wells expressed what all were thinking: 'This is no longer, from the military point of view, an inaccessible island.'

Germany's airship industry was pioneered by Count von Zeppelin, who was committed to the development of rigid airships and, in July 1900, successfully test-flew one of his own design. This flight, over Lake Constance, demonstrated that rigid airships were not only a practical proposition but also the only type of aircraft that offered reliability, safety and the promise of carrying large numbers of passengers or heavy cargoes.

The first Zeppelin – Luftschiff Zeppelin 1 – established the principles followed in later, larger, Zeppelins. It was 420 feet long and contained a number of hydrogen-filled gas cells set within a strong but lightweight aluminium frame, which was covered with fabric. LZ1 was powered with petrol engines and could reach a speed of only 16 miles an hour. In 1907 Zeppelin received a government grant to develop his airship technology and, in the same year, the army ordered a craft. The airship as a machine of war had arrived.

By the outbreak of war in 1914 both the German army and navy had their own airship fleets comprising Zeppelins with aluminium frames and Schutte-Lanzs (SLs) with plywood frames. By this time airships were significantly larger and thus capable of carrying heavy bomb-loads and flying faster (around 50 mph) and higher (10,000 feet and over in good conditions).

The first German air attack against Britain took place on 21 December 1914. The target was Dover; two 20-pound bombs were dropped from an Albatross seaplane. No one was injured, but the myth of Britain as an island fortress safe from the assault of the enemy was shattered. Having enjoyed centuries of relative

137

safety during times of war, Britain's civilians were now to be the first in the world to undergo the ordeal of systematic, regular and long-term aerial attack. The first airship raid came on the night of 19 January 1915. The target was East Anglia with twenty-three bombs dropped, most effectively on Great Yarmouth. These caused the first casualties from aerial attack suffered in Britain during the war: four dead and sixteen injured.

To the German public the Zeppelin was a technological wonder, a source of great national pride and a war-winning machine. But the German military was more sceptical and no senior commander seems to have had a clear idea how this new weapon of war should best be used. Should the airship fleet merely play a tactical role scouting and supporting the army and navy in their initiatives, or should it develop a strategic role of its own and become a genuine third arm – equal to the army and navy – and launch independent attacks deep into the enemy's rear?

Caution and conservatism suggested the tactical role, while vision and confidence in the destructive future of aerial warfare made it clear that airships should be used in a strategic role to attack enemy communications, military depots, harbours and factories, and – ultimately – to cause terror among the enemy workforce and population. Inevitably, a compromise solution was followed, with the German high command requiring its airships to fulfil both tactical and strategic tasks. This meant that raids on England, when they started, were generally undertaken by too few ships with long intervals between raids. In addition, the terror factor was diluted by Germany's initial reluctance to unleash such an inaccurate weapon against centres of civilian population. And the airship was a very blunt weapon indeed. It was difficult to navigate with any accuracy so pre-selected targets were nearly impossible to find, and bombs could not be dropped with any accuracy. Clearly, all attacks were more or less random, and the use of such a weapon over a large city could have horrible implications for the civilian population. As the German commanders realized, a bombardment that missed military targets but killed women and children and destroyed historic buildings could turn world opinion against the German cause. For this reason the German Chancellor, Theodore von Bethmann-Hollweg, was opposed to the idea of bombing civilian targets while the Kaiser, during the first year of the war, ordered that German airships must not attack the London area.

But pressure mounted for the more aggressive use of this new wonder weapon. In January 1915 Admiral von Tirpitz had argued that 'if one could set fire to London in thirty places, then what in a small way was odious would retire before something fine and powerful'. The Kaiser caved in and on 12 February that year issued an Imperial Order which permitted attack on military establishments, oil and petroleum tanks and the docks in London. Given the inaccuracy of the airship's bomb aiming technology and the close integration in London of civilian housing with the declared German targets, this order did in fact, if not in theory, permit the German airship squadrons to unleash the horror of total war on the population of east London where the German targets were located.

The first attack on the heart of the British Empire – an act of aggression that many Germans saw as potentially war-winning – came on the night of 31 May 1915. LZ38, commanded by Hauptmann Karl Linnarz, took off at dusk from Brussels-Evere. The target was industrial east London. The LZ38 passed over the English south-east coast near Southend at 10,000 feet. By 10.50 p.m. it was over east London, and 120 high explosive and incendiary bombs cut a swathe from Stoke Newington and Dalston through Hoxton and Whitechapel to West Ham and Leytonstone. There was some resistance but, as was usual at this time, anti-aircraft fire was inaccurate or incapable of reaching the height at which the airship glided, searchlights were easily thrown-off and fighters – straining to reach the heights inhabited by airships – merely groped around in the dark. Seven Londoners were killed and twenty-five were injured: a tiny number of casualties in the context of the Western Front, but these were civilians, surprised and killed in their homes. For the first time

An image to chill the hearts of any Englishman. Published in the Illustrated London News *in 1913 the picture shows the German threat to Britain, as the Dreadnought of the air – the Luftschiff Zeppelin 1 - floats over and aids the Dreadnoughts of the sea.*

since the Dutch raids of 1667, the London area was under attack by a foreign force and its population was suffering.

The consequences of this raid were immense. At a stroke the German military felt almost omnipotent – LZ38 had thrown off all attackers and returned home safely – while the British felt dreadfully vulnerable. What next, they wondered, was to come since the Germans had demonstrated that London was, apparently, an open target? Yet there were also worrying and unfortunate consequences for the Germans. If the raid was intended as an exhibition of German military prowess to impress the world, it had backfired. No military targets had been hit but, in Stoke Newington, a baby was burned to death while in Dalston a harmless middle-aged couple had been incinerated beside their bed 'in an attitude of prayer'. So the Germans were, as their enemies had long portrayed them, nothing more than frightful Hun barbarians.

British response to the airship threat changed after this raid. In 1913 Winston Churchill had dismissed the Zeppelin as an 'enormous bladder of combustible and explosive gas' and mocked the vulnerability of 'these gaseous monsters', but in June 1915 nobody felt like laughing. Churchill himself – in his role of First Lord of the Admiralty – warned the Cabinet early in 1915 that 'there is no means of preventing the airships coming, and not much chance of punishing them on their return'. These unlikely, lumbering, over-size balloons were, it seemed, about to prove themselves lethal and efficient machines of war.

German reaction to the raid was mixed. It was promoted by the press and hailed by the population as a great triumph – a master-stroke of German technical ingenuity and military skill that promised to help win the war.

But the commanders took a more realistic view. Destruction was relatively minor and – more to the point – virtually random and certainly not of military significance. Prohibition against attacks on clearly non-military targets in London was maintained and it was not until 11 July 1915 that the Kaiser – under great pressure from his military commanders and politicians – gave permission for attacks on London as a whole. But the Kaiser still insisted that St Paul's Cathedral and Westminster Abbey – historic buildings closely associated with his English royal relatives – must be spared.

Despite the removal of this prohibition, the next significant German airship attack against London did not come until the night of 7/8 September 1915. Twenty-two people were killed and eighty-seven were injured that night as a result of airship bombs. All the craft returned safely to Germany, leaving London shaken. The attack of 31 May had been bad but this was worse. The trail of devastation was appalling. No capital city had ever been attacked in this stealthy and remote manner before. There was hatred for the Germans with their new scientific form of terror warfare – 'Murder by Zeppelin' was how one newspaper described the attack – but no lessening in resolve to continue the war to victory. There was also fury against those who were meant to defend the capital and who were so clearly and lamentably failing in their task. Not only had no substantial damage been done to the enemy but they had not even – it appeared – been deflected from their bomb run right across the heart of the capital. Something had to be done – and quickly – because it was assumed that the airship force would return soon and in increased numbers.

More guns were moved to London and organized as concentric rings of defence and more fighters were stationed around the capital but, slow and still inappropriately armed, they had little chance of catching an airship or destroying it even if they got within striking distance. The chance to test the new defences came on the night of 13/14 October 1915 when the German Navy Zeppelin force renewed the great offensive against London. Not all the airships got through to London but all returned safely to their bases, leaving in England seventy-one dead and 128 injured. The Germans had clearly won the battle but there were fragments of hope on which the British could build. With advance warning, the coastal guns did succeed in driving off a raider; the guns positioned along the approach route had seemingly confused the raiders and drawn the bombs intended for the capital.

Although this battle appeared to have been won by the Germans, they did not attempt to consolidate their victory. For the next three months no airship entered the airspace over Britain. But the German airship service was far from idle. It was not only pondering new tactics but designing, testing and building more – bigger – craft. Two ships of the larger L20 class – 585 feet long with a speed of 55–60 mph – were already in service by October 1915 and more were in production. But Peter Strasser, the head of the Naval Airship Division, put his faith in ultimate victory for Zeppelin power in the massive six-engined L30 class – the 'super-Zeppelins' – which were due to be in operation by mid-1916.

In late 1915 Strasser and Admiral Reinhardt Scheer, the Commander-in-Chief of the German High Seas Fleet, agreed a co-ordinated attack on Britain that would involve submarines, surface vessels and the navy's fleet of airships. The plan included the comprehensive bombing of Britain which was divided into three zones of attack: the northern, with the principal targets of the Forth and Clydeside; the Midlands, in which attacks would be focused on Liverpool, the Humber area, Birmingham and Sheffield; and the southern, with London as the main target.

On 31 January 1916 nine Zeppelins, including a number of the new powerful L20 class, flew from Germany to launch this new phase of the grand attack on Britain. The plan was to attack the Midland and southern zones but chaos reigned – among attackers as well as defenders – for the weather was terrible with freezing rain, snow and fog. The airships were buffeted in the winds. The freezing rain made them lose height and caused

Zeppelin raids on Britain meant that the civilian population was for the first time in the front line. Bombs – although relatively small and dropped virtually at random – did much damage, usually to non-military targets such as this house in King's Lynn which was hit in January 1915.

engine problems and the fog and snow prevented accurate navigation as landmarks were obscured or transformed. In addition communications and radio direction-finding devices failed. Bombs were scattered across a wide area of England but no targets of real importance were hit although seventy-one people were killed and 113 injured. So the old problems of inaccuracy, poor navigation and unreliable communications continued to dog the German effort. And – to make things worse for the Germans – one of their ships was missing.

L19 had wandered over the Midlands trying to find Liverpool, dropped its bombs over Burton-on-Trent and the suburbs of Birmingham and then passed over the English coast at 6.41 a.m., when its commander told headquarters, by wireless, that he was on his way home. L19 never made it. The engines failed, the ship lost height, was hit by Dutch gun-fire and then staggered north to crash into the North Sea. Airships were grounded because of high winds so German ships went in search of the missing airship – but an English trawler, the *King Stephen* of Grimsby, found it. What took place next gave rise to one of the greatest controversies of the war.

The master of the trawler refused to take the crew on board although abandonment meant almost certain death. The trawler left and the crew were never seen alive again. Their fate only came to public notice because – incredibly – a bottle bearing two notes about the incident was washed ashore six months later in Sweden. One note was a technical account of the crash written by its commander, which ended: 'February 2, towards 1 p.m., will apparently be our last hour.' The other note was from a crewman: 'My greetings to my wife and child. An English trawler was here and refused to take us on board. She was the *King Stephen* and hailed from Grimsby.' The master of the trawler later explained that he feared the sixteen-strong crew of L19 would seize his ship if he took them aboard. The Germans accused the master of a war crime and Britain of breaking the Geneva Convention. Things were only made worse when the Bishop of London gave it as his opinion that leaving the 'German baby-killers' to drown was understandable – shocking perhaps, but in the context of the time the Bishop was only expressing a commonly held opinion. The First Sea Lord, Lord Fisher, suggested killing one captured German civilian for every British civilian killed in a raid, a proposal supported by the public in letters to the press. The hatred the British felt for the 'unsporting' German airship crews was strong indeed.

Admiral Scheer and Strasser assessed the 31 January raid and decided that the weather had been largely responsible for its shortcomings. They were aware of the clamour in Britain that the raid had caused – the demand for the return of guns from the Western Front was a victory in itself. The pressure must be kept up. On 31 March an attack on London started that was to be spread over five successive nights. This was to be the body blow to the capital, but it was a fiasco with the airships dumping their bombs virtually at random as they were blown all over Britain with one – the L15 – being brought down off the coast by gunfire. But despite failing to achieve any predetermined strategic or military objectives, the airship had sustained its reputation as a terror weapon: eighty-five people were killed and 217 injured during this chaotic attack.

The German airship service made great – but empty – claims about the success of this series of raids. To have done otherwise would have been to admit that one of the German legends of the war – the vaunted Zeppelin – was a sham.

But Strasser was nothing if not a gambling man. He was now in too far, too deep in fantasy and lies to go back. It was all or nothing – and he still believed the Zeppelin could, with luck and courage, win the war. The next roll of the dice came on the night of 2/3 September 1916, with sixteen airships – including four army craft – all attacking London simultaneously. The raid was more confused than usual with craft turning back, getting lost and dropping their bombs at random. Four people were killed and sixteen injured: not a lot to show for such a mighty effort. The night, however, is memorable in the annals of the airship campaign. For the first time Britain's new secret weapon – the answer to the airship problem – was put to operational use. This was the explosive-incendiary bullet. The army airship SL11 was caught over the north-east edge of London by Second Lieutenant William Leefe-Robinson flying a BE 2c. Three drums of the new ammunition were emptied into the hull of the craft, which suddenly burst into flames and fell to earth. Much of the population of north London had seen the historic battle. This was the first time an airship had been shot down over Britain and the first time people had seen one destroyed. The nation was ecstatic. At last a fighter, properly armed, proved that these monsters of the air were not invulnerable after all. Leefe-Robinson was rapidly awarded the Victoria Cross – the grateful nation demanded it.

Six airship crews had witnessed the horrifying sight of the blazing craft falling to earth while its crew burned alive. It was essential that morale in the force was maintained and the only way to do that was through action. The next attack came on the night of 23/24 September – and it was an attack with a difference. The new super-Zeppelins – the 'big thirties' – were now ready to be used in force. This was the action that would finally make or break the airship as a war-winning force.

The raid of L33

The L33 took off for its first mission on 23 September 1916. It was only a few months old. The L30 series Zeppelins each had a length of 649 feet, a diameter of 78 feet and a gas capacity of 1,949,000 cubic feet. They were powered by six Maybach 240 hp Hslu engines, had a maximum speed of about 60 mph and a maximum ceiling of 17,700 feet, although the operational ceiling was round 13,500 feet. These 'big thirties' could carry a bomb load of 5 tons and had been ready for action since July 1916.

The L32 in flight. One of the new generation of massive 'super-Zeppelins' that came into service in mid-1916, the L32 – along with its sister ship the L33 – was shot down on the night of 23 September 1916. This catastrophe put an end to the German belief in the Zeppelin as a war-winning machine.

A fleet of eleven naval Zeppelins left Germany on the afternoon of the 23rd and flew towards England. Eight were to attack targets north of the Wash while three others were to deliver the greatest blow that London had yet felt during the war. This London-bound force consisted entirely of new super-Zeppelins – the L31 commanded by Heinrich Mathy, the L32 commanded by Werner Peterson and the L33 commanded by Alois Bocker. All these commanders were veterans. Great things were expected of these craft – the pride of the German airship service.

The L33 took off from Nordholz at 3 p.m. GMT, carrying nearly 3 tons of bombs. At ten o'clock at night it was the first of the Zeppelins to cross the coast. It passed over the Thames Estuary and then headed north-east so as to avoid the well-defended eastern approach to London. At about this time the L31 and the L32 were crossing the English coast together near Dungeness on a more indirect – and thus more unexpected – route to London. While his companions were making their indirect approach, Bocker in L33 was flying in from the north-east. At 11.50 p.m. he dropped six high-explosive bombs on Hornchurch and was then picked up by a searchlight but escaped its beam before guns could be brought to bear. At 12.10 a.m. L33 was over West Ham. As the crew was later to admit, after reaching the outskirts of London they used the banks of the Thames as the aiming point for their bombs. It was now that the craft became 'entangled', as the crew put it, by searchlights and gunfire – the first land-based anti-aircraft fire of the night. This fire was rapid and soon got the range of the Zeppelin despite its height of 12,000 feet. But Bocker continued on his bomb-run, releasing a clutch of bombs over Bromley-by-Bow. One 100kg high-explosive bomb and five incendiaries landed on St Leonard's Street and Empress Street. Four houses were damaged, six people were killed and eleven were injured. Bocker then penetrated further east towards the City and unloaded bombs over Bow.

The crew of the L33. The commander, Alois Bocker, sits in the centre. All survived the crash of the Zeppelin in September 1916.

But L33 was in trouble. Some of the east London guns had been very accurate and several shells had exploded near the airship. Fragments had hit the craft and punctured at least one of the gas cells. L33 was slowly losing hydrogen and thus was also losing its greatest defence – height. At 12.19 a.m., L33 was seen over Buckhurst Hill and was clearly in difficulties. Escaping gas had brought the craft down to 9,000 feet and the craft was under attack again from a gun and searchlight team at Kelvedon Common. To escape this fire, Bocker attempted a fast climb by dumping a large amount of his water ballast. For the moment he was successful but at 12.30 he was confronted by a new and far more dangerous menace: a British fighter.

The pilot of the fighter, Second Lieutenant Alfred de Bathe Brandon, was a man up to the opportunity that presented itself, for he had managed to attack and damage L15 back in March 1916. After overcoming a number of difficulties – including his Lewis gun coming adrift – Brandon emptied a whole drum, over fifty explosive-incendiary bullets, into the stern of the airship. Nothing happened. Brandon reloaded and attacked the stern again but this time the machine-gun jammed after about ten shots. So L33 had escaped an apocalyptic end, but it had been further damaged and continued to lose height at a faster rate. At 12.45, when over Chelmsford, Bocker gave orders for non-essential objects to be jettisoned in an attempt to retain height. At 1.10 the airship passed over the Essex coast at Mersea Island heading towards Belgium. But it quickly became clear that the craft could not make it. The decision was between a crash at sea or a return to England and, with luck, a controlled descent and captivity.

Bocker and his crew chose the latter option. The craft was turned round and crept back to the Essex coast. The craft steered well until the very last and then, when less than three miles inland, descended rapidly. The time was 1.20 and the landing site was a field between Peldon and Little Wigborough church. The crew barely had time to get clear of the ship before fire swept forward, devouring the whole envelope. But there was no explosion – the remaining hydrogen burned quietly. The structure of the ship was largely undamaged and this bothered Bocker greatly. He ordered his men to destroy all papers and attempted further destruction of the craft to stop the secrets of its technology and construction falling into British hands. But the destructive actions of the crew achieved little. By the time the British authorities arrived at the crash scene, the frame of the Zeppelin was still virtually intact. Bocker was proved right in his fears. The British did use the information they gleaned from the wreck of the L33, which served as the model for the British post-war airships R33 and R34.

Having failed in their attempt to destroy their craft, Bocker and his men made for the coast, hoping to find a craft in which to escape. It must have been a somewhat half-hearted effort for when apprehended by a single special constable, Edgar Nicholas, the crew surrendered in a most orderly manner. Meanwhile, people from all over England were making their way to Little Wigborough to gawk at the stricken terror of the sky – the fallen giant. Within the week an estimated 250,000 people had come to see the thrilling carcass as it was being methodically examined and dismantled by British scientists and technicians. Such was the excitement that a local couple, Mr and Mrs Clark of Little Wigborough, felt compelled to christen their new-born daughter Zeppelina.

This relatively civilized end to the war for the crew of L33 was not shared by its sister ship L32. The Zeppelin was attacked by Second Lieutenant F. Sowrey and crashed near Basildon at Great Burstead, Essex. Oberleutnant Werner Peterson and his crew of twenty-two all died in the blazing wreck.

The crew of L33 was questioned at length by British military intelligence. The interrogators were not only seeking information about Zeppelin construction, manning and bombing tactics but were, it seems, also attempting to form a psychological profile of the team of men who operated this killing machine. The British intelligence officers seemed to have reached no very firm conclusion about the mental make-up of a typical Zeppelin crew. No distinguishing characteristics unite the members of the crew of one of the fleet of airships that – for over a year – had been dealing out indiscriminate death to the inhabitants of British cities. These 'baby killers' were clearly just ordinary men. If these terror fliers were not especially sinister characters, did it mean that anyone was capable of flinging bombs at innocent women and children? This question was to be answered just over twenty years later in the most forceful manner.

The crash of the L32 and L33 was effectively the end of the delusion that the airship was a war-winning weapon. Airship raids continued – indeed, the last raid took place on the night of 12/13 April 1918 when seven people were killed and twenty injured in Norfolk and the Midlands – while the last time a Zeppelin crossed the coast of England was on 5/6 August 1918. The Germans remained convinced that the aerial bombardment of Britain was of great strategic importance, but in May 1917 this task was given over to aircraft. As weapons, the Gotha and Giant bombers – flying in formation, undisturbed by gusts of wind and initially raiding by daylight – were more deadly and accurate than airships had ever been. The death toll and damage they inflicted in Britain's cities was horrifying. In one raid on London and Kent on 13 June 1917, 162 people were killed and 432 injured – including eighteen children killed and forty-five injured in an East End school.

To a horrified British public, war had plumbed new depths. A report in *The Times* the following day summed up the general mood in Britain: 'If it were possible at this time of day for the enemy to increase the utter and almost universal detestation in which he is held by the people of this country, he did it yesterday.' Within the German state, the strategic bombing policy continued to be characterized by division, and yet somehow arguments based more on emotion than objective fact provided sufficient 'justification' for these attacks. In a letter to Bethmann-Hollweg dated 7 July 1917, Field Marshal von Hindenburg concluded: 'I do not think that

The mighty and majestic wreck of the L33, which crashed at Wigborough in Essex, is inspected by the British military. The frame of the Zeppelin was little damaged by the crash and inspired the British post-war airships, the R33 and the R34.

the English nature is such that anything can be done with them by conciliation or revealing a desire to spare them. The military advantages are great… It is regrettable, but inevitable, that they cause the loss of innocent lives as well.'

In Britain the bomber raids brought increased popular pressure for more protection and the government acted. It instigated a primitive early warning system for London that included policemen carrying placards reading 'Take Cover' and boy scouts blowing bugles to sound the 'All Clear', and more fighters were brought from France – much to the army's annoyance.

By the autumn of 1917 the British Government had come to the conclusion – somewhat reluctantly perhaps – that the most effective defence against German bombing was retaliation. But, despite the rising death toll among British civilians, this policy faced tough opposition from religious leaders who remained 'convinced that this country will sacrifice an advantage of an importance which we cannot now estimate if it surrenders its power of entering on peace negotiations with clean hands'. This was not, however, the dominant mood.

The increasing demand for a British strategic bombing campaign led to the merging of the Royal Naval Air Service and the army's Royal Flying Corps to form, in April 1918, the Royal Air Force. The RAF achieved little in the way of strategic bombing before the war ended but some experimental strategic bombing had already taken place during the autumn of 1917. The activity was limited and yet sufficient to provoke a delegation of Rhineland mayors to petition German authorities to stop their strategic bombing and thus put an end to these frightening reprisal raids. This was, indeed, a sign of things to come.

TERROR FROM THE SKIES: STRATEGIC BOMBING 1918–45

On 11 November 1918, the long-awaited peace finally became a reality. Yet for a shaken British populace, the memory, and the fear, of air power would not die. Britain's true vulnerability to strategic bombing – that is, bombing waged as an end in itself to destroy industry, infrastructure, material and morale of the land – had been exposed on all points. As, ironically, a German representative of the Inter-Parliamentary Union was to point out thirteen years later, geographically Britain's nerve centre was too close to the Channel; demographically she was population dense; and she relied heavily upon an urban-based and industrial economy. Conditions were perfect for a decisive air attack, and London was expected to be a key aerial target.

Many generals and politicians were convinced that the next war would be an air war and that invasion – if it came – would come from the sky. Many had great faith that science would bring forth 'new devices from the air whose nature could only be guessed at'. In his maiden speech in the House of Commons in February 1924, Anthony Eden described aerial bombing as 'the greatest peril of modern war'.

The doctrine of strategic bombing waxed and waned during the interwar years, depending on the influence of its proponents. In the early years of debate, the British Chief of Air Staff, Sir Hugh Trenchard, added weight to the argument for an independent air force with his passionately held belief in strategic bombing as a decisive war-winning weapon. His views were a key element in establishing a government policy of strategic bombing policy to be used as a defensive, deterrent measure, and until the mid-1930s debate on air policy continued to be characterized by visions of the 'knockout blow'. Defence against attack was considered anathema, as key figures such as Winston Churchill gloomily predicted that mankind had the means at hand 'to accomplish its own extinction'. Fighter planes were considered a mere sop to public morale, and Stanley Baldwin famously summed up the conclusions of this era when he declared in the House of Commons in November 1932: 'The bomber will always get through.'

The international political climate only served to fuel British anxieties. Tensions between England and France deteriorated in the early 1920s, reaching their lowest point when France occupied the Ruhr in response to German defaults on reparation repayments. These were also the years of the 'Red Scare'. In 1919 the communist threat was taken seriously enough for Winston Churchill to circulate a 'Secret and Urgent' War Office memo regarding the prospect of military service against the Soviet Union. But above all, 'war clouds' could still be seen above Germany. Under the terms of the Versailles Treaty German military capability was severely limited, and yet the German air industry continued to develop using neutral countries for production facilities. There is some evidence to suggest that Germany began arrangements to clandestinely rebuild her military air fleet, mainly in Soviet Russia, as early as 1919.

Motivated by a public fearful of terror attacks from the sky, the government prepared for the worst. Throughout the interwar years, civil defence programmes were developed to prepare for bombing, including chemical and biological warfare. A general programme of education in air raid protection began all over Europe and air raid building regulations became statutory requirements in most major European countries in the 1930s, although little of any significance or coherence happened in Britain until war actually broke out. Then, since there were no strong, large, public deep shelters available when the London Blitz started in late 1940, the public had to shelter in flimsy brick-built surface shelters, in slit trenches, in reinforced basements, under railway arches or, from September 1940 – initially against Government orders – in underground railway stations. The best the Government itself could do was to issue from December 1938 corrugated steel Anderson shelters for those with access to gardens, and from late 1941 steel cage-like Morrison 'table' shelters for use in the home. It was an extraordinary state of affairs considering how long the Government had feared – and anticipated –– a German strategic bombing campaign against Britain. But there was a kind of reason lurking within this apparent madness. Before the war certain powerful politicians and senior civil servants were convinced that, if offered safe and comfortable protection, the public would develop a dangerous 'deep shelter' mentality and refuse to return to the surface and to productive working life.

Although anti-aircraft and passive defences initially developed slowly, air defence was revolutionized in the late 1930s by rapid technological advances. Fighter planes were developed with growing performance superiority and radar was invented, greatly improving the defender's power to plot an attacking bomber and direct fighters to intercept it. Thus the balance began to shift away from bomber-dominated 'Trenchardism' towards a mixed air doctrine of defence and offence. In 1935 the RAF accepted the 'Re-orientation Plan': defences were strengthened and efforts were directed towards rebuilding Britain's position of geographical immunity from large-scale invasion. Long-distance offensive (bombers) combined with local defensive (fighters) was considered the best safeguard against foreign aggression and invasion. Ramsay MacDonald put it succinctly in 1934: 'Since the day of the air the old frontiers are gone. When you think of the defence of England, you no longer think of the chalk cliffs of Dover; you think of the Rhine.'

The interwar pacifist movement was strong and influential and, in the hope that air war might not break out at all, effort continued to be directed towards reaching agreement on multilateral disarmament. Even Hitler, anxious to avoid the bombing of German civilians, told British diplomats in 1935 that 'the German Government particularly liked the idea of the prohibition of the indiscriminate bombing of densely populated regions'. Plans were drawn up for a conference on air arms limitations but, in the face of mounting political insecurities, the conference never took place. On the eve of war, Hitler announced through

Opposite: Children enter an Anderson shelter. Made of corrugated steel and issued in vast numbers from December 1938, these flimsy air raid shelters proved surprisingly effective. But they were miserable to use – damp, cold and terrifying because their thin walls and exposed garden sites made the occupants all too vulnerable to the noise of bombardment.

intermediaries that the Luftwaffe would 'limit aerial attacks to aerodromes and fortifications' and make no attack on the civil population, if the RAF would do the same. With hindsight, this concern seems difficult to reconcile with a man who in years to come, despite repeated requests, would not once visit his burnt and broken cities in the wake of Allied attacks.

The crucial factor in the instability of the interwar air doctrine – uncertainty as to the true nature and capabilities of air warfare – continued after the Second World War began in September 1939. In 1937 the Air Staff had produced an estimate, extrapolated from First World War data, that there would be fifty casualties per ton of bombs dropped and that around 700 tons of bombs could be expected to fall on London per day with up to 3,500 tons in the first twenty-four hours of attack. However, the feared 'knockout blow' did not happen. Neither side was adequately equipped to carry out such an attack, and the estimate of casualties per ton of bombs was wildly pessimistic. Terrified by its own alarming estimates and deeply impressed by the apocalyptic possibilities of a powerful bomber force, Britain from 1934 put the bulk of its military spending into bomber production. In May 1935 the Cabinet approved plans to create a front-line strength of 1,000 bombers by May 1939 – a target increased in 1936 to 1,736 aircraft by the same date. Yet few funds had been used to test equipment under operational conditions, and for a while Bomber Command remained blind to its own shortcomings and failed to realize that its much vaunted heavy bomber fleet could not do the job for which it had been built. It is a bitter irony that Britain, which had spent years formulating a defence policy based on decisive strategic air attack, found when invasion loomed that its preparations and plans to bomb the enemy into submission were fundamentally flawed.

Germany meanwhile had a clearer strategy, and progressed rapidly through mainland Europe by adopting the highly successful tactic of blitzkrieg or 'lightning war', using air power in a tactical role to weaken the incumbent air force prior to invasion and to support German land forces in their offensives. This use of co-ordinated air and land forces proved spectacularly successful for Germany, with the defeat of first the Dutch and Belgian armies and then of the French and British armies being achieved in six weeks in the spring of 1940.

However, German air strategy proved far less successful during the coming months – in the action later to be known as the Battle of Britain – as its airforce attempted to soften up Britain in readiness for a German seaborne invasion. In the initial period of battle, the Luftwaffe concentrated on British shipping targets in the Channel, and radar stations, which proved difficult to hit, and even more difficult to put out of action for any length of time. Despite an aircraft loss ratio of just over 2:1 in favour of the RAF, on 1 August 1940 the Luftwaffe was ordered to step up its offensive and 'overpower the English Air Force'. Consequently, on 13 August the Luftwaffe launched a total of 1,485 sorties against Britain, hitting ports, naval bases and airfields. Thus began a new phase of hard-fought air battles that was to continue without a break for the next six weeks. At no time, however, did the attack on Fighter Command seriously weaken it, and although there were shortfalls from time to time, in general the manufacture and repair of fighters kept pace with losses. More serious were the losses in trained fighter pilots, but here again, the odds were in favour of the British. For each RAF pilot killed or wounded, it cost the Luftwaffe five or more aircrew killed, wounded or taken prisoner. In view of the Luftwaffe's failure by mid-September to win air superiority, Hitler postponed his plan to invade England – indefinitely, as it turned out.

With their British strategy in confusion, the German military planners searched around for yet another policy with which to wear down the enemy. Various phases of assault did not follow each other in clear-cut sequence, but from September 1940 onwards the daylight offensive began to give way to nightly raids on London in an attempt to produce the quick surrender of the British Government. In November this assault spread to other British cities and centres of industry, alternating between attempts to break the nation's morale and strategic assaults on supply and production. From the time the Blitz began to the time it ended in May 1941, nothing changed as a result of the campaign, other than perhaps the Luftwaffe's opinion about its own effectiveness as a long-range attack force. One key reason for this failure was Hitler's policy of committing industrial capacity only to weapons of direct battlefield efficiency. So tanks, infantry light machine-guns and dive-bombers were built but heavy bombers were not. When it needed it, Germany discovered in 1941 that it did not have a bomber force capable of carrying out effective strategic aerial warfare.

By this time, however, Hitler was motivated by yet another factor: revenge. In 1940 Churchill had been forced to bring war to Germany with whatever inadequate means were at his command. In July, he wrote to Lord Beaverbrook:

> When I look around to see how we can win the war I see that there is only one sure path. We have no Continental Army which can defeat the German military power… But there is one thing that will bring him back and bring him down, and that is an absolutely devastating, exterminating attack by very heavy bombers from this country upon the Nazi homeland. We must be able to overwhelm him by this means, without which I do not see a way through.

The defeat of France offered the first opportunity for Britain to pursue a bombing offensive, and it was initiated in a desperate attempt to stem the flow of German forces. On 15 May 1940, Bomber Command commenced its first bombing campaign against the Ruhr, to attack oil and railway installations. These early attacks soon revealed a horrible truth. Bomber Command's highly expensive fleet could not achieve the task for which it had been designed. The twin-engined Wellington (in service from 1936) and the lumbering four-engined Stirling (which entered active service in March 1941) were too vulnerable to operate by daylight as planned, and so were forced to bomb in the relative safety of the night. This meant that the bomber force became a very brutal and blunt weapon indeed, since operating at night meant precision bombing had to be abandoned. Consequently, to have a role in the early stage of the war and to carry the terror and destruction to Germany that Churchill planned, Britain's bombing fleet had to attack targets it could damage through relatively indiscriminate bombing rather than attack the well-defended and hard-to-hit strategic targets – such as military or industrial installations – that it was designed to destroy. And so was launched, through sheer necessity, the controversial British policy of blanket or 'area' bombing of Germany's cities.

In February 1942, under the influence of the ruthless new head of Bomber Command, Air Marshal Arthur Harris, this pragmatic muddling-through took the form of a firm policy. As a British Air Staff directive of 14 February 1942 puts it, operations 'should now be focused on the morale of the enemy civilian population and in particular of industrial workers'. This policy legitimized as a war aim the mass butchering of civilians as they slept in their beds, and the wholesale destruction of the residential areas of German cities as a means to an end. But in 1940 and 1941 Bomber Command's chaotic, and then far from destructive, efforts were the only means Britain had of hitting back at Germany. The pursuit of a policy of strategic bombing – no matter how flawed – confirmed Britain's conviction that the best defence is offence and reflected its hope that such raids were doing something to undermine, or at least delay, Germany's invasion plans.

Although circumstances changed, throughout the war Britain maintained a continual bombardment of Germany, the ferocity of which increased with time. In May 1942 the RAF launched its first 'Thousand Bomber' raid against Germany with the target – Cologne – offering a shocking spectacle to German

Above: *The twin-engined Vickers Wellington bomber – in service from 1936 – was the backbone of bomber command during the early years of the war until gradually superseded by the heavier four-engined bombers such as the Short Stirling and the Avro Lancaster.*

public and politicians alike. The bludgeoning continued with both the German public and the RAF suffering terrible casualties: by the end of the war 55,500 Bomber Command crew had died, out of a service personnel of approximately 125,000. In July 1943, for example, came the grimly named 'Operation Gomorrah' during which RAF Bomber Command attempted to obliterate Hamburg. The bombers raided four times in ten days, whipping up the most ferocious firestorm of the Second World War and killing an estimated 42,000 people, almost entirely in residential districts of the city. As Germany became more desperate, it responded by unveiling its 'secret' vengeance weapons: the V1 'flying bomb' and the V2 rocket.

It would be difficult to maintain, however, that a strategic bombing policy was pursued with any clear objective on either side, other than a belief that in time the pounding would somehow bring about success. Air Marshal Harris believed, at the end of the war, that his brutal methods had made a significant contribution towards victory and so were justified. Few would now be so complacent in their judgement. Harris's conclusion was based on the notion that massive urban destruction would undermine morale, halt

Above: *A German V2 rocket being readied for launch against London. This 'vengeance' weapon – along with the earlier V1 – was intended merely to punish the British and had no larger strategic purpose. Its high speed, which meant that it arrived and exploded before it could be heard, and its inability to be aimed at any precise target made the V2 the ultimate Second World War terror weapon.*

or retard war production, smother the economy, and divert precious resources from the front to the rear theatres of war. The Lancaster bomber – the most effective of the RAF's heavy bombers – was, wrote Harris in 1945, 'the greatest single factor in winning the war'. But air bombardment was a very inexact military science, as was revealed by the number of policy changes in which both Allied and Axis forces indulged during the Second World War.

Although the relative merits and contributions of air power at each stage of the Second World War continue to bear scrutiny, the use of the atomic bomb against Japan in 1945 unquestionably achieved success in terms of direct destruction. Whatever the wider diplomatic and strategic purposes surrounding its use, the nuclear strike represented the culmination of a bombing policy initiated by Britain and Germany before the Second World War began. Thus it is a fitting end to this chapter of history that the nuclear attack should confirm what so many strove to prove: that after adequate research and preparation, following the build-up of air superiority and under the best possible conditions for attack, strategic bombing should act decisively to end a war on its own. The knockout blow had finally proved its inhuman point.

CHAPTER FIFTEEN

OPERATION SEALION

The rapid fall of France in June 1940 meant that Britain suddenly had to confront the possibility of a German invasion force landing not along the east coast, where preparations had been made, but along the south coast. Until the end of May – when the British Expeditionary Force was expelled from mainland Europe at Dunkirk, and north-west France fell into German hands – the south coast of England had appeared secure. It looked across the Channel to its French ally and the worst that could happen, calculated the British in early 1940, was a rerun of the First World War with the opposing armies locked in northern France. But now the unthinkable had happened. France had collapsed and on 22 June – just six weeks after the Germans launched their attack in the west – the French signed an armistice with Germany and German troops had access to the French Channel ports. Suddenly the formerly safe south and south-east coastline of England was transformed into the most likely target for a German invasion and thrust to London.

But this sudden opportunity to invade Britain from France also wrongfooted the German high command. When it appeared that, despite the surrender of France, Britain intended to fight on, Germany was forced to contemplate the unpleasant task of mounting a seaborne invasion. But no invasion plan had been prepared. The occupation of the Channel Islands on 30 June had involved no military action since the islands had been 'demilitarized' by the British and the Germans merely sailed in and took possession. In late June Hitler still hoped that the war with Britain could be concluded without further violence. The British had to be made to face the impossibility of their position and this could be achieved, believed Hitler, by a combination of military threats and diplomatic negotiations.

The most effective military pressure would come from the threat of invasion, and on 1 July Hitler initiated discussions with his military advisers about the preparation of an invasion plan. No date was given for its completion and no target date set for invasion. General Franz Halder, the Chief-of-Staff of the German Armed Forces Supreme Headquarters, was made responsible for drafting the plan. He appears to have been supremely confident and – like Napoleon before him – regarded crossing the Channel as no more than an extended river crossing. He planned to attack a 200-mile-wide stretch of English coast with divisions from Army Group A heading out from Boulogne, Calais, Dunkirk, Ostend and Le Havre to land on the Kent coast around Ramsgate and Dover and on the Sussex coast near Worthing, while units from Army Group B sailed from Cherbourg to land on the Dorset coast around Lyme Regis.

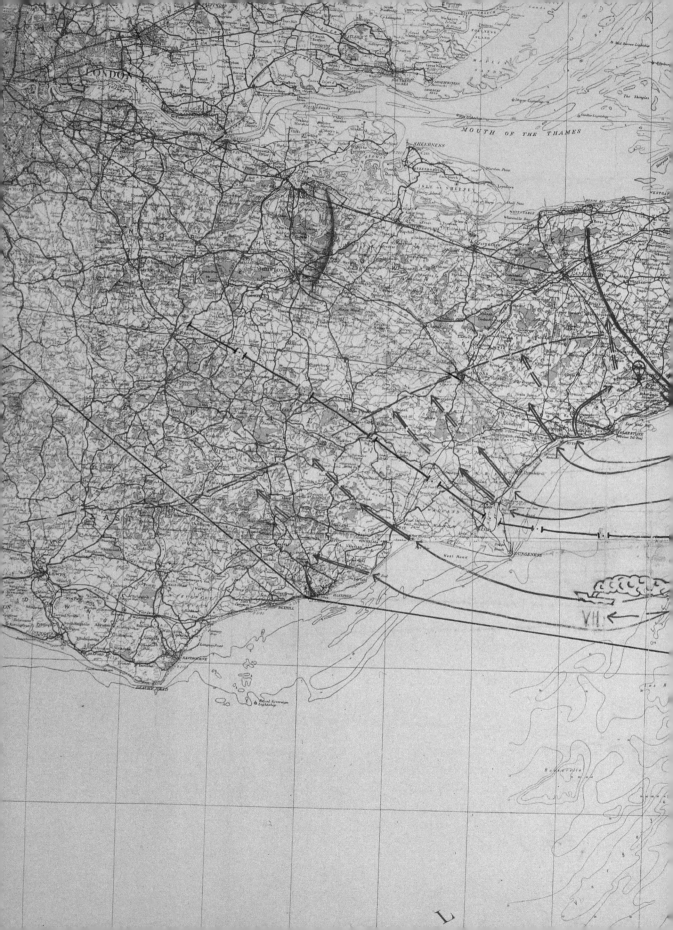

Op. Karte Chef.

Geheime Kommandosache! „Chefsache!"

However, German navy planners did not share Halder's optimism. Grand Admiral Eric Raeder, the naval commander-in-chief, objected to Halder's plan, arguing that the navy was not strong enough to guarantee the security of a German invasion fleet attacking a 200-mile front. His forces had been badly mauled by the Royal Navy during the recent Norwegian campaign, and with no landing craft the navy could not possibly organize the simultaneous landing of 90,000 fully equipped and supported troops as envisaged.

Hitler either did not believe Raeder or, more likely, did not care. At this stage the invasion was a bluff anyway and practical objections did not matter. The fact that an invasion was being planned – at speed and on a large scale – was, hoped Hitler, enough to bring Britain to heel. Consequently, Hitler ignored Raeder's objections, accepted Halder's plan in principle and on 16 July issued his Directive Number 16. It began:

> As England, in spite of the hopelessness of her military position, has so far shown herself unwilling to come to any compromise, I have decided to begin to prepare for, and if necessary to carry out, an invasion of England. This operation is dictated by the necessity of eliminating Great Britain as a base from which the war against Germany can be fought, and if necessary the island will be occupied…

The invasion plan was codenamed Operation Sealion. The political rather than the military nature of the invasion plan at this time is revealed by the timing that Hitler imposed. He wanted the plan completed and the invasion force ready to sail by 15 August – in one month's time. This was clearly a practical impossibility but timing was an essential part of the game of bluff that Hitler was playing. When the British realized what was coming their way – and their reconnaissance aircraft could not fail to observe the massive build-up of troops, arms and barges in the invasion ports – their will to resist would crumble. To keep the military pressure up, the Luftwaffe started from mid-July to attack the Channel ports and shipping, to establish command of the Straits of Dover, while German heavy guns were installed around Calais to bombard the Dover area where the first shells started to fall during the second week of August. By the end of July the Royal Navy had to pull all its larger warships out of the Channel because of the threat from German aircraft. All seemed to be going to plan; perhaps this mounting military pressure and the prospect of invasion would break British spirits and make Operation Sealion unnecessary.

Hitler's other tactic was to offer Britain the prospect of an 'honourable' peace achieved through peaceful negotiation. On 19 July – just three days after launching Operation Sealion – Hitler directed an appeal to Britain during a speech to the Reichstag in Berlin: 'If the struggle continues it can only end in annihilation for one of us. Mr Churchill thinks it will be Germany. I know it will be Britain. I am not the vanquished begging for mercy. I speak as a victor. I can see no reason why this war must go on. We should like to avert the sacrifices, which must claim millions.' The British response was quick. On 22 July Churchill replied through his Foreign Minister, Lord Halifax: 'We never wanted the war… but we shall not stop fighting till freedom for ourselves and others is secure.'

So by the end of July neither the threat of imminent invasion nor the offer of peace had done the trick. The ghastly reality now confronted the German high command: it would actually have to plan for real and

Previous spread: *A German map details the proposed invasion of England, codenamed Operation Sealion. This map shows part of the plan as revised by September 1940. The 16th Army was to leave from the Calais/Antwerp area and land in the Folkestone/Dungeness area and around Rye, and then press inland towards London. Elements of the 9th Army, not shown on this map, were to land in the Brighton/Worthing area.*
Opposite: *Members of the Home Guard in training. They are armed with Canadian Ross rifles.*

probably execute one of the most difficult military operations imaginable – an invasion, launched across at least 20 miles of water, culminating in a landing on a fortified and desperately defended coastline. It was immediately clear that this could not even be attempted until the Royal Navy – still one of the most formidable fighting forces in the world – had been either destroyed or diverted and after the Royal Air Force had been eliminated. And, as the German planners started to work out the details of the invasion, no one in Germany had any idea how, when – or even if – the Royal Navy and Royal Air Force could be destroyed.

The first reaction of Hitler and the German high command, when it appeared that a real rather than a bluff invasion would have to be organized, was to change the schedule. On the last day of July Hitler held a meeting at the Berghof. He was told of the difficulty in obtaining barges suitable to carry invasion troops and about the problems of massing troops and equipment. Raeder again argued for a reduced invasion front and for a postponement of the invasion until May 1941. These were realistic demands but Hitler was no realist and Halder's bold, broad front attack plan was again agreed. But even Hitler accepted that a real invasion could not take place in two weeks' time. He postponed the start date to 16 September. After this meeting it was decided that the job of clearing the Channel of British warships and the skies of south-east England of British aircraft belonged to the Luftwaffe. Hermann Goering saw no problems. He would sweep British aircraft from the skies, destroy them on the ground, attack radar stations and also bomb aircraft factories. With no air protection, British warships would not dare to enter the Channel and if they did German aircraft would sink them. The attack was to start immediately but bad weather delayed the German air offensive against Britain until 12 August.

Meanwhile in Britain anti-invasion defences of all types had been planned and executed with incredible speed since late May. At the same time a new force had been organized to help defend the country. The Local Defence Volunteers had been raised on 14 May 1940 and comprised men too old or too infirm to join the regular army, or in protected occupations and thus exempt from conscription. On 23 July the force became known as the Home Guard after Churchill coined the phrase during a BBC broadcast. By the end of July one and a half million men had volunteered – a huge figure that reveals the seriousness with which ordinary people took the threat of invasion in the summer of 1940.

On 27 May Churchill had put General Sir Edmund Ironside, Commander-in-Chief Home Forces, in charge of organizing Britain's defence. Ironside acted quickly. He had a large force at his disposal, but one that was poorly armed and equipped and generally poorly trained. Only about 60,000 men had been lost in France (11,000 killed and 50,000 captured) but most of the British army's heavy weapons and equipment – including artillery and tanks – had been abandoned. Ironside's only option, given these limitations, was to set up a static system of defence which, he hoped, could delay German invasion forces after landing and so give Britain time to bring its small mobile reserves into play. If the Germans could be delayed on the beaches and then delayed as they pushed inland, their timetable could be thrown off balance, they could lose impetus, direction and initiative and the British army might be able to counter-attack effectively.

The key to Ironside's pragmatic plan was defence in depth. Much as the trench system along the Western Front had been organized during the latter part of the First World War, with a series of defence zones set behind the front line in case of an enemy breakthrough, south-east England was to offer a series of barriers or stop-lines. These lines, formed by concrete pillboxes, gun emplacements, anti-tank obstacles, trench systems, minefields and barbed wire

Opposite: *Leaders of the battle of France and of the following defence of Britain in May 1940. From left to right: Winston Churchill; General Maurice Gamelin, Commander-in-Chief of the French Army; General Ironside, Chief of the Imperial General Staff; General Alphonse Georges, French commander of the north-east front, and General Viscount Gort, Commander-in-Chief of the British Expeditionary Force in France.*

Above: *A type 22 infantry pillbox constructed in the summer of 1940 on the east coast at Shingle Street, Suffolk. This formed part of General Ironside's defensive 'coastal crust'.*

entanglements – and utilizing natural and man-made features such as rivers, canals and railway embankments – were to ensnare and delay the Germans. At best, these defences would channel the attackers into prepared killing grounds where the British army's limited artillery could be brought into play. If the British army could 'script' the battle in this manner, and impose its will on the attacking German army, then victory could be possible.

The Germans, of course, had their own script for the battle and their detailed air reconnaissance of Britain in early 1940 meant that the stop-lines would have held few surprises for the attackers. But, whatever happened, Ironside was determined that this would be a battle of attrition. At the very least the Germans would be made to bleed before they achieved their objectives and – since the British had more men than the Germans could land rapidly – it was worth sacrificing a lot of defenders to kill relatively few Germans. This was to be bloody warfare, with the defenders manning their positions to the last to inflict maximum delay and casualties on German forces. Only when further resistance was impossible were the defenders to pull back to the next prepared line of defence where the battle of attrition would start all over again.

By 25 June Ironside's anti-invasion plan was complete and presented to the War Cabinet as Home Forces Operations Instruction Number 3. This Instruction gave detail to Ironside's defence theory. There was to be a coastal 'crust' that would consist of a thin screen of infantry – supported by pillboxes and a limited number of defence works – deployed along the beaches. This crust, on which work had been started in mid May by Ironside's predecessor General Kirke, was to disrupt enemy landings long enough to allow the arrival of local reinforcements. Behind the coastal crust a network of stop-lines of various strengths and significance were constructed (these were designated Command, Corps and Divisional Stop-lines according to their status) to

Above: *A photomontage published in a German military magazine in November 1940 shows a German Messerschmitt 109 fighter in pursuit of a Spitfire.*

slow down and contain or channel any German advance. Each line was constructed in some depth to prevent it being too easily penetrated or outflanked by enemy mobile forces. The final and main position of resistance was the General Headquarters Anti-tank Line (the GHQ Stop-Line). This was the backbone of Ironside's co-ordinated defence plan. The line was planned to stretch from around Bristol in the west, then east to Maidstone and running south around London, passing just south of Guildford and Aldershot, then north-east to the Thames Estuary. It then ran north through Cambridge and the fens and up the length of England – running inland parallel with the east coast but able to defend the major industrial centres of the Midlands and the north – and up to central Scotland. An auxiliary GHQ Line was also to be established around Plymouth.

These lines were surveyed, planned and constructed with astonishing speed – work began, ahead of official War Cabinet approval, in the second week of June. This was a tumultuous week in British history; it was a time for dramatic and speedy action if the nation was to be saved. The evacuation from Dunkirk had been completed the week before, and on 4 June Churchill had made his memorable speech in which he told the British people that 'we shall go on to the end... we shall fight on the seas and oceans... we shall defend our island whatever the cost might be, we shall fight on the beaches, we shall fight on the landing grounds, we shall fight in the fields and in the streets, we shall fight in the hills; we shall never surrender.' The nation was galvanized into action.

The GHQ Stop-Line at Waverley Abbey

The thirteenth-century ruins of Waverley Abbey stand in the centre of a wide and pleasant meadow, embraced to the north and east by the River Wey and defined to the west by a large lake. Overlooking all from the north is the richly wooded hill that forms part of the highlands of the Hog's Back. It is an idyllic place – but in the summer of 1940, if the German army had invaded, this secluded and tranquil meadow in Surrey would have been transformed into a frightful killing ground.

Waverley Abbey is only a few miles south of Guildford and Aldershot – the heartland of the British Army – and astride one of the main axes of approach to London. The high ground of the Hog's Back and the meandering River Wey formed potential natural defences of the kind that military engineers sought to fortify against German advances inland towards London. In addition, the British wanted to hold the Hog's Back at all costs: if it had fallen into enemy hands then the Germans would have dominated the approaches to south-west London and outflanked the North Downs section of the GHQ stop-line. So the fortifications around Waverley Abbey – one of the designated 'strong points' – formed a vital part of the main defence line around London.

Building work started on 20 June and was completed by September 1940. The Waverley Abbey works illustrate how strong points on the main stop-line itself were formed, and how the standard types of fortifications were adapted to utilize local building materials and to fit as harmoniously as possible into the surroundings. Immediately to the north, next to a small bridge over the Wey, is the main position: a modified Type 28 pillbox. This type was designed originally to house a 2-pounder anti-tank gun but here the standard built-in mountings have been slightly but significantly adapted. Aldershot Command was short of modern 2-pounders (most had been abandoned in France) and so this particular Type 28 was built to house an obsolete First World War 13-pounder field gun issued with twenty-five rounds of solid shot for use against armoured vehicles. The pillbox, low of profile and with a wide embrasure to allow the gun a wide arc of fire, commands the abbey meadow, a substantial length of the river and a distant river crossing. The substantial abbey ruins would have been rapidly demolished by the British to deny cover to the enemy once the invasion had actually taken place.

The pillbox is located beneath a grove of trees that were obviously intended to hide it from the air, and the concrete-roofed portion of the pillbox is flanked by extensive and irregular walls topped with roughly hewn battlements. Clearly this picturesque profile was intended to give the pillbox – the walls of which are clad with local red brick over a concrete core – the appearance of an eighteenth-century Gothic folly. The flank walls themselves are articulated and fitted with loopholes for a variety of weapons, and were apparently intended to be manned by troops who would both defend the gun from flank attack and offer fire to protect adjoining works.

Mutually supporting defence was a crucial consideration when placing the individual works forming a strong point. Following this principle, the east flank of the Type 28 anti-tank pillbox is defended by a polygonal Type 24 pillbox, which would have housed a six-man garrison under the command of a sergeant. This squad would have been armed with rifles and one machine-gun. This type of pillbox was intended only as proof against infantry and light shellfire and could not have withstood heavy artillery attack. Consequently, once fighting started and after the pill box had revealed its position, its garrison would have moved into slit trenches and joined other troops operating in field works with the pillbox acting only as a command post.

All trace of these field works – along with evidence of barbed wire entanglements and minefield – has disappeared, so it is now very difficult to estimate the original defensive strength of strong points such as this. For example, in front of both pillboxes was a deep anti-tank ditch – now long filled-in – running from the river to the

Above left: *Anti-tank blocks mark the site where the anti-tank ditch reached the river. The blocks on each side of the river had steel cables stretched between them to prevent enemy vehicles advancing along the riverbed to outflank the British defences. In the distance are the thirteenth-century ruins of Waverley Abbey.*

Above right: *A modified type 28 pillbox dominates the defences of the strong point. It was designed to house a 2-pounder anti-tank gun but adapted to contain an antiquated First World War 13-pounder field gun. The pillbox was built beneath trees – which still survive – and topped with picturesque battlements to help it fit into its park-like setting.*

lake. At each end the ditch was replaced or strengthened by large, concrete, pyramid-shaped anti-tank blocks. Those by the lake have now been moved but those by the river remain in position.

The river had to be blocked to prevent German troops and vehicles travelling along it to outflank the anti-tank gun, but this blocking could obviously not be achieved by continuing the ditch across the riverbed. Instead, concrete anti-tank blocks were placed on each side of the river to prevent vehicles travelling along its sloping banks, and then stout steel cables were stretched across the river itself. The metal eyes through which these cables were fixed and anchored survive on the top surfaces of a number of the anti-tank blocks. The designers of these defences appreciated that German engineers could cut through steel cables in a matter of minutes, so the river block was to be defended by a very well concealed machine-gun-armed pillbox built into the steep bank rising immediately above the defended crossing.

The primary job of the pillbox was to kill the German engineers, but once it had revealed itself the life expectancy of its occupants would have been very short indeed. It offers no concealed escape route so the small garrison, after a sharp but no doubt short battle, would have suffered near certain death. This would have been fanatically tough warfare in which British defenders literally fought to the finish.

On 14 and 15 June officers from General Headquarters Home Forces made a reconnaissance of the full length of the GHQ Line. Immediately a report and a map were prepared for the various Command Headquarters involved in the construction and development of the line and they were issued with Home Forces Operations Instruction Number 3. These local commands were given reasonable latitude to vary the routes and organization of the line if, given their local knowledge, they could do so to tactical advantage. By the end of July the key elements were complete. By the end of September 18,000 pillboxes and thousands of batteries – built to a set of standard patterns but displaying a vast number of regional variations to reflect the availability of building materials, abilities of construction teams and preferences of local commanders – had been completed throughout Britain. These masonry and earth constructions, supported by anti-tank obstacles and ditches, field works of all sorts and utilizing natural and man-made features with various degrees of ingenuity, were ready to do their job if the Germans came.

During August, as the stop-lines were nearing completion, the Luftwaffe's battle for control of the air over England and the Channel continued. But the assault on the RAF started to go awry as Goering changed the emphasis of attack from radar stations and airfields to aircraft factories and more peripheral targets, thus giving RAF front-line squadrons a much needed breathing space. While what became known as the Battle of Britain started to reach its climax, the debate about Operation Sealion also continued to rage during August between the German navy and the army. A meeting between the army and the navy on 7 August revealed irreconcilable differences. 'I utterly reject the Navy's proposals [for landing on a narrow front],' exclaimed Halden. 'I might just as well put the troops through a sausage machine.' Eventually a compromise was reached. On 13 August Hitler agreed that the invasion front should be narrowed – but not as much as Raeder wanted – with the most westerly landing area being around Worthing. This meant that only one German Army Group – Army Group A – would carry out the invasion. The revised invasion plan was issued by the German High Command on 30 August.

The attack group of the 9th Army (part of Army Group A) was to leave from Le Havre and land in the Brighton/Worthing area of Sussex. The first assault wave was to consist of the VIII Corps, made up of two infantry Divisions and one Mountain Division – who were elite troops – to serve as a special assault unit. This wave was to secure the beachhead. The second wave was to consist of the XXIV Corps, and this wave packed the real punch for it was made up of two Panzer Divisions, each composed of tanks, artillery, mobile troops and Panzer grenadier assault infantry, and one motorized division. The role of the panzers was to break out of the beachhead and then sweep west towards Portsmouth.

The attack group of the 16th Army (also part of Army Group A) was to leave from the Calais/Ostend/Antwerp area and land in the Folkestone/Dungeness area around Rye and at Bexhill/Eastbourne. Three infantry divisions and one motorized division from the XIII and VII Corps were to take part in the Folkestone/Dungeness and the Rye attacks while the main force was to land in the Bexhill/Eastbourne area. The first wave here, made up of XXXVIII Corps, was to consist of two infantry divisions, while the second wave was to contain two infantry divisions, two panzer divisions and one motorized division. The panzers were to break out of the beachhead and advance north to destroy the main reserves of the British army and establish crossings over the River Medway.

These landings were to be supported by parachute troops. It was intended to land these on the Downs above Brighton, to assist in the securing of the beachhead for the Brighton/Worthing assault group, and north-west of Folkestone in Kent to seize the Royal Military Canal of Napoleonic war vintage. The Germans saw this canal – built to stop French invaders storming across Romney Marsh on their way to London – as a significant anti-tank obstacle that could, if not bridged, stall the advance of their panzers.

A battery observation tower set behind an emplacement for heavy guns on the Suffolk coast, near Bawdsey. The utilitarian and functional nature of the design and construction gives the tower a rough beauty,

The initial objective for both assault groups was to establish a front from the Thames Estuary to Portsmouth. Then the build-up would begin, with additional supplies and troops being brought in. When the build up was complete, the panzers of the Brighton/Worthing assault group would attack towards Basingstoke, Newbury and Oxford to secure crossing points over the Thames and to encircle and isolate London and the south-east in a great pincer movement. General Erwin Rommel was to lead one of the 7th Panzer Division attack columns, and he intended to inflict on the British defences the blitzkrieg tactics – rapid tank advances supported by dive-bombing aircraft – which had so rapidly unhinged and defeated the French and British forces in France. The remaining German forces, located around the Medway and on the Thames estuary, would then thrust towards London: the ultimate target of the invasion force. When London had been taken and the British army in the south-east destroyed, armoured formations were to take selected industrial centres and seaports, and a general line from Maldon in Essex to Gloucester was to be established.

If all this went according to plan, and if the Royal Navy had been neutralized, elements of Army Group B were to be ferried across from Cherbourg into occupied Weymouth and Lyme Regis and then advance on Bristol and into Devon and Cornwall.

Field Marshal Gerd von Rundstedt, in command of Army Group A, had little faith in Halder's Sealion plan. He observed that Napoleon had failed to invade and the difficulties that confounded him did not appear to have been solved by the Sealion planners. Probably von Rundstedt observed that one of the plan's main weaknesses was the small scale of the initial assault and the slow build-up. The first wave assault was to be carried out not by nine complete divisions but only their leading echelons, numbering in each case around 6,700 men. So only the equivalent of three divisions, around 60,000 men, would have been involved in the first wave assault. About 250 tanks and very little artillery would have supported them. This force would no doubt have penetrated Ironside's coastal crust but could well have suffered huge casualties if British resistance was determined and if British coastal artillery, pre-targeted on likely landing sites, had operated efficiently. In a disorganized state this force might have been further fatally delayed by the stop-lines so, if luck was on the side of the British, Halder's invasion plan might well have stalled.

An added factor worrying von Rundstedt was, no doubt, the amateur and ad hoc nature of the sea transport. It was formed of barges requisitioned from the rivers of north-west Europe, hastily adapted and in many cases to be towed across the Channel or powered by inappropriate aeroplane engines. The consequence would be troops landed at the wrong place or at the right place at the wrong time – or not landed at all if British sea and air power had not been completely destroyed. And these same problems of transport would apply to – and slow down – the build-up of reinforcements unless a number of major ports were captured quickly and intact, which was highly unlikely.

Hitler appeared to agree with von Rundstedt when on 14 August – the day after he had agreed a narrower invasion front – Hitler told his generals that he would not attempt to invade Britain if the task seemed too dangerous. There were, said Hitler, other ways of defeating Britain. It could be slowly starved by the U-boat campaign, which denied it much needed supplies, or isolated by the neutralization of potential allies. When Britain was famished and alone, it would surrender.

As Hitler started to back away from invasion, the battle for dominance of the skies over England and the Channel reached a new peak of fury. By the end of August Luftwaffe statisticians calculated that over half of RAF Fighter Command was destroyed yet, strangely, every day the fighters appeared in undiminished numbers and Bomber Command started to attack concentrations of barges moored around French, Belgian and Dutch invasion ports. On 3 September this perplexing state of affairs led Field Marshal Keitel, head of the Armed Forces High Command, to delay Sealion until 21 September. It seems that the German high command still had faith in Goering's ability to win command of the air over the Channel. But then on 14 September Sealion was postponed again, this time until 27 September – the last time the tides would be right before the end of the year.

The day after this last postponement was announced, 15 September, Goering launched his final major offensive to destroy RAF Fighter Command in daylight action. It was a dismal failure, with the Luftwaffe losing twice as many aircraft as the British. Through his ineptitude, Goering had lost the battle for Britain even before the invasion was launched. On 17 September – two days after Goering's defeat – Operation Sealion was postponed indefinitely. The plan was never to be revived. Hitler turned his attention east and in June 1941 invaded the Soviet Union. If he had delivered a rapid knockout blow and removed the Soviet Union from the war then, no doubt, Hitler would have returned to the problem of invading Britain. But the Soviets did not crumble and their extraordinary resistance during the following three years meant that Britain was never again threatened by German invasion.

CHAPTER SIXTEEN

BRITAIN'S
SECRET ARMY

If the Germans had invaded in 1940, the British response would have been complex. There is no reason to believe that General Ironside's policy of defence in depth would not have been conducted with vigour, his stop-lines delaying the German advance. It is possible that these delays would have allowed the British mobile reserves to be gathered in the right place and at the right time and, with skill and luck, counter-attacks may have been successful. Reinforcements coming from abroad may have avoided the German U-boat and aircraft screen and helped to roll the invader back into the sea. We will never know – we can now only speculate. But when all factors are considered, including the great military skill, daring and tenacity later displayed by German formations (for example in Crete, North Africa, Russia and at Monte Cassino, Italy), it must be assumed that German forces – if well lodged in a large portion of England with re-supply organized – would have been incredibly difficult to contain or expel.

But the British Government did have a response to a substantial German occupation of part of its territory: the 'secret' army. This Auxiliary Force, as it was called, was set up during the summer and early autumn of 1940. Its role was simple if daunting. It was organized so that it could go to ground if invasion took place and then stay behind in areas overrun by the German forces. Auxiliaries were then to act as a guerrilla force, slowing down the enemy advance, blowing up railway lines and bridges and doing all they could to help give the regular British army time to manoeuvre and to launch counter-attacks.

The British Government was the first in modern times to organize a guerrilla army, but such a force was not without precedent in recent British military experience. In 1899 and 1900 the British regular army had been badly mauled in South Africa by Boer Kommandos – formed by highly motivated farmers – which operated effectively behind British lines. In 1916 Sinn Fein irregulars in Ireland greatly troubled the British army and in the same year, in Arabia, T. E. Lawrence showed what a British commander could do with irregular forces. Partly because of the achievements of these irregular forces, much was expected from Britain's secret army in that desperate summer of 1940. Certainly Churchill was a supporter. In a letter to Anthony Eden of

25 September 1940 he wrote: 'I have been following with much interest the growth and development of the… "Auxiliary Units" [which] are being organized with thoroughness and imagination and should, in the event of invasion, prove a useful addition to the regular forces.'

The idea for the force appears to have come during a meeting on 30 June at Chequers between Winston Churchill and Lieutenant-General Andrew Thorne. Thorne was commander of XII Corps, which had the responsibility for the defence of Kent, Sussex, parts of Hampshire and Surrey and the coastal strip from Hayling Island to Greenwich in south-east London. This was the invasion heartland, but XII Corps was incredibly weak in weapons and personnel. It contained only one fully trained division, the third, which was due to be sent to Northern Ireland, had no anti-tank regiment and few modern anti-tank guns. The meeting must have been a gloomy affair. Churchill's Private Secretary, Sir John Colville, mentions some of the points discussed in his book *The Fringes of Power*. Thorne said he believed that the Germans would land 80,000 men between Thanet and Pevensey, while Churchill was 'not sanguine about our ability to hold the whole expanse of beaches' and pointed out a Napoleonic maxim 'that a river line has never proved a real obstacle to an enemy'.

The meeting had two dramatic consequences. The same day Churchill sent a memo, now in the Public Record Office, to his representative on the Chiefs of Staff Committee, General Ismay, about the possibility of using poison gas and other chemical weapons against an invasion army: 'Let me have a report upon the amount of mustards or other variants we have in store, and whether it can be used in air bombs as well as fired from guns…' Mustard gas was a particularly vicious, potentially lethal substance that blistered the skin and destroyed the throat and lungs when inhaled.

The second result of the meeting was the creation of Britain's secret army. Thorne's experiences must have been crucial in the evolution of this idea. As a British military attaché in Berlin in the mid-1930s, Thorne had been impressed by locally based German peasant militias. These irregular forces, first formed in the eighteenth century, were to contribute to the fight against invasion by utilizing their intimate knowledge of the region being fought through, and by the use of secret arms caches that would allow militia members to infiltrate an enemy front and then transform themselves from peasants into armed fighting men. Thorne got in touch with Ismay who, as it happened, had been thinking alone similar lines, as a memo of 22 June 1940 to the Cabinet makes clear.

The memo is from Ismay's deputy at the Committee of Imperial Defence, Major Leslie Hollis. It records that Ismay agreed with 'sentiments' expressed in memos to him that it was 'essential to instil into the civilian population a thoroughly offensive spirit and a determination to attack the enemy by every means in their power, even after he may have succeeded in occupying some of our territory'. Ismay outlined ways in which civilians could help the military, including recruiting the services of scoutmasters who, after receiving a 'refresher course' on the realities of scouting, could mobilize the Scout organization for the purpose of 'obtaining and passing information'. More potentially rewarding perhaps was Ismay's reflections on 'the action by the civilian population in subjugated areas'. He recommended that 'a study of the Irish in the bad times from 1920–1922 should help us here. Our object would be to keep the enemy continually on the jump as we were in Ireland during that period. There seem to be three main roles: (1) Intelligence. (2) Sabotage. (3) Assassination.' Quite correctly, Ismay observed that 'training would be required for all three roles'.

Intelligence would 'necessitate building up a considerable organization to enable information obtained to be passed through the enemy lines to our side'. Sabotage inside the enemy lines would, conceded Ismay, 'be very difficult to carry out to any co-ordinated plan' but 'a great deal of good work could be done unco-ordinated which would give the enemy an immense amount of trouble. I have in mind such things as "hot boxes" on the railway lines, sugar in petrol, cutting of communications.' Assassination, thought Ismay, could well be organized 'on the Irish model… We found it very difficult to stamp out. Poison as well as the pistol could be employed.' Regarding the personnel to carry out these various duties in the subjugated areas:

we should have a nucleus in the LDVs [the Local Defence Volunteers which became the Home Guard in July 1940] who would presumably disappear into the civilian population when the tide of battle moved forward across them. Selected characters should be trained in the use of the pistol and the hiding of their weapons. The same sort of man could be valuable for sabotage work, but he must be trained in carrying out his job so that it appears as much like an accident as possible.

This was total war for national survival and for world freedom and in 1940, as far as leading British military personnel and politicians were concerned, the techniques of terrorism were legitimate weapons.

Ismay dispatched a young intelligence officer to discuss ideas with Thorne. This officer was Peter Fleming – adventurer, journalist, author and brother of Ian Fleming, the creator of James Bond. Peter Fleming must have been, at least in part, the model for his brother's hero. Peter, an old Etonian and a former Guards officer, worked for Military Intelligence Research (MIR), had travelled to, and written about (for both newspapers and for military intelligence), remote and rough areas of the world. Clearly this was the man, believed Military Intelligence, to set up guerrilla units that would merge into the ordinary population by day, kill and destroy by night and, if necessary, live off the land in secret locations and fight to the death.

Fleming's first task was to set up a prototype training centre where the possibilities of the new secret army could be identified and developed. Soon this 'stay-behind' force expanded into a national auxiliary army and in early July 1940 was given its own commander, Major Colin Gubbins, with Captain Peter Wilkinson as Chief-of-Staff. Gubbins was an inspired choice. Although a forty-four-year-old regular gunner, he was a member of MIR, and the author of books on guerrilla and partisan warfare and on the use of high explosives; in 1921 he had direct experience of guerrilla warfare against the IRA in the Irish Free State, and in early 1940 had led special forces during the Norway campaign.

Recognizing that the most likely location for the main German effort was the 300 miles of coast between Norfolk and Hampshire, Gubbins concentrated on giving a high level of training to those groups in the southeast located between the coast and the GHQ stop-lines running south and east of London.

By July, Fleming, Gubbins and Wilkinson had established the operational structure for the Auxiliary Units. Each unit – of around six men under a patrol-leader – had an operational base (OB), usually underground and secreted in woodland or rough and overgrown land so that it would be virtually invisible to enemy patrols and air reconnaissance. These hides were generally constructed to a standard design and size, with local command centres being somewhat larger. The standard hide had an arched main room formed by a cylinder of corrugated steel sheeting. Within this main room – about 10 feet underground and entered via a vertical shaft – were bunks with storage places for arms and explosives. Beyond the main room was a smaller, brick-lined vestibule, where the Elsan lavatory, the cooking and washing facilities and the entry to the escape tunnel were located. Nothing of this would be visible from the surface – the flue for the fire and the cover to the water tank would be disguised, obscured or camouflaged, as would the main entry and escape hatch.

Here, in the event of invasion, the auxiliaries would hide during the day. Security was all-important. Members of each auxiliary patrol would know only their colleagues and the location of the OBs of neighbouring patrols. Each patrol was to be self-sufficient and operate in isolation. The benefits of this

Above: *A long-abandoned underground hide, or 'Operational Base', at Rise, East Yorkshire. In the summer of 1940 – when this hide was constructed – it formed the hidden headquarters for one six- or seven-man patrol of Britain's 'secret' army.*
Opposite: *Charlie Mason and his wife. In 1940 he was a member of a 'secret' army patrol based in a hide near Kingston-upon-Hull. 'We were lawless then, we destroyed anything that we wanted to destroy. It didn't matter if it affected our own people.'*

lonely approach were to be highlighted during the following years by the fate suffered by many French resistance groups, which were often sprawling and fatally insecure organizations that proved relatively easy for German counter-espionage agencies to infiltrate and destroy.

By late August 1940 secret army bases stretched from the east coast of Scotland to Land's End in the south and to Pembroke Docks in the west. The force was divided into three battalions: 201 based in the north and Scotland, 202 in the Midlands and 203 in the London area and the southern counties. Uniforms were worn, usually Home Guard-style khaki denims, with badges either of the local county regiments or of the Home Guard. The uniform and military insignia were intended as a defence against immediate execution as a spy or terrorist if captured, but few auxiliaries could have believed that any fate other than death awaited them if they fell into German hands while operating behind the front line.

Personnel were generally drawn from outside the ranks of the regular army, which itself had a massive manpower shortage and was unwilling to let men go to fight in a dubious auxiliary army. Most volunteers came from the Home Guard and from reserved occupations. A central training establishment was soon established by Gubbins to serve the rapidly enlarged force. This was based in the spectacular (and now destroyed) 1650s Coleshill House near Swindon in Wiltshire. Some ordinary patrol members were sent to the training centre, but it was mostly used by intelligence officers and regular army officers and technicians who had been seconded to serve in auxiliary units. The course consisted of lectures, technical training on the use of explosives and on the construction of hides (the prototype OB still survives within the grounds) and instruction in unarmed combat.

The instructor was Captain W. E. Fairburn, late assistant commissioner of the Shanghai Municipal Police, expert in oriental fighting techniques, author of the authoritative *All-in Fighting* and co-inventor of the lethal Fairburn-Sykes fighting knife which became the standard silent killing tool not just for auxiliary units but for commandos and the SAS. *All-in Fighting* contains a preface that reveals the ruthless ethos of this new special force. It is a direct defence of fighting to win by any methods available and a rejection of the concept of fair play.

> There seems little doubt that one of the causes of our failures during this war comes from the cricket... mentality. Every soldier, sailor, airman, and in many cases every man and woman, may be called upon to defend their lives in sudden emergencies. This defence can only be achieved by killing or disabling the enemy. To conquer our ingrained repugnance to killing at close quarters is essential... the principal value of the [Fairburn] training lies not so much in the actual physical holds or breaks, but in the psychological reaction which engenders and fosters the necessary attitude of mind which refuses to admit defeat and is determined to achieve victory.

The battle for survival taking place in 1940 was a deadly serious business and Gubbins and his staff were determined to produce men who had the technical ability and the willpower to dispatch Germans in any and every manner that came to hand. And if this meant teaching a recruit to hate his enemy enough to be able to pummel him to death, to silently break his neck with bare hands or to stab him with a stiletto-like Fairburn knife, then so be it. Mental strength was not only necessary when it came to killing the enemy in hand-to-hand fighting. The auxiliary also had to be able to deal with other pressures that came with the job. If invasion took place, the auxiliaries would have to leave – effectively abandon – their families to the mercies of the invader. They would have to accept the reprisals that the German army would, no doubt, inflict on the civilian population following guerrilla activity, and they would have to reconcile themselves to the prospect of being hunted and a violent death – perhaps under torture – if taken alive.

A surviving member of the Secret Army offers an insight into the way in which men were selected and trained for the role of underground fighter.

In 1940 Charlie Mason was a young married man in his early twenties living near Beverley, Yorkshire. He was in a protected trade (an aircraft engineer working with the RAF) when in late 1940 he was approached by a friend and asked if he would be interested in joining a special unit. Mason had no military training – he was not in the Home Guard – but, as he explains, 'I was recruited because of my knowledge of the local area. I knew the woods round about because I liked to poach and we – I was one of five brothers – always sort of liked guns. It was the poaching at night, being able to hide and move into a wood and also being able to understand animal noises that got me in.'

Mason's motives for accepting the invitation to join the auxiliaries were simple. 'I was absolutely certain an invasion was coming. Because I was connected with the RAF I was getting information that the public didn't know about. The pilots told me they had been on raids bombing barges and boats and that they had seen German troops embarking and disembarking. "Rest assured they are coming," the pilots said, so I was convinced.'

Mason was trained at an army HQ at Middleton. 'Regulars trained us and we had to go there and they showed you what to do, unarmed combat, and we practised night operations in daylight. We wore dark glasses but the trainers didn't so they could see all the mistakes we made.' The training appears to have been extremely successful and it was not long before the auxiliaries were able to run rings around regulars when joint exercises were held. Training was gratifying, even amusing, but when eventually posted to their hide near the Yorkshire coast Mason's patrol knew their mission was, potentially, deadly serious. 'Oh yes, we weren't playing games. When we were on duty we had live ammunition. When we went out we knew that the invasion could happen that night – any night. It was total war. When we were out of a night doing exercises, there were our bombers going out and I wished I were up there with them. Life to me didn't matter. You had a job to do and you didn't fear any dangers.'

The particular job assigned to Mason's seven-man patrol was to help bottle-up Hull.

> We expected that the Germans were going to want the port of Hull to land their heavy stuff. That's what we had to keep back. Our job was to keep blowing up the railway continually. We wouldn't operate until our troops had left the area so we could blow up anything that we thought could help the Germans. Once we were cut off behind German lines there would be no information coming in. We were on our own; we would make our own decisions. We were lawless then, we destroyed anything that we wanted to destroy. It didn't matter if it affected our own people. If you were blowing up a railway you would blow up the cabin because in that cabin would be a German guard with the signalman so you'd blow the lot up.

Mason is no less ruthless when describing the fate that would befall wounded comrades.

> It was agreed that you never left anyone behind injured. We'd killed him and then booby trap the body – you hadn't to leave him alive for the Germans to capture because it was information about the units that they wanted. They would torture you for information and then kill you. If there was any danger of being captured you shot yourself and the rest of the unit. We were told all this before we signed on. We were told that the expectation of life on operations was two or three weeks.

Charlie Mason is thankful that he was never put to the test. He remained operational until 1944, when the auxiliary force was stood down. By then it had, finally, become certain that Germany – following massive defeats in Russia and the successful allied invasion of Europe – could not reverse its fortunes and could not mount an invasion of Britain.

If Germany had invaded in 1940, would the auxiliary units have played a significant role in the defence of Britain? All that can be said now for certain is that the auxiliaries were motivated but their training was limited. Few had combat experience of any kind, equipment was ad-hoc and often antiquated, the pressure under which they would have operated would have been immense and they were up against an implacable enemy that, within a few years, was to prove itself expert in dealing with all manner of irregular forces. They were a desperate solution for a desperate time.

CONCLUSION

In 1944 Britain's defences against sea-borne attack were scaled down. By that date it was finally certain that the German army, fatally mauled in Russia, was in no position to invade. But Britain's coastal defences were not dismantled. As the war ended there were those who believed that the Soviet Union would be the next enemy, and in anticipation of this, NATO was formed in 1947 for the defence of Western Europe and North America. But even if the Soviets were the new enemy, it gradually became clear during the early 1950s that a Soviet invasion – if it came – would not be launched against the coast of Britain, and from 1956 coastal defences around the British Isles were gradually decommissioned. So after nearly a thousand years of fortification, Britain's shoreline was undefended.

But the legacy of a millennium of fortification had not only a profound influence on British attitudes to foreign powers, but also on the culture of the country, especially on its architecture. In particular this had been the case in the twentieth century, when aerial bombardment had demonstrated the apparent advantages of modern materials and means of construction – steel and reinforced concrete frames – over traditional masonry and timber buildings. This laid the ground for the enthusiastic support of Modernist architecture in Britain after the Second World War: in the 1950s and 1960s whole quarters of cities were redeveloped utilizing the concrete mass-building systems developed for the construction of wartime fortifications and bomb shelters. Public housing at Spa Green in Finsbury, north London – designed by Berthold Lubetkin with the engineer Ove Arup in the 1940s and early 1950s – was not only built of robust modern materials but also designed to withstand the shock of bomb-blasts. Modern materials and construction techniques seemed to be the only sensible way in which to build for a future which would – inevitably it seemed – include ever more violent aerial attack.

Even after the official decommissioning of Britain's coastal defences, anti-invasion works of a kind were still constructed. As late as the mid 1980s a replica of a north German village was built in the Thetford Battle Zone in Norfolk, where NATO troops were trained to defeat an invasion of Western Europe's frontier by Soviet troops. Britain's front-line was no longer its own coast but, as in the twelfth century, in mainland Europe: this time in north Germany and along the banks of the Elbe, by an ironic twist of fate the Anglo-Saxon heartland. But even as preparations were made to withstand a conventional land invasion, both western and eastern powers knew that if all-out war came, it would not be confined to the traditional tussle between land forces fighting for terrain. It would be a war of the air with aircraft and rockets carrying awe-inspiring payloads of nuclear death and destruction.

Opposite: *An aerial photograph of an atomic bomb test on Bikini Atoll in the Marshall Islands, 12 July 1946.*

It was clear that a new – total – war would not be a war of invasion but of obliteration. Territorial conquest was no longer the aim in this new terrifying form of ideological conflict. Now the defender's ambition was not to build structures that could repel an invader, but to build deep, environmentally controlled shelters – for people and machines – that offered a chance of survival against blast and radiation, and a chance of launching raids of retaliation. The structures of the Cold War years – bunkers, regional command centres buried deep in the earth and early warning systems – are, in their massive and elemental forms – among the most extraordinary and powerful of man's built creations. And, as these strongly defensive buildings proclaim, the aim of battle in the Cold War era was not the possession of an enemy's country but its utter destruction. The age of invasion was over: the age of oblivion had dawned.

BIBLIOGRAPHY

Primary Sources

Alsop, V., *God in the Mount: a sermon upon the wonderful deliverance of His Majesty from assassination, the nation from invasion* (1696) (British Library 4477.cc.2).

Anonymous, *Address to the People of England on Napoleon's Threatened Invasion* (1803) (British Library 8140.a.50).

Anonymous, *Rise in Defence of your Country: as Address to all Ranks* (1803) (British Library 1851.c.3(20)).

Baker, J., *A Brief Narrative of the French Invasion Near Fishguard, Pembrokeshire* (self published, 1797) (British Library 1560/2095).

Berney, T., *The Battle of the Channel Tunnel and Dover Castle Forts* (1882) (British Library 10106.h.26).

Bisset, J., *Patriotic Clarion: Songs on the Threatened Invasion* (1803) (British Library 79.c.33).

Bradbury, T., *Sermon on Occasion of French Invasion in Favour of the Pretender* (1707/08).

Briellat, T., *The Trial of Thomas Briellat for Seditious Word 1793* (1794).

'Britannia', *Proclamation on Expected Invasion* (J. Asperne, 1803).

Calendar of State Papers (HMSO).

Coad, Jonathan G. and Lewis, P. N., 'The Later Fortifications of Dover' in *Post-Medieval Archaeology* 16 (1982).

Collier, B., *The Defence of the United Kingdom* (1957) (British Library B.S.68/33.b(8)).

Collinson, T. B., *On the Present Facilities for the Invasion of England, and the defence thereof* (1877) (British Library 8822.e.7.(12)).

Daubeny, C., *A Sermon on his Majesty's call for the united exertions of his people against the threatened invasion: preached at Christ's-Church, Bath* (1803) (British Library 4476.999.34).

Davies, A. S., *Aberdovey and the Spanish Invasion in 1597* (reprinted from *Archaeologia Cambresis*, 1932) (British Library 7711.c.30.(3)).

Day, H., *Thanksgiving Sermon for the Salvation of the King from Assaination Prior to French Invasion* (Richard Baldwin, 1696).

Defoe, D., *The Apparent Danger of an Invasion, briefly represented in a Letter to a Minister of State* (A. Baldwin, 1701).

Dirom, A., *Plans for the Defence of Great Britain and Ireland* (1797) (British Library 1103.i.29).

Digges, T., *England's Defence: a treatise concerning invasion...to the Earl of Leicester* (1558) (British Library 534.m.23.(6)).

Donnelly, J.A., 'A Study of the Coastal Forts built by Henry VIII' *Fort* vol. 10 (1982).

Drummond, H., *A Letter to the People of England on Invasion* (1859) (British Library 8138.a.23).

Duane, W., *Account of the proceedings of a meeting of the people, in a field near Copenhagen House* (Tree of Liberty, 1795).

Elliot, E., *The Downfall of Despotism; or, the last act of the European tragedy: showing...the invasion of Britain* (1853) (British Library 3187.c.43).

Elizabeth I, Queen of England, *Speech made in Parliament regarding invasion* (1593).

Gifford, G., 'The Giffords' *Historical Collections of Staffordshire*, 5th Series II (Staffordshire Record Society).

Goodall, J., 'Dover Castle and the Great Siege of 1216' *Chateau Gaillard XIX, Actes du Colloque International de Graz (Autriche), 1998* (2000).

Mead, Cdr. H., 'Sussex Martello Towers' *Sussex County Magazine* (1952).

Ormonde, Duke of, *The Jacobite Attempt of 1719. Letters of James Butler the second Duke of Ormonde relating to Cardinal Alberoni's project for the invasion of Great Britain on behalf of the Stuarts, and to the landing of a Spanish expedition in Scotland* (1719) (British Library Ac.8256(19)).

Proclamation by the King and Queen (appointing the times and place for holding the next Assizes, postponed on account of the French Invasion. 19 July 1690 (British Library 816.m.3.(93)).

Round, N. G., '1595 as International Incident' paper given at July 1995 *Invasion 1995 Commemorative Conference* (1995).

Victoria County History, *History of Sussex* vol. 9 (1937).

Williams, H. L., *An Authentic Account of the Invasion by the French Troops under General Tate on Carrig Gwastad Point near Fishguard* (1842) (British Library 10369.bb.40(1)).

Public Record Office documents:

PRO SC11/676 (cited on p. 31)
PRO SP53/22 (cited on p. 53)
PRO SP12/213 (cited on p.55)
PRO W01/627-9, 633, 783, WO30/65, 56 (cited on p. 112, 116-8)
PRO ADMS51/1497 (cited on p. 114-5)
PRO WO30/71 (cited on p. 123)
PRO AIR/1/539/16/15/1 (cited on p. 139-40)
PRO WO178/1 (cited on p. 162)
PRO PREM.3/88/3 (cited on p. 170)
PRO CAB/21/1476 (cited on p.170)

Secondary Sources

Ackroyd, P., *Blake* (Minerva, 1995).

Adair, R. A. S., *The Organisation and Duties of Militia of the United Kingdom Considered with Reference to Invasion* (James Ridgeway, 1860).

Adams, H., *Signal for Invasion* (Collins, 1942).

Alexander, C., *Ironside's Line* (Historic Military Press, 1999).

Allan, J., *Berthold Lubetkin: Architecture and the Tradition of Progress* (RIBA Publications, 1992).

Allmand, C. T., *The Hundred Years' War: England and France at War c1300-1450* (Cambridge University Press, 1988).

Anonymous, *A Narrative of what passed at Killalla in the County of Mayo...during the French Invasion in the Summer of 1798* (J. Wright and J. Hatchard, 1800).

Anonymous, *The Female Association for Preserving Liberty and Property upon Napoleon's Invasion* (J. Asperne, 1803).

Anonymous, *The Duke of Shoreditch, or Barlow's Ghost (an address on the threatened invasion)* (J. Asperne 1803) (and other invasion ballads and pamphlets in the British Library, folio 806 k. 1.).

Anonymous, *The Country in Arms, by an Old Soldier* (Jones, 1803).

Ashley, M., *The Glorious Revolution of 1688* (Hodder & Stoughton, 1966).

Avery, C. H., *In Days of Danger: The Tale of Threatened French Invasion* (T. Nelson & Sons, 1909).

Banse, E., *Invasion of Britain* (Friends of Europe Publications, 1934).

Barrington, J. T., *England on the Defensive: The problems of invasion critically examined* (Kegan Paul, 1881).

Barrow, W. Rev., *The Right of Resisting Foreign Invasion. A sermon preached at the Collegiate Church of Southwell... before the Southwell Loyal Volunteers* (S.& I. Ridge, 1803).

Bartlet, T. et al, *Rebellion: a television history of 1798* (Gill & Macmillan, 1998).

Beadon, G., *Ten Minutes Reading of Plain Observations upon Canals and Navigable Rivers...and upon the question of the national defence of Great Britain from foreign invasion* (Chapman & Hall, 1848).

Berners, J. B., *From the Chronicles of Froissart* (Tern Press, 1986).

Beeler, J., *Warfare in England, 1066-1189* (Cornell University Press, 1966).

Blunt, H., *Perils and Panics of Invasion in 1796, 97, 98, 1804-05 and at the present time* (T. C. Newley, 1860).

Boynton, L., *The Elizabethan Militia, 1558-1638* (Routledge & Kegan Paul, 1967).

Bowman, M.W., *RAF Bomber Stories* (Patricia Stephens, 1998).

Brodrick, G. C. and Fotheringham, J. K., *The History of England from Addington's Administration to the Close of William IV's Reign 1801 -1837* (Longmans & Co., 1906).

Brown, I. et al., *Twentieth Century Defences in Britain: an introductory guide* (Council for British Archaeology, 1995).

Brown, R. A., *English Medieval Castles* (Batsford, 1954).

Brown, R. A., 'The Battle of Hastings' in R.A. Brown, (ed.), *Proceedings of the Battle Conference on Anglo-Norman Studies, III, 1980* (Boydell, 1981).

Brown, R. A., *The Norman Conquest* (Edward Arnold, 1984).

Burridge, D., *A Guide to the Western Heights Defences, Dover, Kent* (Kent Defence Research Group, 1993).

Campion, E., *The Campion-Parsons Invasion Plot, 1580. The Jesuit Edmund Campion martyr or traitor? Queen Elizabeth's Secret Service vindicated after 350 years by the recently discovered Vatican Archive documents* (Protestant Truth Society, 1937).

Carradice, P., *The Last Invasion: the story of the French landing in Wales* (Village Publishing, 1992).

Carroll, M. J., *A Bay of Destiny: a history of Bantry Bay and Bantry* (Bantry Design Studios, 1996).

Castle, H.G., *Fire over England: The German air raids in World War I* (Secker & Warburg, 1982).

Childers, E., *The Riddle of the Sands. A record of secret service recently achieved* (Smith, Elder & co., 1903).

Childs, J., *The Army, James II and the Glorious Revolution* (Manchester University Press, 1980).

Chesney, G.T., *The Battle of Dorking. Reminicences of a Volunteer* (W. Blackwood, 1871).

Christiansen, R., *Tales of the New Babylon. Paris, 1869 -1875* (Sinclair-Stevenson, 1994).

Churchill, W. S., *The World Crisis 1911-1918* (2 vols. Odhams Press, 1939).

Clarke, S., *England's Remembrancer* (John Rothwell, 1657).

Clayton, T. and Craig, P., *Finest Hour* (Hodder & Stoughton, 1999).

Clements, B., *Towers of Strength – The Story of Martello Towers* (Pen & Sword, 1998).

Coad, J. G., *Historic Architecture of the Royal Navy* (Gollancz, 1983).

Coad, J. C., *Dymchurch Martello Tower, Kent* (English Heritage, 1990).

Cocroft, W. D., *Dangerous Energy: the archaeology of gunpowder and military explosives manufacture* (English Heritage, 2000).

Coleridge, S. T., *Fears in Solitude, written in 1798 during the alarm of an invasion* (Johnson, 1798).

Colvin. H. M., *The History of the King's Works* (HMSO, 1963).

Cooper, D., *The History of Winchelsea, one of the ancient towns, added to the Cinque Ports* (John Russel Smith, 1850).

Cousins, G., *The Defenders: A history of the British volunteers* (Muller, 1968).

Creasy, E. S., *The Invasions and the Projected Invasions of England from the Saxon Times, with remarks on the present emergencies* (Richard Bentley, 1852).

Cronin, S., *Irish Nationalism. A history of its roots and ideology* (Academy Press, 1980).

Curling, H., *A few words in recommendation of the formation of volunteer rifle corps, as a guarantee against the risk of invasion* (W.N. Wright, 1852).

Cruickshank, C., *Henry VIII and the Invasion of France* (Clarendon, 1969).

Curry, A. and Hughes, M. (eds.), *Arms, Armies and Fortifications in the Hundred Years War* (Boydell Press, 1994).

Daunton, M. J., *Progress and Poverty: an economic and social history of Britain 1700-1850* (Oxford University Press, 1995).

de Beer, E. S., *The Diary of John Evelyn* (Oxford University Press,1959).

de Chair, S., *Napoleon on Napoleon* (Brockhampton Press, 1992).

Defoe, D., *Advice to the Electors of Great Britain; Occasioned by the Intended Invasion from France* (Heirs and Successors of Andrew Anderson, 1708).

D'Egville, H., *The Invasion of England* (Hodder & Stoughton, 1915).

Devereux, R. Earl of Essex, *Opinion…on the alarm of invasion from Spain in 1596 and the measures proper to be taken on that occasion* (A. Strahan, 1794).

Dickinson, R., 'The Spanish Account of the 1595 raid on Mousehole' *Journal of the Royal Institution of Cornwall* (1988).

Dobinson, C., *Fields of Deception… Britain's Bombing Decoys of World War II* (Methuen Publishing Ltd., 2000).

Duffy, C., *Siege Warfare: The Fortress in the Early Modern World, 1494-1660* (Routledge & Kegan Paul, 1979).

Fairbairn, W. E., *All-in Fighting* (Faber & Faber, 1942).

Farrell, S., *The Last Invasion, 1066* (Dragon, 1986).

Featherstone, D., *Weapons and Equipment of the Victorian Soldier* (Blanford Press, 1978).

Flanagan, T., *The Year of the French* (Holt, Rinehart & Winston, 1979).

Fleming, P., *Operation Sealion* (Simon & Schuster, 1957).

Forth, C., *The Surprise of the Channel Tunnel. A sensational story of the future* (Wightman & Co., 1883).

Fowler, K. (ed.), *The Hundred Years' War* (Macmillan, 1971).

Garmonsway, G. N., *The Anglo-Saxon Chronicle* (J.M. Dent & Sons, 1972).

Glover, R., *Britain at Bay: Defence against Bonaparte, 1803-14* (George Allen & Unwin, 1973).

Goodwin, J., *Fortification of the South Coast – The Pevensey, Eastbourne Defences 1750-1945* (1994).

Gush, G., *Renaissance Armies, 1480-1650* (Stephens, 1982).

Hainsworth, R and Churches, C., *The Anglo-Dutch Naval Wars 1652-1674* (Sutton Publishing, 1998).

Hanna, H. B., *Can Germany Invade England?* (Methuen & Co., 1912).

Hassall, A., *The Life of Napoleon* (Methuen & Co., 1911).

Hastings, M., *Bomber Command* (Joseph, 1979).

Hillier, C., *The Bulwark Shore* (Eyre Methuen, 1980).

Hogg, I. V., *The Coast Defences of England and Wales, 1856-1956* (David & Charles, 1974).

Holmes, G. (ed.), *Britain after the Glorious Revolution 1689-1714* (Macmillan, 1969).

Horne, A., *The Fall of Paris. The siege and the commune, 1870-1* (Macmillan, 1965).

Horne, P., *The Last Invasion of Britain, Fishguard, 1797* (Preseli, 1980).

Howarth, D., *Trafalgar: The Nelson Touch* (Collins, 1969).

Howarth, D., *Sovereign of the Seas: The Story of British Sea Power* (Quartet, 1980).

Hozier, H. M., *The Invasions of England. A history of the past with lessons for the future* (2 vols. London, 1876).

Hughes, Q., *Military Architecture. The art of defence from earliest times to the Atlantic Wall* (Beaufort, 1991).

Hussey, F., *Suffolk Invasion: The Dutch Attack on Landguard Fort, 1667* (Dalton, 1983).

Hutchinson, G., *Martello Towers* (G. Hutchinson, 1994).

Ireland, D., *Patriot Adventurer: extracts from the memoirs and journals of Theobald Wolfe Tone 1763-1798* (Rich & Cowan, 1936).

Johnson, P., *Elizabeth I: a study in power and intellect* (Weidenfield and Nicolson, 1974).

Jones, P., *Memoirs of Rear-Admiral Paul Jones* (Edinburgh, 1830).

Kelly, T., *Radical Tailor: life and work of Francis Place, 1771-1854* (Birkbeck College, 1972).

Kent, P., *Fortifications of East Anglia* (Terence Dalton, 1988).

Kenyon, J. R., *Castles, Town Defences and Artillery Fortifications in Britain and Ireland: A bibliography 1945-74* (Council for British Archaeology, 1990).

Kightly, C., *Strongholds of the Realm* (Thames and Hudson, 1979).

Knox, C., *The Defensive Position of England* (London, 1852).

Lampe, D., *The Last Ditch* (Cassell, 1968).

Lavery, B., *Nelson's Navy: The Ships, Men and Organisation, 1793-1815* (Conway Maritime, 1989).

Lecky, W. E. H., *Democracy and Liberty* (Longmans & Co., 1896).

Lecky. W. E. H., *A History of England in the Eighteenth Century* (8 vols. London, 1878-90).

Lemmon, C. H., 'The Campaign of 1066' in C.T. Chevalier, (ed.), *The Norman Conquest: Its Setting and Impact* (Eyre & Spottiswoode, 1966).

Lenman, B., *The Jacobite Risings in Britain, 1687-1746* (Eyre Methuen, 1980).

Le Patourel, J., *Feudal Empires: Norman and Plantagenet* (Hambledon, 1984).

Longmate, N., *The Bombers: The RAF Offensive Against Germany* (Hutchinson, 1983).

Longmate, N., *Defending the Island* (Hutchinson, 1989).

Longmate, N., *Island Fortress. Defence of Great Britain, 1603-1945* (Grafton, 1993).

Ludwig, E., *Napoleon* (G. Allen & Unwin, 1927).

Markham, F., *Napoleon* (Wiedenfield & Nicolson, 1963).

Massie, R. K., *Dreadnought* (Pimlico, 1993).

Marcus, G. J., *Heart of Oak* (Oxford University Press, 1975).

Marquand, D., *Ramsay MacDonald* (Cape, 1977).

Mattingly, G., *The Defeat of The Spanish Armada* (Cape, 1983).

McLynn, F., *France and The Jacobite Rising of 1745* (Edinburgh University Press, 1981).

McLynn, F., *Invasion: From The Armada to Hitler, 1588-1945* (Routledge & Kegan Paul, 1987).

Middlebrook, M. and Everitt, C., *The Bomber Command Diaries, 1939-45* (Penguin, 1990).

Morillo, S. (ed.), *The Battle of Hastings: Sources and Interpretations* (Boydell Press, 1996).

Morison, S. E., *John Paul Jones: A Sailor's Biography* (Faber & Faber, 1960).

Murphy, J. A., *The French are in the Bay* (Mercier Press, 1997).

Neillands, R., *The Hundred Years' War* (Routledge, 1990).

Overy, R. J., *The Air War, 1939-1945* (Europa Publications, 1980).

Pepys, S. *The Diary of Samuel Pepys* (Unwin Hyman, 1987).

Plowden, A., *The Elizabethan Secret Service* (Harvester Wheatsheaf, 1991).

Pocock, T., *Horatio Nelson* (Bodley Head, 1987).

'Posteritas' *The Siege of London* (Wyman & Sons, 1885).

Poole, A. L., *From Domesday Book to Magna Carta, 1087-1216* (Oxford University Press, 1955).

Poolman, K. E., *Zeppelins Over England* (Evans Bros., 1960).

Pounds, N. J. G., *The Medieval Castle in England and Wales: a social and political history* (Cambridge University Press, 1990).

Powers, B. M., *Strategy Without Slide-Rule: British Air Strategy, 1914-1939* (Croomhelm, 1976).

Pratt, M., *Winchelsea: A Port of Stranded Pride* (Malcom Pratt, 1998).

Price, A., *The Battle of Britain* (Daily Express/Arms and Armour, 1990).

Richmond, H. W., *The Invasion of Britain: an account of plans, attempts and counter-measures from 1586-1918* (Methuen & Co., 1941).

Rodger, N. A. M., *The Wooden World: an anatomy of the Georgian Navy* (Collins, 1986).

Rodger, N. A. M., *The Safeguard of the Sea. A naval history of Britain* (Harper Collins in association with the National Maritime Museum, 1997).

Rogers, P. G., *The Dutch in the Medway* (Oxford University Press, 1970).

Rowse, A. L., "The Expansion of Elizabethan England" *The Elizabethan Age* (Macmillan & Co., 1955).

Saunders, A., *Fortress Britain: Artillery Fortification in the British Isles and Ireland* (Beaufort, 1989).

Saunders, A., *Channel Defences* (Batsford/English Heritage, 1997).

Scarisbrick, J. J., *Henry VIII* (Yale University Press, 1997).

Selby, J. M., *Over the Sea to Skye: The Forty-Five* (Hamilton, 1973).

Sinclair-Stevens, C., *Inglorious Rebellion: The Jacobite Risings of 1708, 1715 and 1719* (Hamilton, 1971).

Starkey, D., *The Reign of Henry VIII: Personalities and Politics* (George Philip, 1985).

Stenton, F. M. (ed.), *The Bayeux Tapestry: A Comprehensive Survey* (Phaidon Press, 1965).

Sumption, J., *Trial by Fire* (Faber, 1999).

Sutcliffe, S., *Martello Towers* (David and Charles, 1972).

Szechi, D., *The Jacobites: Britain and Europe 1688-1788* (Manchester University Press, 1994).

Taylor, W., *The Military Roads in Scotland* (David and Charles, 1976).

Telling, R. M., *Handbook on Martello Towers* (CST, 1998).

Thale, M. (ed.), *The Autobiography of Francis Place* (Cambridge University Press, 1972).

Thompson, E. P., *The Making of the English Working Class* (Penguin Books, 1968).

Thompson, M. W., *The Decline of the Castle* (Cambridge University Press, 1987).

Thompson, M. W., *The Rise of the Castle* (Cambridge University Press, 1991).

Todd, J., *The Secret Life of Aphra Behn* (Andre Deutsch, 1996).

Tone, W. T. W., *The Life of Theobald Wolfe Tone* (Dugeur Editions, 1998).

Trevor-Roper, H., *From Counter-Reformation to Glorious Revolution* (University of Chicago Press, 1992).

Urquhart, D., *The Invasion of England* ("Free Press" Office, 1860).

Usherwood, S. (ed.), *The Great Enterprise: The History of the Spanish Armada as Revealed in Contemporary Documents* (Bell & Hyman, 1982).

Vine, P., *The Royal Military Canal* (David and Charles, 1972).

Ward, A., *Resisting the Nazi Invader* (Constable, 1997).

Wheeler, H. F. B. and Broadley, A. M., *Napoleon and the Invasion of England: The Story of the Great Terror* (2 vols. John Lane, 1908).

Whiting, R., *The Enterprise of England: The Spanish Armada* (Sutton, 1988).

Williams, P., *The Tudor Regime* (Clarendon Press, 1979).

Wills, H., *Pillboxes: A Study of UK Defences 1940* (Lee Cooper in association with Secker and Warburg, 1985).

INDEX

Acknowledgments

Making the television series *Invasion* and writing this book were, in many ways, daring military operations in their own right with the weather and time being the implacable enemies. There were moments of true despair and of terror – scaling the near vertical coastal cliff at Fishguard during filming comes readily to mind, as does the moment the desperately tight deadline for the production of this book was first revealed. But there were also many moving moments – Charlie Mason's evocation of the invasion summer of 1940 remains unforgettable – and much sheer delight. Like most military campaigns the making of the *Invasion* programmes and the writing of this book have only been concluded (successfully I hope) with the aid of a number of stout and stalwart allies – all of whom deserve very special thanks. First comes Sarah Barratt who not only helped me with research but took prime responsibility for a number of chapters. From the BBC I must thank Jane Root (Controller of BBC2) and Roly Keating (Controller of Arts Commissioning for BBC Television) for their tremendous enthusiasm for the idea from the first, and Basil Comely (Executive Producer for *Invasion*) who managed to turn my long-time obsessions about military architecture, warfare and remote parts of Britain's landscape and history into a television series. The producers of the individual programmes – Ed Bazalgette, Julian Birkett and Tim Dunn - provided research, insights, enthusiasm and encouragement that proved invaluable during the making of the programmes and which has provided a firm foundation for the production of this book, while the four researchers – Melisa Akdogan, Nick Barratt, Jane Mayes and Robert Murphy will, if they read this book, realise just how deeply indebted I am to their discoveries and perceptions. Additional advice and support has come also from Roger Bowdler, Matthew Hill, Freddie Nottidge and – especially – from Linda Dalling who proved her usual tower of strength when confronted by the difficult logistical problems of organising a shoot, at speed, in desperate and difficult winter conditions. Many of the people interviewed for the television series will find some of their facts and opinions emerging in this book. My apologies if all the ideas that I have appropriated are not adequately acknowledged. I would like to thank especially: Peter Barber for his enthusiastic explanation of invasion maps in the British Library; Colin Breen for his revelations about the history concealed below the waters of Bantry Bay; Major John Conway of the Small Arms Museum at Warminster for information about the finer points of military weaponry; Colin Digby for instructing me on the art of firing nineteenth century firearms; Colonel Fairie and the men of the Royal Highland Fusiliers for their instructive hospitality at Fort George; Bill Fowler for accompanying me on my landing in the footsteps of the French Legion Noire in Fishguard; Richard Gardner for access to the wondrous world of the former Royal Aircraft Establishment at Farnborough; Norman Garnish for his insights into twentieth-century military engineering; Bob Garrett for his help in recreating an Elizabethan beacon early-warning system; Major Gladen RE for showing me how to bridge and cross a river under fire; John Goodall for his description of the siege of Dover Castle; Peter Goodwin of HMS *Victory* for his tales of Nelson's navy; Nicholas Hall for detailed information on blackpowder ordnance; Colonel Harvey for allowing me to fire a number of fascinating weapons on army land; Colin Herriett for showing me how to fire a trebuchet and other early and alarming weapons; Colonel Hughes-Wilson for his wise comments about a wide range of military history and intelligence; Jack Jones for information about the French invasions of the Isle of Wight; Shaun Maguire for access to Spitbank Fort; Charlie Mason for an evocation of the invasion terrors of 1940 and tips on unarmed combat; Peter Mooney and the 2nd Battle Group for helping with the invasion and occupation of Whitehall; Andrew Mullin for initiating me into the secrets of the Napoleonic Volunteer movement; Professor John A Murphy for his insights – and songs – about the French in Ireland in 1796 and '98; Malcolm Pratt for information about the rape of Winchelsea; Sam Seaton for his evocation of the terror – and the thrill of being under Zeppelin attack; Lord St. Leven for his revelations about the Spanish raid on Mousehole and Mount's Bay; Roger Thomas of English Heritage for his ready advice on Second World war fortifications; Commander Alistair Wilson RN retired for his explanation of the significance of HMS *Warrior*; Chris Wren for his explanation of the operations room at RAF Uxbridge. Also, the Army's 17 Port and Maritime Operation and the men and women of the Royal Logistic Corps for showing me how to survive an assault by landing craft; the staff at RAF Cranwell for allowing me access to the building and its archives; the Ordnance Survey for giving me a bird's eye view of the invasion coast from its balloon; and English Heritage and The National Trust for the generous use of many of their properties. From the publishers, I would like to thank Emma Marriott, Christine King and Dan Newman for the incredibly fast and professional manner in which this book has been produced. For her patience at times of trouble and stress and for information about the Spanish view of Sir Francis Drake I must thank Eugenia Sartorius.